Children's Theories of Mind:
Mental States and Social Understanding

Children's Theories of Mind:
Mental States and Social Understanding

Douglas Frye
Yale University

Chris Moore
Dalhousie University

LEA LAWRENCE ERLBAUM ASSOCIATES, PUBLISHERS
1991 Hillsdale, New Jersey   Hove and London

Lawrence Erlbaum Associates, Inc., Publishers
365 Broadway
Hillsdale, New Jersey 07642

Library of Congress Cataloging-in-Publication Data

Children's theories of mind : the development of the social
  understanding of self and others / [edited by] Douglas Frye and
  Chris Moore.
      p. cm.
    Includes index.
    ISBN 0-8058-0417-X. — ISBN 0-8058-0418-8 (pbk.)
    1. Philosophy of mind in children. 2. Social perception in
children. I. Frye, Douglas. II. Moore, Chris, 1958–   .
    [DNLM: 1. Self-Concept—in infancy & childhood. 2. Social
Perception—in infancy & childhood. WS 105.5.S3 C536]
BF723.P48C45 1990
155.4'18—dc20
DNLM/DLC
for Library of Congress   90-3702
                                                                        CIP

Printed in the United States of America
10 9 8 7 6 5 4 3 2

Contents

Preface

Recent work on children's theories of mind has refreshed the study of the mental life of the child. The new research acknowledges the child's conceptions of intention and belief, as well intention and belief themselves, and considers the explanations they provide for the developing abilities of the child. Effects of the child's theory of mind spread across cognitive, language, and social development. The topic, therefore, holds the promise of bringing a unifying influence to developmental psychology. This book on the child's theory of mind began its life as a study group that met for several days in March, 1988 at Yale University. Sponsorship by the Society for Research in Child Development and the Foundation for Child Development was critical to the success of the project. It allowed the group to be international in composition; a necessity when laboratories in Canada, the United States, England, and Europe are all engaged in the research. It also permitted us to meet and talk before committing our thoughts irretrievably to paper. This procedure, we believe, was responsible for the new speculations on the acquisition of theories of mind that made their way into the contributions between the first discussions and the final drafts. We thank Judi Amsel and Debra Ruel at Lawrence Erlbaum Associates for their excellent supervision of the published result.

CHAPTER 1
The Acquisition and Utility of Theories of Mind

Chris Moore
Dalhousie University

Douglas Frye
Yale University

Imagine that the following story is acted out for a child: A boy comes home, places some chocolate in a cupboard, and then leaves the room. While he is gone, his mother comes in and happens to move the chocolate to another cupboard. Later, the boy returns and wants to eat the chocolate. Where will the boy look?

Notice that a correct answer to this question depends on the child knowing something about the beliefs of the boy in the story. In other words, it depends on the child having a "theory of mind" (Astington, Harris, & Olson, 1988), that is, an understanding that people have mental states including thoughts, beliefs, and desires.[1] In this instance, the child must realize that the boy's beliefs do not match reality. Wimmer and Perner (1983), who devised the false belief paradigm, found that younger children say that the boy will open the cupboard

---

[1]The terms *folk psychology* or *commonsense psychology* may more adequately capture what is being developed during the preschool years. The child is not really developing a theory in anything like its scientific sense (Johnson, 1988) but rather a way of thinking and talking about self and others that involves mental states. Unfortunately, however, these phrases have acquired somewhat pejorative connotations through their adoption by instrumentalist and reductionist philosophers of mind (e.g., Churchland, 1984; Stich, 1983), who have claimed that such psychology is, at best, an inadequate way of understanding mental states, that its constructs have no ontological reality, and that it will ultimately be replaced by a true neuroscientifically based account. We, therefore, somewhat reluctantly retain the phrase theory of mind.

where the chocolate actually is. It is not until 4 or 5 years of age that their results indicate that the boy will look in the original cupboard. Subsequent studies (Baron-Cohen, Leslie, & Frith, 1985; Gopnik & Astington, 1988; Perner, Leekam, & Wimmer, 1987) have confirmed these findings.

There has been a sharp increase over the past several years in the amount of research conducted on what children know about their own and other people's minds. The increase would seem to be justified for two basic and related reasons. A theory of mind makes an enormous difference to the child. As the preceding example illustrates, it transforms the way children are able to see other people and make sense of what they are doing. Of course, it also makes a difference to our understanding of the child. If the results of the false belief task are a guide, then making sense of "the child's theory of mind" will be important for explaining developmental changes in the child's responses to situations where they must consider what other people are actually doing—in other words, almost all social situations.

The contributors to this volume discuss several aspects of the child's theory of mind. They present research that illuminates the young child's theory of mind and how it changes. That research stands well on its own. They also provide discussions of the utility of a theory of mind to the child and to developmental psychologists trying to understand children. Finally, new explanations are offered for how children acquire such a theory in the first place. The question of acquisition is a very difficult one. Because the mental states of others cannot be observed, how does the young child ever come to postulate their existence? Some background to the questions of the utility of the child's theory of mind and how theories of mind may be acquired is sketched in the following section.

THE UTILITY OF A THEORY OF MIND
TO THE CHILD

The major ways in which the development of a theory of mind enters the life of the child can be placed in two familiar categories. A theory of mind, is firstly and most obviously, a powerful social tool.[2] It allows the

---

[2]It is worth pointing out that the idea that human intelligence evolved as social intelligence appears to be gaining ground over the possible competitors, namely that intelligence evolved for increasingly sophisticated tool use or foraging (see, e.g., Byrne & Whiten, 1986). Thus, the view that the investigation of the child's theory of mind is central to our understanding of child development is one that fits with recent thinking on hominid evolution.

explanation, prediction, and manipulation of the behavior of others. Secondly, acquiring a theory of mind may well be instrumental in the development of particular forms of reasoning and, as such, may represent a significant step in cognitive development.

Social Function

At its most basic, social behavior can be broken down into cooperation and competition. We either try to work with others to achieve goals of mutual benefit or we try to improve our position at the expense of others. (Often, of course, cooperation and competition become combined, as when we form alliances to compete with others; examples can be found throughout social behavior, from friendships to team sports to war.) The common elements of mental state psychology—belief, desire, and intention—play central roles in competitive and cooperative social behavior. For example, competition requires recognizing when other people's desires conflict with our own so that those desires can be blocked or overcome. One of the first competitive strategies that makes its way into the child's behavioral repertoire is deception, including lying (Chandler, Fritz, & Hala, 1989; Lewis, Stanger, & Sullivan, 1989; Shultz & Cloghesy, 1981; Sodian, in press; Wimmer & Perner, 1983). Although deception can occur at a number of different levels (Mitchell, 1986), the more effective variants depend entirely on mental state psychology. The point of lying is to give someone else a false belief, a misrepresentation of reality. Effective lying means telling them something they are likely to believe. Thus, lying well requires knowing that others can have false beliefs and having some idea of which ones they are likely to embrace.

A form of cooperation that is noteworthy, both because it carries such powerful social force and because it provides an intriguing puzzle for theories of social behavior, is altruism. In order to behave altruistically, it is, by definition, necessary to take into account the needs and desires of others. It is probably also important to be able to assess the beliefs that others have about us; for example, knowing that others will think well of us if we act altruistically but poorly if we do not. Certainly, the middle stages of moral reasoning which Kohlberg and his followers (e.g., Colby, Kohlberg, Gibbs, & Lieberman, 1983) have claimed characterize most adolescents and adults seem to be based on the ability for such an assessment.

Lastly, in a social world where both competition and cooperation are possible, the judgment of intention appears to be particularly useful. Ascribing intention to others allows one to look for the goals in the other's actions (Premack & Woodruff, 1978). In addition, the assessment of other people's intentions provides an index of the valence of their attitudes towards us. For example, if someone performs an action with deleterious consequences for another, then it is to the latter's advantage to know whether that action reflected a negative attitude on the part of the actor and may be repeated, or whether it was essentially a mistake. Dunn (see chapter 6, this volume) presents some examples that may reveal the developmental origins of this process.

Cognitive Function

It is becoming reasonably well established that a theory of mind turns on the ability to represent mental states and processes. Terms such as metacognition and metarepresentation are often used in this context, and it is worth explicating these further. Metacognition usually denotes knowledge about the cognitive system, including, perhaps most obviously, memory. Since the 1960s, it has been known that children's understanding of memory changes with age and that their memory performance appears to be tied to their knowledge of mnemonic strategies. For example, Flavell and his colleagues (e.g., Flavell, 1970; Keeney, Cannizzo, & Flavell, 1967; Moely, Olson, Halwes, & Flavell, 1969) showed that, although young children tended not to employ strategies such as rehearsal on short-term memory tasks and consequently performed poorly, this failure could be construed as a production deficit rather than a mediation deficit. Teaching the children to use memory strategies greatly improved memory performance.

Metarepresentation is a term more commonly employed in the literature on the theory of mind. Two usages of this term need to differentiated. Firstly, metarepresentation can be taken to mean merely embedding one representation within another. Thus, one can think about a thought that another person has. Conceivably, such embedding can occur to an infinite extent. Secondly, metarepresentation can mean modelling the representational process (Perner, 1988a) so that, for example, one can think about another's belief as false. In the latter case, we are talking about representing a representation as a representation of reality or, in other words, judging how the person's representation relates to the world.

The development of metarepresentation in the second sense results in an important change in the way the child thinks about the world. Acquiring such a theory of mind involves the simultaneous recognition that there is a single reality but that different people, or the same people at different times, may have different representations of that reality. In other words, the child develops a distinction between subjective and objective (Russell, 1984). Such a distinction is crucial if the child is ever to gain an understanding of the difference between facts and values, in that facts are objective and not open to argument, whereas values and opinions are subjective and may differ between people (Russell, 1982). Similarly, in order to appreciate the notion of "correctness," the child must be able to recognize that there is "only one world against which alternative representations must be assessed" (Forguson & Gopnik, 1988, p. 239). Without standards of truth, it is easy to see why, since Piaget's time (Piaget, 1928), young preschoolers have been described as illogical (Forguson & Gopnik, 1988).

If the arguments of the previous paragraphs are correct, then one might expect that individuals without a theory of mind would suffer severe social and cognitive problems. It is possible that such individuals do exist. A number of studies have shown that autism may well be the result of a specific deficit in the cognitive abilities involved in the construction of a theory of mind (Baron-Cohen, Leslie, & Frith, 1985, 1986; Leslie & Frith, 1988; Perner, Leslie, Frith, & Leekam, 1989). For example, Baron-Cohen, Leslie, and Frith (1986) found that, compared to mental age matched retarded and normal children, autistic children perform particularly badly on tasks that require the subject to impute intentional states to others, while they perform as well as controls on problems that require causal or simple behavioral reasoning.

THE UTILITY OF A THEORY OF MIND TO DEVELOPMENTAL PSYCHOLOGY

Theory of mind is becoming a valuable approach in the study of child development. It furnishes a framework for generating new research and, at the same time, for looking at various traditional issues in developmental psychology. The fertility of the approach is evident in the mass of new empirical work produced in the last few years. However, the issues that are considered in this approach have a history as long as any within developmental psychology, dating back to the earliest work of founders such as Baldwin (see Bretherton, chapter 4, this volume) and Piaget. In order to illustrate these two points, it may be instructive to glance at the history of the "theory of mind" construct.[3]

The modern beginnings of theory of mind research are easy to find.

---

[3]We acknowledge Janet Astington's contribution to our reading of the early history of the theory of mind construct.

A clear starting point is Premack and Woodruff's (1978) article, "Does the chimpanzee have a theory of mind?" published in the *Behavioral and Brain Sciences*. Premack and Woodruff investigated the ability of the chimpanzee to predict what a human would do in certain goal-directed circumstances, and they claimed that the animals exhibited skills that required an understanding of the mental states of the human actor. As shown in the commentaries on the article, the work generated intense interest in what would be required as firm evidence for such an understanding. That interest spread into developmental psychology, where Wimmer and Perner (1983) were the first to begin to test the issue with children, using their false belief paradigm.[4]

It did not take long for a number of correspondences and controversies to appear. Various researchers showed that a number of other developments seem to occur at about the same age as the recognition of false beliefs. The work on understanding false belief was extended to include self-knowledge. Gopnik and Astington (1988; Astington & Gopnik, 1988) showed that at about the same time children develop the understanding that other people may have beliefs that are false, they also start to recognize that they themselves may previously have had beliefs that turned out to be wrong. In addition, the recognition that objects can, in reality, be different from how they appear also shows a similar developmental progression (Flavell, Flavell, & Green, 1983; Gopnik & Astington, 1988; Moore, Pure, & Furrow, 1990). All of these developments seem to rest on the understanding that mental representations may differ from reality (Astington & Gopnik, 1988; Flavell, 1988; Forguson & Gopnik, 1988).

It soon became recognized, however, that young children do not simply have difficulty with representations that differ from reality. From about 2 years of age, children are quite capable of engaging in pretend play, or, in other words, manipulating representations that differ from the way the world is (Leslie, 1987, 1988). The apparent discrepancy between young children's ability to pretend and their ability to pass experimental tasks such as that of Wimmer and Perner created favorable conditions for further theorizing and experimentation. Perhaps the crucial distinction that came out of this controversy was the distinction drawn most clearly by Perner (1988a), and outlined earlier, between having a representation of a representation, which pretense requires, and having a representation of a representation as a representation, or

---

[4]It should be noted that Bretherton and her colleagues have priority in terms of introducing the phrase "theory of mind" into the developmental psychology literature (Bretherton, McNew, & Beeghly- Smith, 1981).

a representational theory of mind, which is required in order to recognize the existence of false beliefs.

More recently, others have claimed that false belief may not be the best way of investigating the child's theory of mind. Wellman and his colleagues have shown that even though children younger than 4 years old may not perform successfully on false belief tasks, they do, nevertheless, have considerable knowledge about mental states and processes (Wellman, 1988). For example, 3-year-olds know that mental images of objects are different from real objects (Wellman & Estes, 1986), and they are able to predict other people's behavior on the basis of the other's desires (Wellman & Bartsch, 1988). Naturalistic observations reveal that children appear to be thinking and talking about mental states some time before they are successful in false belief tasks (Bretherton, McNew, & Beeghly-Smith, 1981; Shatz, Wellman, & Silber, 1983). Although such observations are always open to more reductive kinds of explanations (Perner, 1988b), they are at least suggestive of a sensitivity on the part of the young preschooler to the existence of mental life. Chandler and colleagues (Chandler et al., 1989) have criticized the apparently demanding nature of the false belief task and argued instead for deception as the criterion of understanding mental states. They have reported that 2- to 3-year-old children are capable of behaving deceptively in a novel game-playing situation. However, this result contradicts much of the rest of the available evidence on deceptive behavior in children, and, consequently, urgently requires replication for validation (e.g., Shultz & Cloghesy, 1981; Sodian, in press).

Up to this point, we have dealt only with what children know about the nature of belief. Another growing topic has been children's understanding of how information is passed between minds and between world and mind. The study of children's understanding of communicative efficacy has been studied at least since Piaget's early work (Piaget, 1926) and continues to intrigue researchers (e.g., Beal, 1988; Bonitatibus, 1988; Flavell, Speer, Green, & August, 1981; Robinson, 1981). Piaget, of course, claimed that young children were egocentric and therefore unable to communicate effectively. More recent studies have considerably refined Piaget's notions in showing that, even into the early grade school years, children are poor at judging the adequacy of messages either sent or received and that they have no clear distinction between actual message meaning and speaker's intended meaning (Beal, 1987; Beal & Flavell, 1984; Robinson, Goelman, & Olson, 1983).

According to Piaget, another manifestation of the egocentrism of preschool children's thought is an inability to take the perspective of another and a tendency to claim that others see the same view as one's own (Piaget & Inhelder, 1956). Research on perspective taking has been plentiful since Piaget. Much of it has demonstrated that under different conditions preschool children can take the perspective of another, especially when the children are asked to report what object another can see, as opposed to how the object appears (Masangkay et al., 1974). Flavell and his colleagues (Flavell, 1978; Flavell, Everett, Croft, & Flavell, 1981) developed this notion into a distinction between level I and level II perspective taking, with the transition coming at about 4 years of age. Level I perspective taking entails the ability to recognize that another person can see something different from oneself. Level II perspective taking entails the further ability to recognize how something appears to someone else. Flavell showed that, developmentally, level II perspective taking is correlated with understanding of the appearance-reality distinction (Flavell, Green, & Flavell, 1986). Again, the theory of mind approach has brought greater coherence to the literature. Flavell has recently extended the distinction between level I and II perspective taking to cover other aspects of children's theories of mind, such as the understanding of false belief (Flavell, 1988).

Most recently, a new line of work has emerged on children's understanding of the origins of beliefs. Young preschoolers seem to know that perceptual contact, a direct line of sight, is necessary for something to be seen (Yaniv & Shatz, 1988). It is not until age 4 to 5, however, that children recognize that acquiring a belief will depend on comparable kinds of access to relevant information (e.g., Gopnik & Graf, 1988). Even then, the story is not complete, because it is not until later in development again (age 6 to 8) that children recognize that informational access interacts with an observer's pre-existing knowledge in order to determine current knowledge (Taylor, 1988).

THE PRESENT VOLUME

The chapters that follow give evidence that theory of mind research touches cognitive, social, and linguistic development from infancy onwards. To date, there has been little attempt to answer the question of how these important developments come about. Because the mental state of another is the very prototype of an unobservable, explaining how the child becomes aware of their existence is not a simple task. The chapters in this book propose a variety of possibilities while extending what is known about the implications of the development of a theory of mind.

The question of developmental precursors is directly addressed in several chapters. Frye (chapter 2) argues that the ability to act intention-ally is a prerequisite for a theory of mind and, further, that being able to act intentionally allows the child to draw a clear distinction between the social and physical worlds. The infant comes to understand that certain kinds of means (e.g., gestures) are appropriate for achieving social ends, whereas other means (e.g., physical manipulation) are more appropriate for achieving physical ends. Identifying means and ends allows the child to recognize that others are also acting intentionally, or doing one thing in order to achieve something else. Not until such understanding is in place will the child be capable of intentional social interaction resulting in cooperation and competition.

Premack (chapter 3) describes a very different possibility for the origins of the child's theory of mind. He proposes that infants are able to perceive intention directly from patterns of movement. Only objects that are self-propelled will be identified as agents or as capable of having goals. He is able to show, just from an analysis of an agent's move-ments, how the infant might put a value on what the agent is doing. The infant's perception of intention and interpretation of the valence of the agent's movements are not sufficient to support a full theory of mind. They will not, for example, allow the infant to understand beliefs, but they are the bottom rungs in the climb from perception to interpretation to conceptual understanding of others.

Communication and language offer other explanations of the devel-opment of the theory of mind. In a systematic review of the early communication literature, Bretherton (chapter 4) finds evidence that infants begin to be aware of the mental states of others when they begin to communicate at about 9 months. Communication requires intersub-jectivity, or shared representation and reference. As Bretherton puts it, infants must make a "rich interpretation" of adult messages as much as adults must make one of infant messages. That there is successful communication at this age implies that the infant has some awareness of the point of view of the other. Bretherton goes on to link the changes in the child's theory of mind with the increasing precision and power of the child's fast-developing linguistic abilities.

Beckwith (chapter 5) comes to the child's theory of mind through another aspect of language. He asks how it is possible for children to learn terms with abstract reference. The example he considers is that of emotion. How do young children learn terms for emotions when the feelings of another cannot be directly perceived? To answer, he intro-duces the perspective of nominalist bootstrapping, which says that children initially learn about the behavioral and situational aspects of emotions; later, this knowledge deepens into an understanding of others' emotions as mental states through reasoning about the child's own emotions. In other words, children form a theory of other minds by analogy with their own.

The relevance of theory of mind to social development has remained largely unexplored to date, despite the apparent importance of a theory of mind as a social tool. Two general issues are prominent here. Firstly, what, if any, is the role of the social world in the development of the child's theory of mind? Secondly, what does the developing under- standing of mental states do for the social life of the child? The answers to these two questions will almost certainly be inextricably linked, and several chapters go some way toward unravelling these issues.

Dunn (chapter 6) considers the social life and world of the family from this perspective. The ability of young children to read and react to the emotions and intentions of family members seems to be in advance of what they are able to do in experimental laboratory conditions. Dunn furnishes diverse examples from episodes of teasing, giving of excuses, and cooperative pretend play. She advances the idea that children may make early strides in understanding the feeling states and actions of family members because what happens in the family is of real affective significance to the child. Moreover, there is evidence that children from families who talk about inner states and motives are themselves likely to do so earlier on.

In one part of her chapter, Hay (chapter 7) demonstrates how children might learn the use of mental terms from older models. Her extensive line of studies on imitation have shown it to be a form of learning that is selective, sociable, and creative. When young children imitate, they do not just copy others' movements but seem to take into account the point of the action. Hay offers a new analysis of imitation and of the early formation of the child's theory of mind based on the child's attempts to recognize and act on their own and others' desires.

The relationship of children's understanding of beliefs to their under- standing of nonepistemic mental states, including desire and intention, generates further puzzles in metarepresentation, especially with respect to the watershed at 4 years. Previous results have shown that children seem to understand the nature of desire before belief (Wellman & Bartsch, 1988; Yuill, 1984). These results do not fit well with the logical structure of belief–desire reasoning, in that beliefs and desires appear to be symmetrical components of a theory of mind (Wellman & Bartsch, 1988).

In the present volume, Perner (chapter 8) attempts to resolve this issue by arguing that, in fact, the distinction established in the research is not between belief and desire but between different types of repre- sentation. Perner analyzes the various tasks to show that some require the child merely to represent situations, whereas others require the child to think about representations themselves. Most tasks testing desire have only called for reasoning about situations, whereas those testing belief—including the false belief task—depend on reasoning about representations. Perner's analysis explains early theory of mind development in terms of these different types of representation, including the major change that seems to occur at about 4 years.

Astington (chapter 9) evaluates this same problem. She agrees that in order to assess adequately whether young children recognize the intentional nature of intention, it is necessary to use problems that are logically analogous to the false belief problem in what they require of the child's representational abilities. She devises an unfulfilled intention task to meet this criterion. With the task, she empirically demonstrates that children do not appear to understand the representational nature of intention until about the same age as they understand false belief.

Moore and Furrow (chapter 10) present evidence that the understanding of various mental state terms also develops at about the same time as the understanding of the nature of belief. Various writers have claimed a significant role for later language in the development of the child's theory of mind. Feldman (1988), for example, hypothesized that the process of recursion in language, whereby mental state comments may themselves become the topics for further comments, could allow the development of metarepresentation. And Olson (1988), advocating the view that language is the primary phenomenon, proposed that the awareness of mental states depends on the acquisition of a metalanguage for talking about propositions (which themselves express mental states). Here, Moore and Furrow show how children's understanding of the pragmatics of mental terms such as *think* and *know* is related to their developing theory of mind.

Finally, Shultz (chapter 11) offers a new approach to understanding children's theory of mind through artificial intelligence modelling techniques. He presents programs to model false belief, deception, and strategic game playing. Changes in the level of embedding of intentional descriptions in the production rules of these programs are shown to be capable of simulating developmental changes in children's responses in these domains. Shultz's computationally precise approach allows a careful specification of the capabilities necessary to support a theory of mind. It even begins to give clues to how transitions between less and more sophisticated theories of mind could occur.

ACKNOWLEDGMENTS

The authors thank John Barresi and Phil Dunham for helpful comments on an earlier version of the manuscript.

REFERENCES

Astington, J. W., & Gopnik, A. (1988). Knowing you've changed your mind: Children's understanding of representational change. In J. W. Astington, P. L. Harris, & D. R. Olson (Eds.), *Developing theories of mind* (pp. 193–206). New York: Cambridge University Press.

Astington, J. W., Harris, P. L., & Olson, D. R. (1988). *Developing theories of mind.* New York: Cambridge University Press.

Baron-Cohen, S., Leslie, A. M., & Frith, U. (1985). Does the autistic child have a "theory of mind"? *Cognition, 21,* 37–46.

Baron-Cohen, S., Leslie, A. M., & Frith, U. (1986). Mechanical, behavioral and intentional understanding of picture stories in autistic children. *British Journal of Developmental Psychology, 4,* 113–125.

Beal, C. R. (1987). Repairing the message: Children's monitoring and revision skills. *Child Development, 56,* 631–642.

Beal, C. R. (1988). Children's knowledge about representations of intended meaning. In J. W. Astington, P. L. Harris, & D. R. Olson (Eds.), *Developing theories of mind* (pp. 315–325). New York: Cambridge University Press.

Beal, C. R., & Flavell, J. H. (1984). Development of the ability to distinguish communicative intention and literal message meaning. *Child Development, 55,* 920–928.

Bonitatibus, G. (1988). What is said and what is meant in referential communication. In J. W. Astington, P. L. Harris, & D. R. Olson (Eds.), *Developing theories of mind* (pp. 326–338). New York: Cambridge University Press.

Bretherton, I., McNew, S., & Beeghly-Smith, M. (1981). Early person knowledge as expressed in gestural and verbal communication: When do infants acquire a "theory of mind"? In M. E. Lamb & L. R. Sherrod (Ed.), *Infant social cognition* (pp. 333–373). Hillsdale, NJ: Lawrence Erlbaum Associates.

Byrne, R. W., & Whiten, A. (1986). *Machiavellian intelligence. Social expertise and the evolution of intellect in monkeys, apes, and humans.* New York: Oxford University Press.

Chandler, M. J., Fritz, A. S., & Hala, S. (1989). Small scale deceit: Deception as a marker of 2-, 3-, and 4-year-olds' early theories of mind. *Child Development, 60,* 1263–1277.

Churchland, P. M. (1984). *Matter and consciousness.* Cambridge, MA: Bradford Books/MIT Press.

Colby, A., Kohlberg, L., Gibbs, J., & Lieberman, M. (1983). A longitudinal study of moral development. *Monographs of the Society for Research in Child Development, 48* (1–2, Serial No. 200).

Feldman, C. F. (1988). Early forms of thought about thoughts: Some simple linguistic expressions of mental state. In J. W. Astington, P. L. Harris, & D. R. Olson (Eds.), *Developing theories of mind* (pp. 126–137). New York: Cambridge University Press.

Flavell, J. H. (1970). Developmental studies of mediated memory. In H. W. Reese & L. P. Lipsitt (Eds.), *Advances in child development and behavior* (Vol. 5, pp. 181–211). New York: Academic Press.

Flavell, J. H. (1978). The development of knowledge about visual perception. In C. B. Keasey (Ed.), *Nebraska symposium on motivation* (Vol. 25, pp. 43–76). Lincoln: University of Nebraska Press.

Flavell, J. H. (1988). The development of children's knowledge about the mind: From cognitive connections to mental representations. In J. W. Astington, P. L. Harris, & D. R. Olson (Eds.), *Developing theories of mind* (pp. 244–267). New York: Cambridge University Press.

Flavell, J. H., Everett, B. A., Croft, K., & Flavell, E. R. (1981). Young children's knowledge about visual perception: Further evidence for the Level 1–Level 2 distinction. *Developmental Psychology, 17,* 99–103.

Flavell, J. H., Flavell, E. R., & Green, F. L. (1983). Development of the appearance-reality distinction. *Cognitive Psychology, 15,* 95–120.

Flavell, J. H., Green, F. L., & Flavell, E. R. (1986). Development of knowledge about the appearance-reality distinction. *Monographs of the Society for Research in Child Development, 51* (1, Serial No. 212).

Flavell, J. H., Speer, J. R., Green, F. L., & August, D. L. (1981). The development comprehension monitoring and knowledge about communication. *Monographs of the Society for Research in Child Development, 46,* (5, Serial No.192).

Forguson, L., & Gopnik, A. (1988). The ontogeny of common sense. In J. W. Astington, P. L. Harris, & D. R. Olson (Eds.), *Developing theories of mind* (pp. 226–243). New York: Cambridge University Press.

Gopnik, A., & Astington, J. W. (1988). Children's understanding of representational change and its relation to the understanding of false belief and the appearance-reality distinction. *Child Development, 59,* 26–37.

Gopnik, A., & Graf, P. (1988). Knowing how you know: Young children's ability to identify and remember the sources of their beliefs. *Child Development, 59,* 1366–1371.

Johnson, C. N. (1988). Theory of mind and the structure of conscious experience. In J. W. Astington, P. L. Harris, & D. R. Olson (Eds.), *Developing theories of mind* (pp. 47–63). New York: Cambridge University Press.

Keeney, T. J., Cannizzo, S. R., & Flavell, J. H. (1967). Spontaneous and induced verbal rehearsal in a recall task. *Child Development, 38,* 953–966.

Leslie, A. M. (1987). Pretense and representation: The origins of "theory of mind." *Psychological Review, 94,* 412–426.

Leslie, A. M. (1988). Some implications of pretense for mechanisms underlying the child's theory of mind. In J. W. Astington, P. L. Harris, & D. R. Olson (Eds.), *Developing theories of mind* (pp. 19–46). New York: Cambridge University Press.

Leslie, A. M., & Frith, U. (1988). Autistic children's understanding of seeing, knowing and believing. *British Journal of Developmental Psychology, 6,* 315–324.

Lewis, M., Stanger, C., & Sullivan, M. W. (1989). Deception in 3-year-olds. *Developmental Psychology, 25,* 439–443.

Masangkay, Z. S., McCluskey, K. A., McIntyre, C. W., Sims-Knight, J., Vaughn, B. E., & Flavell, J. H. (1974). The early development of inferences about the visual percepts of others. *Child Development, 45,* 357–366.

Mitchell, R. W. (1986). A framework for discussing deception. In R.W. Mitchell & N.S. Thompson (Eds.), *Deception: Perspectives on human and nonhuman deceit* (pp. 3–40). Albany: State University of New York.

Moely, B. E., Olson, F. A., Halwes, T. G., & Flavell, J. H. (1969). Production deficiency in young children's clustered recall. *Developmental Psychology, 1,* 26–34.

Moore, C., Pure, K., & Furrow, D. (1990). Children's understanding of the modal expression of certainty and uncertainty and its relation to the development of a representational theory of mind. *Child Development, 61,* 722–730.

Olson, D. R. (1988). On the origins of beliefs and other intentional states in children. In J. W. Astington, P. L. Harris, & D. R. Olson (Eds.), *Developing theories of mind* (pp. 414–426). New York: Cambridge University Press.

Perner, J. (1988a). Developing semantics for theories of mind: From propositional attitudes to mental representation. In J.W. Astington, P. L. Harris, & D.R. Olson (Eds.), *Developing theories of mind* (pp. 141–172). New York: Cambridge University Press.

Perner, J. (1988b). Higher-order beliefs and intentions in children's understanding of social interaction. In J. W. Astington, P. L. Harris, & D. R. Olson (Eds.), *Developing theories of mind* (pp. 271–294). New York: Cambridge University Press.

Perner, J., Leekam, S. R., & Wimmer, H. (1987). Three-year-olds' difficulty with false belief: The case for a conceptual deficit. *British Journal of Developmental Psychology, 5,* 125–137.

Perner, J., Frith, U., Leslie, A. M., & Leckam, S. (1989). Exploration of the autistic child's theory of mind: Knowledge, belief, and communication. *Child Development, 60,* 689–700.

Piaget, J. (1926). *The language and thought of the child.* London: Routledge & Kegan Paul.

Piaget, J. (1928). *Judgment and reasoning in the child.* London: Routledge & Kegan Paul.

Piaget, J., & Inhelder, B. (1956). *The child's conception of space.* London: Routledge & Kegan Paul.

Premack, D. & Woodruff, G. (1978). Does the chimpanzee have a theory of mind? *The Behavioral and Brain Sciences, 1,* 515–526.

Robinson, E. J. (1981). The child's understanding of inadequate messages and communication failure: A problem of ignorance or egocentrism? In W. P. Dickson (Ed.), *Children's oral communication skills* (pp. 167–188). New York: Academic Press.

Robinson, E. J., Goelman, H., & Olson, D. R. (1983). Children's understanding of the relation between expressions (what is said) and intentions (what was meant). *British Journal of Developmental Psychology, 1,* 75–86.

Russell, J. (1982). Propositional attitudes. In M. Beveridge (Ed.), *Children thinking through language* (pp. 75–98). London: Arnold.

Russell, J. (1984). The subject-object division in language acquisition and ego development. *New Ideas in Psychology, 2,* 57–74.

Shatz, M., Wellman, H. M., & Silber, S. (1983). The acquisition of mental verbs: A systematic investigation of the first reference to mental state. *Cognition, 14,* 301–321.

Shultz, T. R. & Cloghesy, K. (1981). Development of recursive awareness of intention. *Developmental Psychology, 17,* 456–471.

Sodian, B. (in press). The development of deception in young children. *British Journal of Developmental Psychology.*

Stich, S. P. (1983). *From folk psychology to cognitive science.* Cambridge, MA: Bradford Books/MIT Press.

Taylor, M. (1988). The development of children's understanding of the seeing-knowing distinction. In J. W. Astington, P. L. Harris, & D. R. Olson (Eds.), *Developing theories of mind* (pp.207–225). New York: Cambridge University Press.

Wellman, H. M. (1988). First steps in the child's theorizing about the mind. In J. W. Astington, P. L. Harris, & D. R. Olson (Eds.), *Developing theories of mind* (pp. 64–92). New York: Cambridge University Press.

Wellman, H. M., & Bartsch, K. (1988). Young children's reasoning about beliefs. *Cognition, 30,* 239–277.

Wellman, H. M., & Estes, D. (1986). Early understanding of mental entities: A reexamination of childhood realism. *Child Development, 57,* 910–923.

Wimmer, H., & Perner, J. (1983). Beliefs about beliefs: Representation and constraining function of wrong beliefs in young children's understanding of deception. *Cognition, 13,* 103–128.

Yaniv, I., & Shatz, M. (1988). Children's understanding of perceptibility. In J. W. Astington, P. L. Harris, & D. R. Olson (Eds.), *Developing theories of mind* (pp. 93–109). New York: Cambridge University Press.

Yuill, N. (1984). Young children's coordination of motive and outcome in judgments of satisfaction and morality. *British Journal of Developmental Psychology, 2,* 73–81.

CHAPTER 2

The Origins of Intention in Infancy

Douglas Frye
Yale University

Does there come a time in development when babies do things on purpose? This question has natural application to infancy. It asks, for instance, if babies cry as an automatic consequence of distress or if they cry to gain needed responses from caregivers. Similar questions can be posed about crawling into an unfamiliar room, using language, and removing an obstacle to grasp a toy. Any or all of these accomplishments may signal that infants act intentionally—that is, that they knowingly employ means to goals. If so, then it is important to determine how intention fits into or, better yet, helps explain development in the first years of life.

Intention has the potential not only for contributing to well-known changes in the infant's own abilities but also for bringing about changes in the infant's abilities to understand others. At some level, understanding the behavior of others requires understanding their intentions, what they are trying to do (Premack & Woodruff, 1978). Unless you know what someone is trying to accomplish, you will be at severe disadvantage for understanding their current behavior. For example, how much sense can it make to infants to see someone twist the lid off of a jar unless they understand that the person is trying to get access to the jar's contents? Similarly, how much sense can it make to see one person ask a question of another if the observer does not realize that the one wants information or assistance from the other? Recognizing that others have mental states, such as intention and purpose, has come to be referred to as having a *theory of mind*.

The line of argument I take in this chapter is that children come to act intentionally in infancy as well as begin to form a theory of other people's minds. The two developments are related. Together, they bring about a variety of other changes in the infant's abilities. Two that are considered in detail are how intention and a first theory of mind affect the baby's perception of people and how they influence social development itself. It is argued that recognizing intentions in others allows the child to appreciate the difference between people and other physical objects in the world. Intention and a theory of mind further provide for the advent of social development. When infants recognize that other people have goals, then they will be able to help or hinder them, in other words, cooperate or compete in gaining common human desires.

DEFINING INTENTION

A major stumbling block to the psychological study of intention over the years has been defining exactly what it is. Cazden (1977) made the point more than a decade ago that even perfect reliability among observers about the intentionality of an act does not insure the validity of that judgment. Assigning intention would seem to require something more than just observational data. Knowing what else to count as evidence, however, requires an explicit definition of intention.

One such definition can be adapted from the British philosopher, Anscombe's (1957) formative work on the topic. Anscombe (p. 35) says, roughly, that an act is intentional if it is being done in relation to some future state of affairs and if what is being is done is directed towards bringing about that future state of affairs. Both conditions must be satisfied for the act to be described as intentional. The definition can be restated in somewhat more psychological terms by saying that an act is intentional if it is composed of a goal and a means; both must be present for there to be intention.

A benefit that Anscombe identified for this definition is that it makes it possible to judge the intentionality of people's actions. Most of what adults do most of the time is intentional—but not all of it. Anscombe's definition rules out the possibility of judging the intentionality of an act simply by knowing what was done. The action needs to meet the two conditions of the stated definition. Anscombe even invented a simple guide for determining whether what somebody was doing was intentional. The test consists merely of asking, "Why are you doing X?" or

"Why are you X-ing?". If the person is aware that they are doing X and if they give some plausible account that they are doing X in order to bring about Y, then they are acting intentionally.

Anscombe's analysis has the advantage that it can make various important distinctions among different kinds of behavior. The definition excludes from intention some well-known kinds of behavior that should be excluded. For example, someone may have it in their mind that they would like to read a particular book and, quite independently, be given that book to review. This would not be an intentional act but an *accident* or *coincidence*, because the person was not acting to bring about the goal. Similarly, the person, in a run of remarkable luck, might order another book and be sent a new edition of the first one as a bonus. This occurrence might be call a *fortuitous success*. Here, the person is acting intentionally, but receiving the new edition was not intentional, because what the person did was not directed towards achieving that goal.[1]

Without something on the order of Anscombe's definition, the difference between the preceding sorts of behavior and intention would collapse. The examples make clear the shortcomings of simply judging intention by what might be called the success test. At various times when intention has been imported into psychology, there has been the tendency to say that if people are intentional, then when they succeed at something, they must have been acting intentionally. Accidents and fortuitous successes show that this assumption is not warranted. There can be other explanations for success in some instances.[2] Anscombe's more stringent definition, rather than the success test, allows these other cases to be understood and distinguished from intention. It can also allow other behaviors—for example, reflexes and conditioned responses—to be distinguished from intention as well.

The opposite of the success test, that acts that fail must not be intentional, is similarly flawed. Having a goal and trying to bring it about, but choosing the wrong means to do so, is a *mistake*, but the act still can be counted as intentional. Thus, even if we never observed someone's success at achieving a particular goal, as long as what was

---

[1]A related phenomenon is when someone's intentional act produces a long string of consequences (see Anscombe, 1957, and Shultz, this volume, for examples). Anscombe's definition makes it possible to determine how many of the effects were intentional. If the end of the chain of events was unforeseen or, better yet, unforeseeable, then the person cannot take credit for having brought about the outcome intentionally—assuming that the outcome was beneficial and credit would have been sought.

[2]The point is not new in developmental psychology. Topologically similar or even identical responses can have different explanations at different times. Babies can "walk" soon after birth and at 2 years, but, presumably, the abilities that account for the two acts at the two ages are different.

done was directed towards the goal, then the act was intentional. Failed actions can satisfy Anscombe's test just as easily as successful ones.

Anscombe's test for intention is not infallible. When people are asked why they are doing something, they may reply that they did not realize that they were doing it in order to make the act appear unintentional. Or, when asked about an unintentional act, they might quickly invent a reason so that the act appears purposeful. These tangled cases do not arise from an inadequacy in the definition of intention. Anscombe has discussed a number of them and shown that there are times when we should doubt what the person says. In fact, intention is probably necessary for these cases to occur because intention and a relatively sophisticated theory of mind are likely to be needed for someone to be able to lie (Shultz & Cloghesy, 1981). The implications of this aspect of the theory for psychology are discussed later in this chapter.

STUDYING INTENTION

In her analysis of intention, Anscombe's test is applied to adult actions to pick out those that are intentional from those that are accidents, reflexes, fortuitous occurrences, and so on. Investigating the development of intention poses a somewhat different problem. Here, the issue is not so much which of the child's acts are intentional and which are not as when the child gains the ability to act intentionally. Asking children, "Why did you do X?" at various times in their lives might very well provide a profitable avenue for understanding the development of intention. However, this approach can only be used with children who have acquired language; it has obvious limitations for investigating intention in infancy.

It is possible to devise tests for intention in infancy following Anscombe's definition. Recall that the definition specifies that an act is intentional if it has a goal (a desired state of affairs) and a means (the act is directed towards bringing about the desired state of affairs). Tasks can be designed to search for each of these elements in infant behavior. For example, the presence of a goal can be detected by a *changed consequence* manipulation, in which the baby does something several times and then the consequence of the baby's action is unexpectedly changed. If the child was aware of the outcome of the action because it was a goal, then the unexpected change should produce a surprise reaction.

The changed consequence manipulation alone, however, is not sufficient to assess intention. Essentially, it just establishes expectancy. The baby could expect an outcome to follow an action, perhaps just as certain events are commonly expected to follow others in the world, and the child might even be favorably disposed towards the outcome without the child's action actually being directed towards bringing about the outcome, that is, without there being a means present. Detecting the presence of a means can be done through a *mismatch of means and goal* manipulation. In this maneuver, a favorable outcome is presented to the child after a response that should not have produced that outcome. Now, if the baby is surprised, we know that the child recognizes the relationship between what was done and the outcome that it should have produced.

When this general logic for generating experiments is adopted, it becomes possible to elaborate a variety of different tests for intention. For convenience, the tests can be grouped together depending on whether they apply primarily to goals or to means. No matter which category they fall into, however, all of the manipulations will, in one way or another, test for a relationship between means and goal because in an intentional act there cannot be a means without a goal or vice versa.

Goals

There are a number of manipulations for testing for goals in addition to the changed consequence. A related procedure to the changed consequence is to make a change with the subject's awareness. Dickinson (1988) has argued that this sort of manipulation can help distinguish between conditioning and intention. *Change of goal value* manipulations can be effected in several different ways. The goal itself can be changed, as when animals have learned to make a particular response to obtain food and then the food is made toxic in some way. Alternatively, the animal's desire for the goal can be changed, for example, by teaching the animal to respond for water under normal conditions and then testing them when they are very thirsty. Assuming the proper controls, the animal that is acting intentionally will change its response according to the changed value of the goal.

An even simpler manipulation than the two changed consequence ones is where the consequence itself is not changed, but information about the outcome is. In a *knowledge of the consequence* manipulation, an infant could be shown that an action failed to bring about an outcome or be denied information about the outcome of the action, say, by "accidentally" blocking the child's view. If the child's action was directed towards obtaining the goal, then knowledge of the outcome will be an important determinant of the infant's subsequent behavior. When temporarily denied knowledge of an outcome, the infant ought to repeat the action in order to see whether the expected outcome did or did not occur.[3]

A final manipulation related to goals is that of *multiple consequences*. It is possible to find situations where a single action results in a long string of consequences. Shultz (this volume) cites the example of Gavrilo Princip shooting Archduke Ferdinand, which started World War I. In this example, Princip may have intended to kill the Archduke, but he probably did not intend to start World War I, even though that was the effect of his action. A similar sort of situation might be constructed with infants, where one action leads to a number of different outcomes. If only some of the outcomes were intended, then the infant should only show surprise to the unintended ones. Merely watching the same sequence of causes and effects initiated by someone else should not provoke the same pattern of surprise.

Means

Like the goal manipulations, there are several empirical techniques that can be arranged for testing means. The *mismatch of means and goal* itself admits to two variations. The one originally described assessed the reaction to a means that successfully brought about a goal, even though, under normal circumstances, the means should not have been successful. Another possibility is to establish a situation where a means should, by all rights, bring about a goal but does not. A recently reported animal experiment instituted this sort of manipulation to test an unrelated hypothesis. Hershberger (1986) allowed newly hatched chicks to run in a runway containing a food cup that moved in the same direction as the chicks only twice as fast. To solve this problem, the chicks would have had to walk away from the cup to get the food. The results showed that their behavior seemed to be under the control of a simple positive feedback loop because all of the chicks chased the food cup, which, of course, only served to put it out of reach.

Another, more familiar class of tests for means is that of *discovery of new means*. Piaget (1952) pioneered the use of this method in his work on intention in infancy. The baby is given a problem to see if a means will be found to solve it. An attractive object might be put inside a matchbox so that the child has to discover how to open it, or a toy might be placed

---

[3]A conditioning account, on the other hand, would not expect there to be a difference between the two procedures because both are equivalent to extinction trials.

in reach but blocked by an obstacle. For Piaget, the defining characteristic of intention was that the child be able to change means and eventually invent new ones. Requiring that the infant demonstrate several means to a goal has the advantage that it rules out success by the single reflexes or simple conditioned responses that might coincidentally fit a given situation. Observing how the child produces new responses can reveal if these are random responses that are gradually reinforced or new means that have been selected for their relevance to the situation.

Just as one action can result in a chain of consequences, it often occurs that several means need to be carried out, one after another, before a goal can finally be accomplished. It may be unrealistic to expect infants to be able to concatenate multiple submeans-subgoals in order to reach a main goal. However, Anderson (1983) pointed out that there is good evidence of intention, indeed, of planning, when such a sequence can be found. He identified a case—Sacerdoti's (1977) example of painting a ladder and a ceiling in a limited amount of time—where subgoals must be carried out in a particular order or else they will conflict. Anderson argued that if someone can anticipate the conflict before it occurs, then there is clear evidence for planning.

AN EMPIRICAL TEST OF
INTENTION IN INFANCY

To begin to study the development of intention in infancy, two experiments were conducted using a subset of the goals and means manipulations. In the first study, the infants were shown two changed-consequence procedures and one that mismatched means and goal. The babies in the second study were presented with a different mismatch arrangement as well as versions of the choice and new means procedures. The manipulations were given to children in the laboratory in the form of the support task (Piaget, 1952, 1954; Willats, 1984, 1985). In this task, a toy is placed out of reach on a supporting cloth or some other suitably shaped object that is in reach. The infant must pull on the support in order to reach the toy. Babies reliably solve this task at about 8 months of age. The babies in the present studies were 8, 16, and 24 months old. There were 12 at each age in each of the studies for a total of 72 in all. The infants' responses were videotaped so that their looking, manual responses, and surprise reactions could be measured.

Study I

The apparatus for the first study is shown in Fig. 2.1. The baby sat in front of a flat surface that had a cloth and a small plastic toy (one of the Fisher-Price Little People) on it. The toy could be placed directly on the cloth, or it could be attached to a lucite rod that extended away from the child through a short, 6-inch-high wall at the end of the table. If the toy was put on the rod, it looked from the child's angle to be sitting on the cloth. The cloth was connected to the rod by a light string and a hidden pulley arrangement. The pulley arrangement made it possible to change the effect that pulling the cloth had on the toy.

The infants were all presented with the same sequence of manipulations: the two changed-consequence procedures followed by the mis-

FIG. 2.1. Photograph of the toy and cloth used in Study I. Because the toy was attached to a lucite rod and the cloth to a string, the apparatus could be configured so that pulling the cloth would bring the toy into reach, have it remain standing still, or make it move backwards away from the child.

match of means and goal. In the first changed-consequence sequence, the toy was placed on the cloth, and the child was allowed to retrieve it three times in a row, as in the normal support task. On the fourth trial, the toy was inconspicuously placed on the lucite rod. Now, when the child pulled the cloth to bring the toy within reach, the apparatus made the toy move backwards, directly away from the child. In the next changed consequence, the child was allowed to retrieve the toy again on three successive occasions. On the fourth, it was placed on the lucite rod. Now, however, pulling the cloth had no effect on the toy. The cloth moved, but the toy stayed in the same place. Trials of this type were repeated until the infant stopped responding. Finally, in the mismatch task, the cloth was removed. The apparatus was restructured by running a string from the pulley apparatus, underneath the table, to the table top in front of the child. If the baby pushed the end of the string *towards* the toy (which was on the lucite rod), it caused the toy to come into reach.

Each experimental session was videotaped with two cameras. One showed a view of the child and the entire apparatus. The other only recorded a picture of the baby's face. These two views were combined on a single videotape with a split screen generator. The tapes were later scored for the child's looking patterns and surprise reactions by observers who only saw the picture of the baby's face and did not know which trial they were judging. Surprise was judged as in previous experiments (Ramsay & Campos, 1975) with infants. Reactions were rated on a three-point scale, where 1 denoted normal attention by the infant; 2 stood for mild puzzlement as shown by pausing, slight frowning or a sober expression; and 3 was full puzzlement or surprise as evidenced by widening of the eyes, raised eyebrows, pointing or exclaiming. The observers' ratings were reliable ($r^2 = .88$). Scoring of the infants' manual responses was done from the videotape record.

All of the infants produced manual responses for the full sequence of changed-consequence trials. They pulled the cloth and retrieved the toy on the normal support trials. On the changed-consequence trials themselves, they tried to retrieve the toy by pulling the cloth. All three age groups were significantly more surprised on the first changed-consequence trial, when they toy went backwards, than on the preceding support trial. The two older groups also showed characteristic reactions on the changed- consequence trial. Seven of the 24-month-olds and three of the 16-month-olds began to move the cloth back and forth watching the effect on the toy. When they began to pull on the next support trial, six of the 24-month-olds and four of the 16-month-olds looked to where toy had gone on the previous changed-consequence trial as if they were anticipating it going there again. Lesser, but still significant, surprise reactions were observed on the second changed-consequence trial where pulling the cloth had no effect on the toy. After this trial, the 8-month-olds continued to try to retrieve the toy for significantly more trials than the two other groups. The 8-month-olds pulled for an average of five more trials in this situation, whereas the 16-month-olds stopped after an additional two and a half trials, and the 24-month-olds stopped after less than two. The results of the mismatch-of-means-and-goal manipulation were clear-cut. Only the 24-month-olds solved this task, in that 11 of them managed to move the string forward and retrieve the toy, whereas only one of the 16-month-olds and none of the 8-month-olds did so. The younger groups failed the task, even after the experimenter pointed to the string and moved it slightly in the right direction.

Study II

The procedure in the second study partially resembled the first. It attempted to establish a mismatch-of-means-and-goal manipulation that all of the infants would be able to do. The apparatus was modified as shown in Fig. 2.2. Two lucite rods were installed 12 inches apart. The toy and a cloth could be attached to either of these rods. A new pulley arrangement made it possible for a cloth in either position to control either of the rods. The mismatch of means and goal was accomplished by putting the toy on one of the rods (with the side counterbalanced across subjects) and the cloth underneath the other. If the infant pulled the cloth, the toy came into reach, even though the two were separated by 12 inches. The operation of the apparatus was not changed for the choice task. After the baby had obtained the toy three times in the mismatch situation, another cloth was introduced and placed underneath the toy. The infant then had the choice of pulling the cloth that had previously been effective or pulling the new one that was in the normal spatial arrangement found in the support task. Finally, in the new means task, the toy was moved to the other rod, and the apparatus was surreptitiously changed. Both cloths were still present. In this task, the infant still had to pull the cloth that was on the opposite side to the toy, but now the cloth that worked was the one that had never been effective before.

Unlike Study I, all three age groups made the required response in the mismatch-of-means-and-goal task. There were slight differences in how the children reacted to the task, however. A majority of the 8-month-olds spontaneously pulled the cloth and retrieved the toy. The majority of the 16- and 24-months-olds, on the other hand, did not

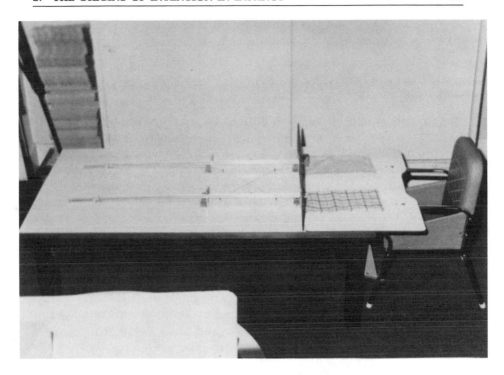

FIG. 2.2 The modified apparatus with the two lucite rods from Study II. The picture shows the two-cloth arrangement where either could be designated to be connected to the toy. The apparatus could also be set up with only one cloth on one side and the toy on the other, so that pulling the cloth would move the toy, even though the two were on different sides of the table.

respond until the experimenter either pointed to the cloth or pulled it slightly. Both the 16-month-olds and 24-month-olds showed significant surprise reactions on the mismatch trial. These were the only surprise reactions shown in the experiment. On the choice-of-means task, when the infants could either pull the spatially disjoint cloth that had previously worked in getting the toy or pull the new cloth that was positioned under the toy, all three age groups pulled the cloth under the toy. In the next three trials, however, 11 of the twelve 24-month-olds returned to pulling the effective cloth, whereas only four of the infants in each of the younger groups did so. A small number of the 24-month-olds showed a characteristic action not exhibited by the other groups. Four of them slowly pulled both cloths, keeping the ineffective one underneath the toy. The new means task tended to differentiate the groups as well. The 8- and 16-month-olds, after the change in the side of the toy and effective cloth, again pulled on the cloth under the toy. In comparison, half of the 24-month-olds managed to switch to the effective cloth on the side away from the toy.

General Discussion

The infants at all three ages (8, 16, and 24 months) were able to pull a cloth in order to bring a toy into reach. The results from the two studies testing this response provide good evidence for intention in the 16- and 24-month-olds and incomplete evidence regarding the 8-month-olds. All three age groups were surprised by the changed-consequence manipulations, whereby the toy went backwards or remained standing still when the cloth was pulled. These reactions show that the infants expected a particular outcome when they pulled the cloth and were surprised when it did not occur. The 16- and 24-month-olds were also surprised by the mismatch of means and goal manipulation in the second study. In this task, pulling the cloth moved a toy that was sitting 12 inches to the side. The surprise reactions of the two older groups showed that they were aware of what means should have brought about the relevant goal, because they were surprised when a means that should *not* have worked nonetheless did. The overall results were less convincing for the 8-month-olds. They were not surprised by the mismatch task. Thus, it may be concluded their actions were not fully intentional. Yet, it is also possible that the support mismatch task did not represent the optimum test of the 8-month-olds. To be valid, a mismatch task must present an incongruous pairing of means and goal, but the 8-month-olds readily pulled the cloth on the first trial. Alternative types of mismatch tasks should probably be tried with this age group.

The other results in the experiment revealed further differences among the groups. A variety of results indicate that the 24-month-olds were the most adept at changing means and adopting new ones. The 8-month-olds continued to respond in the second changed-consequence condition, even though pulling the cloth had no effect on the toy. Neither the 8-month-olds nor 16-month-olds managed to change back to the effective cloth in preference to the ineffective but spatially contiguous one in the choice manipulation. And, in the changed-means task, only the 24-month-olds showed any indication of being able to cope with the switch in the effective cloth. The results of the failed mismatch task in the first study give strong evidence that the 24-month-olds were the only ones to be able to acquire a new, arbitrary means-ends relationship. The 24-month-olds solved the rather bizarre task in which a string had to be moved towards a toy to bring it into reach, whereas virtually none of the younger children were able to do so. In sum, it appears that the 24-month-olds were the only ones who understood how a means should work but were also able to learn a new means if necessary. The four 24-month-olds who pulled both cloths in unison in the choice task furnish the most striking illustration of this phenomenon.

THE DEVELOPMENT OF
INTENTION IN INFANCY

Described in psychological terms, the minimum requirement for acting intentionally is being able to place two actions in sequence, with the first performed in order to do the second. Of course, intention can take very much more complicated forms. It can consist of a long list of actions that must be carried out, step by step, in order to accomplish some remote and obscure goal. Complex planning is probably beyond infants, however. The experiments just described were designed to test for the simplest forms of intention. They sought evidence for infants carrying out one action in order to do another by seeing if a particular outcome was expected from doing something and if the infants understood that doing the first action should make it possible to do the second.

Intention in Later Infancy

The 16- and 24-month-olds' performance met the requirements for intention. Their surprise reactions revealed that they were putting two behaviors in sequence and were aware that doing the first should make it possible to do the second. The developmental changes that were evident in the older infants' abilities were much as Piaget (1952) described. The 16-months-olds, to some extent, and the 24-months-olds, without question, adjusted the means they employed to changes in the situation. Both groups stopped responding when pulling the cloth had no effect. The 24-month-olds were also able to switch back to the effective cloth in the choice situation. Piaget characterized this development as the infant's schemes becoming more *flexible*. The flexibility of the schemes placed in means-end relations is crucial because it is the ability to form these combinations that makes intention possible. When the combinations can be broken up quickly and new ones attempted, the infant will have the chance of pursuing a goal successfully in the face of changes in the environment.

The 24-month-olds seemed to be able to do more than just change means. They were able to adopt new means. In the too ambitious mismatch manipulation in the first study, the 24-month-olds were the only ones who realized that pushing the string forward would bring the toy into reach. They were also the only ones who could cope with all of the switches imposed in the second study. The four 24-month-olds who simultaneously pulled the two cloths in the choice situation seemed to reveal that they could discover a means that worked and also knew the one that should work. These results agree with others that have been obtained with this age group. For example, Koslowski and Bruner (1972) found that it was not until 24 months that infants could push a lever away on a rotating table to bring a toy from the far side into reach. Here, again, the results demonstrate 2-year-olds satisfying a goal by what, at first, must have seemed to be a very unlikely means.

The ability of 2-year-olds to adopt these arbitrary means is rather remarkable. Piaget emphasized that 2-year-olds were adept at discovering new means. Certainly, it seems that they are primed to find a means whenever possible. It may be that intention is so well established at this point that babies can be easily convinced that there should be a means that will work and thus are willing to search for it. Their ability to handle arbitrary means also predicts that they should be able to cope with means that can be nothing but arbitrary. Thus, as has been found (Bates, 1979), infants at this age should have no trouble using a symbol or a word to accomplish a goal, even though the symbol may be entirely conventional and will have nothing but an arbitrary connection with its effect.

Intention at 8 Months

The experimental results for the 8-month-olds were ambiguous. The infants in this youngest group were only surprised when the outcome of their action was unexpectedly changed. They did not seem to show surprise when something they did (pulling the cloth) brought about an outcome that it normally would not (moving a spatially distant toy). These results are consistent with others for this age. Object-hiding tasks are normally considered to be tests of object permanence but can as easily be seen as tests of intention. The infant has the goal of grasping the object and must use the means of removing the cover to do so. A variety of object permanence studies (Appel & Gratch, 1984; LeCompte & Gratch, 1972) have demonstrated that, at about this age, infants react when the outcome of their actions is unexpectedly changed in object-hiding situations. They are puzzled when the toy they are searching for has been secretly removed or if a different one has been surreptitiously put in its place.

Object permanence studies establishing 8-month-olds' sensitivity to the means necessary for retrieving hidden toys do not seem to have been carried out. It might be instructive to conduct a mismatch-of-means-and-goal experiment in the context of object hiding. In this case, something the infant does, for example, waving a hand or touching the table, would have the effect of uncovering the toy. If 8-month-olds were surprised by the mismatch, even though they were not in the gimmicked support task, then there would be more evidence for intention. There is already a modicum of object permanence evidence indicating that, at first, infants are not terribly sensitive to the means that they employ in hiding tasks. The well-known AB error (see Wellman, Cross, & Bartsch, 1987, for a recent review) illustrates that 8-month-olds continue to use the simple means of lifting the cover of the first hiding place, even when it is no longer appropriate because the toy has been moved. A directly comparable result was discovered in the second changed-consequence manipulation when the 8-month-olds repeatedly pulled a cloth even though it stopped having an effect on the toy. Both show the infants' tendency at this age to perseverate in using means that are no longer effective.

Given that the 8-month-olds were not surprised by the mismatch manipulation, it might be argued that their behavior could be better described as an instance of operant conditioning rather than intention. An instrumental conditioning explanation of the support task would specify that infants solve this task because they happened to have made a response that was followed by the pleasant circumstance of the toy coming into reach. This analysis would seem to fit the mismatch and second changed-consequence results. Presumably, the 8-month-olds pulled the cloth even when the toy was displaced because the situation is sufficiently like ones in which that behavior had previously been reinforced. The preservative responding after the cloth stopped working would simply be an example of a longer than usual decline in responding with extinction.

There are a number of features of the results that weigh against this explanation. The most obvious is that the changed-consequence manipulations showed that the 8-month-olds had specific expectations for the outcome of their response. They did not merely show less of a tendency to respond because they had not gotten what they wanted. Operant conditioning only specifies that the reinforcing value of the outcome is important, not any more detailed evaluation of the goal. It is also of interest that the 8-month-olds in the choice situation changed and maintained their responding on the new, ineffective cloth. Because responding on the other cloth was being reinforced by its effect on the toy, it seems that there would be little reason to switch and even less reason to continue to respond on the new cloth, unless the infant thought that it was the one that should work. It is also relevant that infants have not been characterized as acquiring responses in the support and object permanence tasks in the trial and error fashion that conditioning dictates. They tend to shift rather abruptly from not being able to do these types of tasks to solving them (e.g., Diamond, 1985).

Before 8 Months

Selecting the support task to deliver the manipulations in the present experiments made it impossible to test for intention before 8 months because the task is not solved earlier. Of course, Piaget's theory would not find this constraint an accident. It holds that the initial signs of intention appear at about 8 months and that these are what make it possible for the infant to master the support task in the first place. The mixed results for the 8-month-olds in the current studies do not, themselves, give much indication that intention might be present earlier; however, there have been reports of intention at younger ages that should be considered.

The strongest case for early intention comes in neonatal reaching. It is difficult for adults to imagine that reaching could be anything but intentional. Bower, Broughton, and Moore (1970) contended many years ago that infants must be intentional from birth because their early reaching was intentional. Butterworth and Hopkins (1988) have recently re-introduced this argument on the basis of new experimental work. In both cases, the first line of evidence put forward for early reaching is that it is accurate. Bower found that 4- and 5-week-olds could accurately reach for objects. Butterworth discovered that infants at about the same age will accurately place their fingers in their mouths. There is further evidence that the babies might expect the outcome of their action. Bower found that neonates were surprised if the object they reached for was only a "virtual" object formed by a holographic projection. In Butterworth's experiment, the infants were observed to open their mouths *before* their hand arrived.

Unfortunately, subsequent research (Field, 1977) has failed to find that very young infants are surprised when their hands pass through a virtual object. If this aspect of Bower's experiment had been confirmed, then the results for the neonates would have been very much like those for the 8-month-olds. They would have shown that the young baby has specific expectations for the outcome of certain actions. As it stands, the evidence for intention seems to be primarily that the infant has carried out an action accurately (but see also Ruff & Halton, 1978). It has already been argued, however, that success is not sufficient for ascribing intention. It is possible that the young infants' reaches to objects or their mouths are reflexes or early conditioned responses. Neonates reach to two-dimensional pictures as often as to objects (Rader & Stern, 1982). Plooij and Rijt-Plooij (1989) reported that, early on, even blind infants engage in hand regard—slow waving of the hands in front of the face in order to "watch" them. Without more evidence than accuracy, there do not seem to be sufficient grounds to force an explanation of early reaching in terms of intention.

Summary

When the criterion for intention is adopted that a specific outcome of an action must be expected and the action must be directed towards bringing about that outcome, it is difficult to find evidence for the development of intention before 8 months. At 8 months, there is partial evidence for intention. Babies of this age do seem to have expectations for the outcome of actions. It is less clear that they are well aware of the particular means that bring about goals, although perhaps a task giving a more dramatic mismatch between means and goals than has currently been tried would show an effect. There appear to be important developmental changes in intention after 8 months. Both 16- and 24-month-olds give strong signs of having both means and goals. In addition, the 24-month-olds seem to be able to switch between means quickly and acquire new ones, even when the means-goal relations involved are unusual or arbitrary.

SOCIAL VERSUS COGNITIVE DEVELOPMENT AND THE INFANT'S THEORY OF MIND

It would be reasonable to expect that there would be important effects on other aspects of development if babies gained the ability to act intentionally during the course of infancy. I have argued elsewhere (Frye, 1989) that social and cognitive development begin to be differentiated at about 8 months. Their separation is likely the consequence of the change in intention at the same time.

Social and Cognitive Development

A prerequisite for there being a distinction between social and cognitive development is that infants must know the difference between people and objects, given that social development depends on the one and cognitive development on the other. Frye, Rawling, Moore, and Myers (1983) found that 10-month-olds produced differential behavior to people and objects, but 3-month-olds did not. In the first half-year of life, babies tend to show the same "social" responses—smiling, looking, vocalizing, and reaching—to people and objects alike. These responses are sensitive to different kinds of stimulus control—perceptual configuration, familiarity, amount of movement, and contingency—at different points in development. The stimulus factors typically favor people rather than objects, but the reverse can occur (see, e.g., Field, 1979). When the known stimulus factors are controlled for, as in the preceding experiment, early differences disappear. Babies do not appear to show qualitatively different responses to people and objects in the first months of life. Such responses would seem essential for social development.

It may be intention that permits the differentiation of social and cognitive development. When babies begin to act intentionally at 8 months or later, it is likely that they are able to act intentionally towards both people and objects. However, the means that they apply and the goals that they pursue will become different. For example, if infants want to move a person and an object from one place to another, they could push each of them, but it must soon become apparent that with the person it is more effective to try a gesture, a word, or eye contact. By this explanation, then, the infant's capacity for intention does not initially differ in social and cognitive domains, but social and cognitive development begin to diverge because the infant forms different classes of means and ends for each. The most striking example of this separation is early language development, where infants quickly learn to use gestures and words intentionally to affect the behavior of other people. Another example is attachment, which can be interpreted as the infant's intentional use of a variety of means to maintain proximity with a valued caregiver (Frye, 1981). Both of these phenomena occur only with people, so they are examples of qualitatively different responses being shown to people and objects, and both appear after 8 months.

The infant's differentiation of people and objects is suggestive of Strawson's (1958) definition of persons. Strawson showed that the concept of a person requires that both mental and physical predicates be applied to people, whereas only physical attributes can be applied to objects. Of course, babies will be unable to apply predicates to anything for some time. However, they do appear to apply two classes of means to people—roughly, mental and physical—whereas they only apply physical means to objects. Mental, in this case, refers to means that must be understood by another to be effective. This division suggests that infants may make people a special class of entities in the world because they successfully begin to apply a unique class of means to them. People become people for the infant because intention makes it possible for the infant to employ means, including gestures and words, that can only be effective with people and not with objects, thus opening the social world.

Theory of Mind

The natural question that follows is whether the infant's differentiation of people and objects, the social and physical, exists only in the infant's own actions or if the baby also recognizes that other people have mental states—intentions, at least—and objects do not. The question can be put in simpler form: Does the baby have a theory of mind?

When infants begin to act intentionally, they at least gain the chance of recognizing the same intentions in others. Take, for example, the infant pointing to something to draw someone's attention to it. The infant's act is intentional, with a means and goal. Now, when the infant sees someone else point, the infant may be able to recognize that the person is pointing and not just extending an arm. Without intention or familiarity with pointing as a means, however, it is hard to imagine that the baby would be able to identify the other person's arm extension as a means (or as meaningful) and search around for its goal.[4] Without means and ends, the infant should merely see the other's movements, and never consider why they are being done. Seeing intention in other people's acts relies on infants developing means and ends in their own acts.

The proposed explanation that infants begin to recognize means and goals in others from their own means and goals carries a number of implications. The problem of why the infant recognizes mental states in people and not objects does not arise because similarities in actions will

---

[4] It might be argued that infants learn of the intentionality of others merely through observing sequences of events. They see someone point, see what follows, and conclude that the pointing must have been aimed at the successive event. There are many difficulties with this account, including how the infant picks out the correct events from all of the ones that are almost certainly occurring simultaneously. The explanation also will not suffice for perceiving the intentionality of failed actions. When infants see someone try to do something and fail, how could they possibly recognize it as an attempt to bring something about, when the outcome does not follow the act?

only occur between the baby and other people. The explanation also implies that the infant's initial detection of mental states in others will be limited because the infant's own intentional repertoire is far from complete. Certainly, babies will not acquire more than the precursors of a theory of mind. They will be able to employ specific means and goals, and recognize them in the actions of others, but it is unlikely that they will be able to think explicitly about their own or others' mental states. In other words, infants will be able to reason using means and ends without yet being able to reason about them.

Some experimental work relevant to the infant's ascription of mental states to others can be found. Golinkoff and Harding (1980) examined whether infants expected people and not objects to be animate, which, in this case, meant being capable of independent movement. A majority of 24-month-olds and a sizeable minority of 16-month-olds were surprised when they saw a chair (appear to be) moving itself across the laboratory. To test the specific question of whether infants ascribe intention to other people, it would be instructive to conduct an experiment similar to Premack and Woodruff's (1978) with chimpanzees. Babies would be shown a portion of the behavior of another person. They could then choose among several outcomes. If they chose a goal for the behavior, they would be giving it an intentional explanation. Social referencing may be a natural example of this same effect. By a year, infants will either cross or avoid a visual cliff depending on whether their caregiver adopts a facial expression of encouragement or warning (Sorce, Emde, Campos, & Klinnert, 1985). Here, the infant's own action shows a sensitivity to the other's intention.

Social Interaction

Recognizing the intentions of others will open entirely new social developments to the infant. If the baby can act intentionally and begin to be aware of the intentions of others, then it becomes possible for the child to adjust his or her intentions to the other. An unexpected example of a development of this type materialized in the experiments reported previously. In a later phase of the experiments, the infants were meant to touch a button in order to make an effect occur. To get the babies to touch the button, the experimenter and then, if necessary, the baby's mother tried to take the baby's finger and place it on the button. This technique was only effective with three of the 8-month-olds, whereas it worked with 10 and 11 of the 16- and 24-month-olds, respectively. The 8-month-olds did not seem to realize that there was anything more to the situation than their finger being grasped. Consequently, they either did not relax their arms or they pulled away. The older groups, in contrast, appeared to understand that the adults had some further purpose in taking their finger. They allowed their hand to be moved, usually paying close attention to what would happen next.

Meaningful social interaction begins when infants can adjust their intentions to those of others. Intention makes possible the two basic forms of social interaction: cooperation and competition. For cooperation, the infant must be able to pursue a shared goal with another. Competition also involves a particular goal, but achievement of it by one of the participants will interfere with achievement of it by another. There are abundant examples of both in later infancy. Competition can be found in the struggles of two infants for the same toy, as seems to happen when there are few toys available and the infants are in their second year (Hay & Ross, 1982). In these encounters, the babies have the same goal (playing with the toy) so the competition is straightforward. Later, the child may want the toy precisely *because* the other child wants it, so the first child will take it to upset the other (see Dunn, this volume, for examples). Cooperation is also evident in infancy. When babies enter into conversations, they are participating in a form of cooperation. Towards the end of the second year, babies are even able to engage in coordinated play where they will, for example, take turns putting down blocks to build a tower (Eckerman & Didow, 1989; Mueller & Vandell, 1979). This type of advance requires the infants to share a goal and adjust their actions to the other's to bring the goal about.

Intention promises new explanations of social interaction and social development in infancy. It is apparent that for infants to be active participants in a social interaction, they must be able to bring about intended effects in the behavior of others, whether those effects are maintaining proximity with valued caregivers, producing emotional reactions in peers, or gaining the cooperation of adults in accomplishing a goal. With the next step, when the baby recognizes and begins to take into account the intentions of others, the ground is prepared for the meeting of intentions in cooperation or competition. A new analysis of social interaction and social development in the second year would examine the formation of the class of means and ends that babies apply only to people. Then it would assess the exchanges infants have with adults and other babies in order to determine how the intentions of these different actors come to be engaged and adjusted to each other.

THE IMPLICATIONS OF INFANT INTENTION
FOR PSYCHOLOGICAL THEORY

Opening the door to intention has very clear consequences for the kinds of explanations that are warranted in psychology. To say that infants act intentionally is to say that their behavior is, in large measure, under their own control. What they will do at any given point cannot necessarily be deduced from the stimulus conditions and their history. Intention, like language, is creative. It permits the child to show other than already established responses. Even so, it may be possible for a psychological theory to say what children are *likely* to do in a given situation or to build up probabilistic laws for behavior (see Macnamara, Govitrikar, & Doan, 1988, for a similar argument). Taken from the other side, intention for the first time invites rational explanations of behavior. It should be possible to specify what people *ought* to do if their goals are known. What is given up when intention is granted, however, is any possibility of absolute "prediction and control" of behavior. Probably the most that the psychologist will be able to strive for is "understanding and perhaps influencing" the behavior of others.

Developmental psychology is in a position to make a further contribution to psychological explanation in these circumstances. The infant's capacity for intention appears to change. It is developmental psychology's task to determine what means and goals children can have at different points in development, how adept they are at combining the two, if they are able to perform several means in sequence to reach a goal, if they are capable of higher order intentions, and so on. Having the answers to these questions will not restore the possibility of perfectly reliable predictions of behavior. But the answers will outline the infant's capabilities—the lower and upper limits—of intention at important points in development. Our theories may not be able to say what the infant will do at any particular time, but they ought to be able to explain what the infant is capable of doing.

CONCLUSIONS

I have argued that the empirical study of intention is possible through a variety of procedures that test if acts serve as means and goals. When these procedures were applied to infancy, the experimental results and related literature indicated that the ability to do one thing in order to do something else appears towards the end of the first year and is well established in the second. When infants begin to act intentionally, they have the chance of recognizing specific means and ends in the acts of others. Detecting intention in what others do permits the child to place people in a special category relative to other objects in the world. Social development becomes possible when infants are aware of the intentions of others and can act with their own intentions towards them.

ACKNOWLEDGMENTS

The studies reported in this chapter were supported by a 1982-83 grant from the Social Science Research Council of Great Britain. Grateful acknowledgment is made to Jane Taylor for her contributions to the research and to Chris Moore for his comments on the manuscript.

REFERENCES

Anderson, J. R. (1983). *The architecture of cognition.* Cambridge: Harvard University Press.

Anscombe, G. E. M. (1957). *Intention.* London: Blackwell.

Appel, K., & Gratch, G. (1984). Will infants search when "no toy" is hidden? A study of implicit assumptions about the development of object permanence. *British Journal of Developmental Psychology, 2,* 179–188.

Bates, E. (1979). *The emergence of symbols: Cognition and communication in infancy.* New York: Academic Press.

Bower, T., Broughton, J., & Moore, M. (1970). Demonstration of intention in the reaching behavior of neonate humans. *Science, 228,* 679–680.

Butterworth, G., & Hopkins, B. (1988). Hand-mouth coordination in the new-born baby. *British Journal of Developmental Psychology, 6,* 303–314.

Cazden, C. (1977). The question of intent. In M. Lewis & L. Rosenblum (Eds.), *Interaction, conversation and the development of language* (pp. 309–314). New York: Wiley.

Diamond, A. (1985). Development of the ability to use recall to guide action, as indicated by infants' performance on AB. *Child Development, 56,* 868–883.

Dickinson, A. (1988). Intentionality in animal conditioning. In L. Weiskrantz (Ed.), *Thought without language* (pp. 305–325). Oxford: Clarendon Press.

Eckerman, C., & Didow, S. (1989). Toddlers' social coordinations: Changing responses to another's invitation to play. *Developmental Psychology, 25,* 794–804.

Field, J. (1977). Coordination of vision and prehension in young infants. *Child Development, 48,* 97–103.

Field, T. (1979). Visual and cardiac responses to animate and inanimate faces by young term and preterm infants. *Child Development, 50,* 188–194.

Frye, D. (1981). Developmental changes in strategies of social interaction. In M. Lamb & L. Sherrod (Eds.), *Infant social cognition* (pp. 315–331). Hillsdale, NJ: Lawrence Erlbaum Associates.

Frye, D. (1989). Social and cognitive development in infancy. *European Journal of Psychology of Education, 4,* 129–140.

Frye, D., Rawling, P., Moore, C., & Myers, I. (1983). Object-person discrimination and communication at 3 and 10 months. *Developmental Psychology, 19,* 303–309.

Golinkoff, R., & Harding, C. (1980, April). *Infants' expectations for the movement potential of inanimate objects.* Paper presented at the International Conference on Infant Studies, New Haven, CT.

Hay, D. F., & Ross, H. (1982). The social nature of early conflict. *Child Development, 53,* 105–113.

Hershberger, W. (1986). An approach through the looking-glass. *Animal Learning and Behavior, 14,* 443–451.

Koslowski, B., & Bruner, J. (1972). Learning to use a lever. *Child Development, 43,* 790–799.

LeCompte, G., & Gratch, G. (1972). Violation of a rules as a method of diagnosing infants' level of object concept. *Child Development, 43,* 385–396.

Macnamara, J., Govitrikar, V., & Doan, B. (1988). Actions, laws and scientific psychology. *Cognition, 29,* 1–27.

Mueller, E., & Vandell, D. (1979). Infant-infant interaction: An empirical and conceptual review. In J. Osofsky (Ed.), *Handbook of infant development* (pp. 591–622). New York: Wiley.

Piaget, J. (1952). *The origins of intelligence in children.* New York: International Universities Press.

Piaget, J. (1954). *The construction of reality in the child.* New York: Basic Books.

Plooij, F., & Rijt-Plooij, H. (1989). Evolution of human parenting: Canalization, new types of learning, and mother-infant conflict. *European Journal of Psychology of Education, 4,* 177–192.

Premack, D., & Woodruff, G. (1978). Does the chimpanzee have a theory of mind? *The Brain and Behavioral Sciences, 4,* 515–526.

Rader, N., & Stern, J. (1982). Visually elicited reaching in neonates. *Child Development, 53,* 1004–1007.

Ramsay, D., & Campos, J. (1975). Memory by the infant in an object notion task. *Developmental Psychology, 11,* 411–412.

Ruff, H., & Halton, A. (1978). Is there directed reaching in the human neonate? *Developmental Psychology, 14,* 425–426.

Sacerdoti, E. (1977). *A structure for plans and behavior.* New York: Elsevier North-Holland.

Shultz, T., & Cloghesy, K. (1981). Development of recursive awareness of intention. *Developmental Psychology, 17,* 456–471.

Sorce, J., Emde, R., Campos, J., & Klinnert, M. (1985). Maternal emotional signaling: Its effect on the visual cliff behavior of 1-year-olds. *Developmental Psychology, 21,* 195–200.

Strawson, P. (1958). Persons. In H. Feigel, M. Scriven, & G. Maxwell (Eds.), *Minnesota studies in the philosophy of science* (Vol 2, pp. 330–353). Minneapolis: University of Minnesota Press.

Wellman, H., Cross, D., & Bartsch, K. (1987). Infant search and object permanence: A meta-analysis of the A-not-B error. *Monographs of the Society for Research in Child Development, 51* (3, Serial No. 214).

Willats, P. (1984). The Stage-IV infant's solution of problems requiring the use of supports. *Infant Behavior and Development, 7,* 125–134.

Willats, P. (1985). Adjustment of means-ends coordination and the representation of spatial relations in the production of search errors by infants. *British Journal of Developmental Psychology, 3,* 259–272.

CHAPTER 3
The Infant's Theory of
Self-Propelled Objects*

David Premack
CREA Ecole Polytechnique

What are the origins of the child's "theory of mind" (Premack & Woodruff 1978)? In this chapter, I attempt to answer this question by tracing the origins back to the perception of the infant. This is the main hypothesis: The perception of intention, like that of causality, is a hard-wired perception based not on repeated experience but on appropriate stimulation. In the case of causality, thanks largely to Michotte (1963), we can specify the stimulation: Basically, it is temporal and spatial contiguity between appropriate events. What is the analogous stimulation in the case of intention?

Picture the infant as dividing the world into two kinds of objects: those that are self-propelled and those that are not. Self-propelled objects can both move and stop moving without assistance from another object; nonself-propelled objects cannot. The nonself-propelled object can have as its initial state either rest or motion, but in either case it will retain this state unless acted upon by another object.

Induced movements in nonself-propelled objects are what the infant perceives as causal (not all movements, of course, but those that carry out Michotte's temporal and spatial contiguity). On the other hand, it is the movement of self-propelled objects that, I suggest, the infant

*A slightly modified version of this chapter appeared in *Cognition* (1990) 36, 1–16. Reprinted with permission.

perceives as intentional. This, then, is my first argument: Just as causality is the infant's principal hard-wired perception for nonself-propelled objects, so intention is its principal hard-wired perception for self-propelled objects.

Here is a more complete statement of the argument: First, the infant perceives certain properties, for example, one object is moved by the other under conditions of temporal and spatial contiguity, versus the object is self-propelled; second, the infant not only perceives but also interprets, that is, the infant's perception is the input to a slightly higher order device that has interpretation as its output. The interpretations in the two cases in question are causality and intention, respectively.

DIGRESSION: INTERPRETATION

The question of interpretation raises some interesting issues, which I treat more fully elsewhere (Premack, in preparation) and, thus, only mention here. Here are two such issues:

1. We must suppose that only a small proportion of perceived distinctions are simply perceived; they are not perceived and interpreted. The distinction between perceived versus perceived + interpreted is the formal version of the casual distinction we make when speaking of what does and does not "interest" an individual. A study by Roberta Golinkoff (1975) illustrated this point. She habituated infants to a scene in which Mary gave Jane an apple. Then, for half the infants, she reversed the donorship (Jane now gave Mary the apple), whereas for the other half, she changed not donorship but the left/right location of Mary and Jane. The change in donorship produced significantly greater dishabituation than the change in location. I take this to suggest that, whereas location is only perceived, donorship is both perceived and interpreted.

2. Consider the implications of interpretation for species differences. Species that do not differ at all in the distinctions that they can perceive may, nonetheless, differ substantially in those that they interpret. Consider the set of all interpretations in this world. Humans probably enjoy (or suffer from) a larger proportion of this total than any other species; we engage in far more interpretation than other species. But how are the interpretations distributed over other species? Two main alternatives can be depicted by Venn diagrams, using concentric and nonconcentric circles. With concentric circles, every species' interpretations are a subset of another "more interpretive" species, and only the

human or "highest" species has unique interpretations. For example, the ape's interpretations are a subset of the human's, the monkey's a subset of the ape's, and so forth. Alternatively, in the case of nonconcentric circles, the interpretations of different species may not overlap at all or overlap only in part; species have unique interpretations. Indeed (horror of horrors), they could even assign the same interpretations to different perceptual distinctions, and/or vice versa. Obviously, we would have a great deal of difficulty unraveling a mess of this kind. The digression has taken a depressing turn; let's close it and return to our main business.

BDR AND THE PERCEPTION OF
SOCIAL GOALS

Now, suppose we show the infant not one but two self-propelled objects and, in addition, arrange a special relation between the two objects. Specifically, we arrange a BDR sequence, where B stands for base, D for deflection from base, and R for recovery to base. The movements constituting B, D, and R can take innumerable forms, and we have only begun to look at their possible composition rules (there is more about this in a later section). At this point, consider an example instead. Two balls, one larger than the other, appear on the screen and bounce together for, say, 5 seconds; that constitutes base. Next one of the balls gets "stuck" in a virtual hole, that is, stops moving and remains immobile; that is deflection from base. Finally, the other ball "frees" the stuck one, that is, contacts the immobile ball, after which it resumes moving; that is return to base.

My second argument is this: Although the self-propelled object alone leads to the perception of intentional movement, adding the BDR relation leads to a further perception. Specifically, the infant perceives one object as having a goal—that of affecting the other object.

To demonstrate this second argument, Dasser, Ulbaek, and Premack (1989) used habituation/dishabituation in conjunction with a role-reversal paradigm. Our subjects in this experiment were not infants but young children, 3.5 to 5.5 years of age. To demonstrate that BDR leads to the perception of a social goal—that one object intends to affect the other object—we compared the effect of the would-be critical BDR with the reverse, RDB. We divided the children into two groups, and, after habituating one of them to BDR and the other to RDB, carried out a role reversal. The ball that had been the instigator of the action, that is, "rescued" the "stuck" ball, became the recipient, and vice versa. We then showed BDR with role reversal to one group and RDB with role reversal to the other. Role reversal should have a strong effect in the case of BDR and a weak effect in the case of RDB. If one perceives the interaction between the two objects as intentional, then role reversal is important and should lead to considerable recovery from habituation. But if one does not perceive the interaction as intentional, then role reversal is unimportant and should have little effect. As we predicted, role reversal produced significant dishabituation in the case of BDR but not in the case of RDB.

Actually, the results were somewhat more complex. With young children, 3.5 years and less, the results were exactly as described. However, with older children, role reversal produced significant dishabituation with both BDR and RDB. Fortunately, we had obtained similar results some years earlier in a study concerned with the effect of violating the sequence in picture stories. Whereas presenting the pictures out of order to older children had no effect, it had a profound effect on younger ones. When asked to describe the individual pictures, younger children now said things like, "He's here" and "He's over here," rather than, "He's over here because he's afraid," omitting specific reference to the intentional component (Poulsen, Kintsch, Kintsch, & Premack, 1979). We argued that older children already knew the story schemata; therefore, they needed only the elements, being capable of putting them into order themselves. But younger children did not know the schemata; hence, they needed not only the elements but also the properly ordered elements. We now make for the BDR sequence the same argument that we made earlier for the picture story.

BDR AND RECIPROCATION

The perception of first-order social intention—that one object has as its goal affecting the other object—is not the only consequence of the BDR sequence. Indeed, it is the weaker of the two major consequences. In addition to perceiving that one object intends to reciprocate, the infant also perceives that the affected object intends to reciprocate. Specifically, BDR leads the infant to expect that the initial recipient of the action will "reply," acting upon the instigator in a manner that preserves the valence (and possibly magnitude) of the act that was directed at it. That is my third argument.

RECIPROCATION: PRESERVATION OF VALENCE

One could simplify the infant's theory while still granting the infant the perception of intention to reciprocate. One could say the infant expects the initial recipient to reciprocate, applying to the instigator exactly the same act that was applied to it. In other words, a kiss for a kiss, a blow for a blow. But that theory will prove too simple, I think. It will not only underestimate the infant's computational capacity but also miss the heart of reciprocation, which devolves, I think, not around form but around valence.

The infant must be credited, in my opinion, with the ability to perceive and code valence, thus the ability to code some movements as positive and others as negative. (Whether it can also code intensity is a secondary issue that we can leave open here). The theory I grant the infant is this: The infant can code valence and expects reciprocation to preserve valence, not form. A recipient may, in the infant's expectations, apply the very same act that was applied to it; but if it does so, that would be an accident, rather than an essential feature of reciprocation, and would not make the act a more genuine case of reciprocation than one in which the act was totally different.

In claiming that the infant expects reciprocation to preserve valence, and thus that it can code acts as either positive or negative, I do not assume that infants can code all conceivable acts—all those that an adult might code. There is, I assume, a set of canonical acts that the infant can code, and its ability to do so is not dependent on learning.

POSITIVE VALENCE AS THE MAINTENANCE OF LIBERTY

Broadly speaking, "canonical" can be understood in these terms: The infant will code as positive movements of the one object that maintain, restore, or increase the "liberty" of the other object; even as it will code as negative movements of the one object that impair the liberty of the other object. It is more than coincidence, I suggest, that Rawls (1970), in discussing his theory of justice, made liberty his first criterion.

Let us flesh out what is meant by "liberty," using as characters the "balls" that were used in the experiment described earlier. Incidentally, the reader (I'm confident) has already recognized a main characteristic of the infant's theory. It is not a theory of domain-specific features, for example, a theory that cats have intentions but boxes do not. Infants may have domain-specific theories, for example, that only fractals are self-propelled, whereas nonfractals are always nonself-propelled. But if they do, their domain-specific theories are not a part of the present discussion. The only assumption I make here that is even remotely related to domain-specificity is that the infant can perceive objects. Because, in effect, I treat object as a primitive, I have nothing further to say about it (see, e.g., Spelke, 1982, for discussion of infant's perception of object).

Here are some examples of movements that impair liberty in one case and aid it in another. Suppose one object repeatedly deflected the other object from its course of action—that is stopped it when it was moving, induced it to move after it had stopped, changed the direction and/or speed of its motion. The infant will code this action as negative. Conversely, picture an object that was repeatedly deflected from its course of action and another object that just as repeatedly restored the deflected object to its previous course of action. The infant will code the action as positive. In brief, the infant will code as positive those acts that restore an object to its course of action and as negative those acts that deflect it from its course of action. When human adults were shown these cases, they tended to spontaneously label them, using such phrases as "helping," or "trying to help" in the one case, "hurting," or "trying to hurt" in the other (Dasser et al., 1989).

Infants will probably prefer to observe actions they code as positive to those they code as negative. More interesting is the possibility that they will have preferences even for the movement of single objects. Indeed, it seems almost certain that they will, given the premium they place on liberty. In brief, the infant may prefer the object in which it can discern the highest exercise of liberty. Notice that, in order to decide whether a second object is interfering with a first object, one must have some idea of the intended course of action of the first object. What would this object do if left alone? When a second object causes a first one to stop, this could be interference, or, if this is what the first object was about to do, a form of assistance.

If one cannot predict an object's course of action, one cannot compute either facilitations or infringements on its liberty, therefore, infants may prefer objects whose course of action they can discern. For this reason, they could not prefer randomly behaving objects or even objects that behaved with greater complexity than they could decipher. But the infant might also dislike repetitive objects—not merely because they are boring, but because it is not clear that the repetitive object actually exercises liberty.

An object that is not repetitive—that stops, starts, changes directions, and so on—can be perceived as exercising liberty at a high rate; each change is the product of a decision to change. Can the same be said for an object that makes no changes? It is not clear, for an object that continues its course of action may do so either by default or by merit of decisions to continue. Does the infant perceive the nonvarying object as making a decision not to change? If so, it may perceive the nonvarying object as exercising as much liberty as the varying one and have no preference between them. Studies of the infants' preferences should help us understand this matter.

Although the experiment that will determine whether infants perceive intention to reciprocate when shown the BDR sequence has not been done, the form of the experiment is easily described. One can use the standard habituation/dishabituation paradigm with abstract objects of a kind used in the Dasser et al study. The infants are shown two BDR sequences, one that they would code as positive (e.g., a sequence in which, as an observing adult would say, one object "helps" another), and another sequence that they would code as negative (a sequence for which an observing adult would say one object "hurts" or interferes with another). Then, they are shown these same sequences with role reversal, the previous instigators of the action now serving as recipients and vice versa. Thus, reciprocation is shown in all the sequences. But for half the infants, the reciprocation preserves the valence, and for the other half it does not. The predictions made by the theory are clear. Reciprocation that violates valence should disagree with the infant's expectations and therefore produce substantial dishabituation, whereas reciprocation that preserves valence should agree with the infant's expectations and produce little dishabituation.

A simple extension of the experiment would test the hypothesis that the infant's theory of reciprocation depends on preservation of valence but not form. First, we should find that reciprocation that violates form (but preserves valence) should produce only negligibly more dishabituation than reciprocation that preserves both form and valence. But a second, more impressive demonstration of the hypothesis is possible. Consider reciprocation that preserves form but violates valence. For example, an object that "presses" against another object when it is "stuck" in a virtual hole, thus freeing the stuck object, would be said to act positively; but an object that applied the same motion to an object on the edge of a virtual cliff, sending the object hurtling down the cliff, would be said to act negatively. A proper comparison of these cases should tell us whether the infant's theory of reciprocation is one that is based on the preservation of form or of valence.

PERCEPTION, INTERPRETATION, AND CONCEPTION

The elegant work of Tom Shultz (1982), showing that the child can find causal relations in events that are not related by simple temporal and spatial contiguity, does not, I suggest, infirm the basic role of temporal and spatial contiguity in the infant's hard-wired perception of causality.

Rather, Shultz's work underscores the difference between three levels of processing—perception, interpretation, and conception—and calls to mind the necessity of both characterizing these levels and clarifying the relations among them.

How does the notion of causality, which, in its early stages, is evidently highly dependent on simple physical parameters, escape these parameters and become a more general notion? A proper answer to this question will clear up not only ontogenetic mysteries but also phylogenetic ones, for the transition from perception to conception (for lack of better terms) is, almost certainly, uniquely human; we do not expect the ape to make this cognitive journey.

The ape, both in perception and initial (or hard-wired) interpretation, may differ little from the human: The basic habituation/dishabituation data for the two species may be difficult to tell apart. Nevertheless, the cases that 5-year-old children can properly classify as causal are not ones that the ape could recognize. Why? What faculties account for this difference? What are the devices, present in the child, but lacking in the ape, that enable the one species to make the transition from perception-interpretation, with its strong dependence on physical parameters, to conception, with its relative freedom from such parameters? Although I am concerned here with only the perception-interpretation level, and find this difficult enough, I wished at least to acknowledge the conceptual level and to underscore the difficulty of accounting for the transition from the former to the latter. In the next section, I acknowledge this problem again, from a different angle.

LIMITATIONS OF THE INFANT'S
THEORY OF SELF-PROPELLED OBJECTS

It is essential to recognize that the infant's theory of self-propelled objects is a highly restricted one. For example, although I claim that the infant, when shown the BDR sequence, perceives one object as having the goal of affecting the other object, I do not claim that it perceives either object as perceiving that the other object has a goal. That is, I do not claim that the infant can perceive second-order intentions. One has only to look closely at the test requirements that such a claim would impose to see that the infant is highly unlikely to be able to meet such requirements.

Similarly, I do not claim that the infant perceives nonmotivational or informational states of mind, in particular, belief—an uncommonly strong state of mind—or even expectancy—a notably weaker state of mind (see Premack, 1988, for preliminary account of the distinction between belief and expectancy). For instance, the theory credits the infant with expecting (that the recipient will reciprocate) but not with perceiving that the instigator expects the recipient to reciprocate.

Thus, the theory does not grant the infant the perception of either second-order motivational states or even first-order informational states. The infant may perceive such relatively weak informational states as expectancy, but, again, the reason for doubting it are the same as those noted earlier. When one lays out the habituation/dishabituation tests that would be needed to prove such a claim and looks at the requirements that such tests would impose on the infant, one doubts the infant's ability to meet the requirements. To be sure, wisdom councils running the tests, but it is not lack of wisdom that councils doubt.

In effect, the infant's theory of self-propelled objects does not account for most of the basic components that, along with intention, make up theory of mind. This limitation on the perceptual origins of theory of mind is in no way special; it is part of a more general restriction. In proposing that both causality and intention can be traced to perceptual origins, I by no means suggest that all fundamental ideas have similar origins; this would be an extremely risky proposal. Not only is there the time-honored difficulty of identifying "fundamental ideas," but even among the ideas we are intuitively willing to grant such status, there are many for which it is not possible to construct plausible perceptual origins. I return to the example of "belief"—if there are plausible physical parameters that give rise to this interpretation, they are not self-evident.

In identifying possible perceptual origins of "fundamental ideas," and validating these claims with relatively straightforward tests, we make a certain amount of progress; but our success should not cover over the "fundamental ideas" that apparently do not have such origins. Neither should it conceal our inability to distinguish in any principled way between those ideas that do have perceptual origins and those that apparently do not, nor even to know why there should be such a distinction.

REFERENCES

Dasser, V., Ulbaek, J., & Premack, D. (1989). Perception of intention. *Science, 243*, 365–367.

Golinkoff, R.M. (1975). Semantic development in infants: The concept of agent and recipient. *Merrill-Palmer Quarterly, 21*, 181–193.

Michotte, A. (1963). *The perception of causality.* London: Methuen.

Poulsen, D., Kintsch, E., Kintsch, W., & Premack, D. (1979). Comparison of young and older children's comprehension of out-of- order picture stories. *Journal of Experimental Child Psychology, 28,* 379–286.

Premack, D. (1988). "Does the chimpanzee have a theory of mind?" revisited. In R. W. Byrne & A. Whiten (Eds.), *Machiavellian intelligence* (pp. 160–179). Oxford: Oxford University Press.

Premack, D. (in preparation). *Social cognition.*

Premack, D., & Woodruff, G. (1978). Does the chimpanzee have a theory of mind? *The Behavioral and Brain Sciences, 4,* 515–526.

Rawls, J. (1970). A theory of justice. Cambridge: Harvard University Press.

Shultz, T. (1982). Rules of causal attribution. *Monographs of the Society for Research in Child Development,* 47(1, Serial No. 194).

Spelke, E. S. (1982). Perceptual knowledge of objects in infancy. In J. Mehler, M. F. Garrett, & E. C. Walker (Eds.), *Perspectives in mental representation* (pp. 409–430). Hillsdale, NJ: Lawrence Erlbaum Associates.

CHAPTER 4

Intentional Communication and the Development of an Understanding of Mind

Inge Bretherton
University of Wisconsin—Madison

How do human infants come to understand that other people have psychological, not just physical, existence? When do they discover that one mind can be interfaced with another through intentional signals? This topic was of absorbing interest to some of the early students of child development, including Baldwin (1884), Preyer (1888/89), and Stern (1914), to name just a few. However, in response to the rise of behaviorism (Watson, 1928) and later to Piaget's writings on egocentrism (Piaget, 1959, 1962), interest in the early development of psychological understanding waned. Followers of Watson had no use for mental constructs, and, although this was, of course, not true of Piagetians, they were nevertheless persuaded that very young children's understanding of mental phenomena was extremely limited. It is only quite recently, with the advent of the "cognitive revolution," that it has once again become acceptable to ask questions about the infant's understanding of mind.

In this chapter, I briefly summarize Baldwin's arguments on how infants come to understand that others, too, have subjectivity. This review demonstrates that many of the ideas with which we wrestle today were already being pondered at the turn of the century. However, Baldwin's writings, as well as those of his contemporaries in the field of developmental psychology, had a methodological weakness: They were largely based on personal anecdotes. It is, therefore, noteworthy that the more recent literature on infants' understanding of mind provides extensive empirical corroboration for many of Baldwin's ideas. In support of this argument, I review relevant studies of gestural communication and language acquisition, although it should not be overlooked that investigations of empathy, social (especially emotional) referencing, pretend play, and social cognition also shed new light on this topic.

I make the point that 9- to 12-month-olds already possess the ability to intentionally recruit and guide a partner's attention through well-timed and well-directed gestures. During the second year, language comes to play an increasingly important role in infants' communicative interchanges with others, but meaning is still primarily conveyed through intentional gestures. Thus, during the preverbal and early verbal periods, infants' understanding of mind can best be inferred from how they communicate. As their ability to converse increases, a further milestone is passed as they begin to label and discuss inner states. It is now possible to infer something about their "theory of mind" from the content as well as the process of their communications with others.

SUBJECTIVITY AND UNDERSTANDING OTHER SELVES: BALDWIN'S WRITINGS

Baldwin was keenly interested in the emergence of subjectivity and the infant's attribution of subjectivity to others. He contended (Baldwin, 1884) that the self is not the isolate-and-in-his-body-alone-situated abstraction that theories of personality usually lead us to think (he did not specify to which theories he was referring). Understanding self and other are mutually interdependent, because they develop together from infancy, each reflecting on the other.

In observing his own infants, Baldwin had noticed that even 2-month-olds could distinguish between mother and nurse in the dark by touch. On the basis of such observations, he surmised that what the infant had learned were characteristic methods of being picked up, patted, and so forth. He did not go so far as to claim that an ability to differentiate between two persons implied that the young infant could attribute subjectivity to the other. Initially, he postulated, infants understand others only as "projects," people known through their behavior and its effect. A major developmental shift occurs when the child understands others as selves through the realization that "other people's bodies . . . have experiences in them such as mine has. They are also 'me's'; let them be assimilated to my me-copy" (Baldwin, 1906, p. 14). Baldwin coined the term ejection to denote this process: "The child's subject sense goes out by a sort of return dialectic to illuminate the other persons. The 'project' of the earlier period is now lighted up, claimed, clothed on with the raiment of selfhood" (1906, p. 14). Ejecting the self is, in a sense, like calling the self into another.

Conversely, the developing self benefits by appropriating the experiences of others through imitating their behavior. It is crucial to note, in this context, that what Baldwin understood by *imitation* includes much of what we at present call *representation*. Imitation a la Baldwin operates in two ways. He spoke of imitation when one individual uses another individual as a copy or model for his or her own behavior (and experience), but also when the imitator imitates himself or herself by drawing on internal "copies" of the relevant behavior/experience. The first of these phenomena is termed *social imitation*, the second *psychic imitation*. For Baldwin, the process is the same whether an idea originates in the person's mind or is introduced there by someone else.

Baldwin also reflected briefly on the origin of individual differences. In commenting on "the extraordinary variety which the same parental suggestions take on in the active interpretations by different children" (1906, p. 33), he explained that there is "always the fusion of the old self with the new elements coming in from the selves external to it" (1906, p. 33). However, despite individual differences there must be commonalities. Children's games depend on the "sameness of the personal thoughts" of the whole group in each situation (an idea later elaborated by Mead, 1934, and reworked by Rommetveit, 1979a). Without each participant's understanding of others' thoughts, cooperative action would be impossible. The same can be said of the more general social self that is shared by family members (Baldwin, 1906): "But apart from the personal form in which the family suggestions are worked over by each child, we may say that the material of the social life of the family is largely common stock for all the members of the family. This means that the alter to each ego is largely common to them all" (p. 35).

Baldwin's writings on the social origins of mind strongly hinted at an intimate connection between interpersonal communication and shared knowledge, although the precise nature of the link was not made explicit. More recently, the very same topic was taken up by Rommetveit (1971, 1972, 1979a, 1979b) who argued persuasively that the process of verbal communication in adulthood cannot be explained without taking into account the existence of the conversants' shared but unstated presuppositions (shared representations). No matter how precisely they are worded, out-of- context messages are necessarily ambiguous. They acquire specific meaning only within an intersubjectively shared world.

It is important to note that these principles also hold for communication between infants and adults. Indeed, developmental psycholinguists had advanced the view that, in order to make sense of infants' one-word utterances, adults must rely on a special technique known as *rich interpretation* (Bloom, 1970; Brown, 1973). Rich interpretation requires at least two basic assumptions about infants (Greenfield & Smith, 1976): (a) that infants perceive relations between agents and objects more or less like adults (making shared knowledge possible), and (b) that their gestures or words indicate important elements of the communicative situation (establishment of an intersubjective framework). What had been overlooked is that rich interpretation must also be used by infants who attempt to communicate with adults. From around 9 months, they, too, act as if they presupposed a shared framework of understanding with the adult. Without it, their attempts to convey intentional messages would be pointless. To use Rommetveit's (1979a) words: "Intersubjectivity has in some sense to be taken for granted for it to be achieved. It is based on faith in a mutually shared world" (p. 96). What develops during the ensuing years is a gradual realization that intersubjectivity cannot be taken as a given, that it sometimes requires great skill, and that it can never be achieved perfectly.

SUBJECTIVITY AND INTERSUBJECTIVITY: RECENT FINDINGS

Primary Intersubjectivity

After a long hiatus during which Baldwin's ideas lay fallow, we are now witnessing a renewed upsurge of interest in infants' understanding of mind. It was Bruner (1975) who first pointed out that infants are not the profoundly egocentric beings that Piaget's early writings had made us believe (Piaget, 1959, 1962). When Bruner proposed these ideas, evidence about the perspective-taking abilities of *preschoolers* had already begun to accumulate. Some of the relevant studies originated from within the social cognitive tradition (e.g., Flavell, Botkin, Fry, Wright, & Jarvis, 1968); others were inspired by an interest in nonegocentric verbal communication (e.g., Garvey, 1975; Maratsos, 1973). What was new in Bruner's 1975 article was the notion that even infants under 1 year of age might have a rudimentary ability to understand the world from the viewpoint of other persons.

Trevarthen and Hubley (1979) went even further than Bruner, suggesting that a primitive capacity for intersubjectivity (or mutual understanding) exists from birth. Note, however, that Trevarthen and Hubley used the term *intersubjectivity* in two distinct senses. *Primary* intersubjectivity characterizes early mother-child interactions that have no topic other than the interaction itself: The baby shares itself with the caregiver but cannot yet communicate with the caregiver *about* a shared topic (see also Stern, 1985). *Secondary* intersubjectivity, by contrast, refers to interactions in which *both* partners are intentionally exchanging messages about a common topic, although infants are, of course, much less expert at this enterprise than their caregivers.

Trevarthen (1979) pointed out that primary *intersubjectivity* presupposes *subjectivity* or the capacity to engage in voluntary behavior (including the deliberate focusing of attention on an interactive partner). Primary intersubjectivity is also characterized by early precursors of behaviors that later support intentional communication or that indicate an ability to resonate to a partner. For example, Meltzoff and Moore (1977) documented that very young infants imitate the facial expressions and some simple hand gestures of adults as if they recognized the correspondence between the perception of the adult model and their own movements. Along the same lines, Condon (1979) showed that newborn infants, like adults, move their limbs synchronously with a partner's speech rhythm as if it helped to be "on the same wavelength." Trevarthen (1979) noticed that somewhat older infants interacting with their mothers often engage in a phenomenon he called *prespeech*. Prespeech consists of the mouthing of speech sounds unaccompanied by vocalizations but accompanied by gesturing. At around 3 to 4 months, infants readily engage in turn-taking interactions with their caregivers (Stern, Jaffe, Beebe, & Bennett, 1975) and respond with gaze aversion and facial signs of disappointment when the caregiver suddenly ceases to interact (Tronick, Als, & Adamson, 1979). By 6 months, they respond to an adult's negative expressions with negative expressions of their own, thus demonstrating a capacity for empathic intersubjectivity (Charlesworth & Kreutzer, 1973). Although these developments allow the infant to share himself or herself with the caregiver in ever more complex ways, a totally new way of relating become possible at around 9 months.

SECONDARY INTERSUBJECTIVITY:
THE PREVERBAL PERIOD

Nine-month-old infants are no longer limited to sharing themselves with an interactional partner but can intentionally establish and sustain attention on a shared topic. This newfound ability is manifested in many contexts. Consider a behavior that Scaife and Bruner (1975) have termed *shared reference.* They noticed that although four-month-olds occasionally followed their mothers' line of regard, they did so reliably and frequently only around 8 or 9 months. Butterworth's observations (1979, cited in Bruner, 1980) provided further justification for regarding this behavior as intentional search for the goal of a partner's gaze. He showed that 12-month-old infants turned to follow the mother's line of regard only once her gaze had settled on a particular location, but then turned back to check her face if her gaze happened to be directed at a blank space (i.e., when "shared referencing" yielded no referent). It was as if the infant was asking the mother, "Why are you looking up there?". Related studies showed that infants follow their mothers' pointing gestures as well as her line of regard, although this ability was still not fully developed at 9 months (Murphy & Messer, 1977). Nine-month-olds sitting next to their mothers were able to follow the mother's pointing gesture when it was directed to a location ahead or to the side but did not respond correctly when the mother pointed across the infant's body. By 14 months, on the other hand, infants understood pointing gestures directed across their bodies as well. Related phenomena (termed *social referencing*) have been noted in the emotional domain. Infants just under 1 year of age appear to use their mothers as a source of information when faced with ambiguous situations or objects (a toy robot, a stranger, or a visual cliff; e.g., Campos & Stenberg, 1981; Feinman & Lewis, 1983; Klinnert, Campos, Sorce, Emde, & Svejda, 1983). Depending on the nature of mother's emotional reaction, they will respond more positively or negatively to the situation. Feinman (1982) and Campos (1983) interpreted this behavior as deliberate affective information seeking about a joint topic.

In addition to understanding maternal attempts at establishing a common focus of attention, 9-month-olds become skilled at actively producing shared reference through a variety of gestures. Infants' use of gestures with communicative intent has been studied by, among others, Bates, Camaioni, and Volterra (1975); Bates, Benigni, Bretherton, Camaioni, and Volterra (1978); Bruner (1975); and Lock (1980). Communicative intent, in this context, is defined as the sender's prior awareness of the effect that a message will have on the addressee. According to Bates (1979), the communicative intent of infant gestures can be inferred on the basis of three behavioral indices:

1. *Gaze alternation.* In pointing or reaching towards desired objects, infants will often turn to the addressee as if to check that the message is being received (gaze alternation).
2. *Repair of failed messages.* If the addressee does not respond in the intended manner, infants frequently augment the intensity of the

communicative behavior or substitute a new gesture for the first, as if to clarify the message. This substitution of means is an especially telling index of intersubjectivity.

3. *Ritualization of previously instrumental gestures.* Behaviors that previously served purely instrumental functions are now transformed into ritualized signals. For example, infants may ask for an object with empty-handed grasping motions directed toward the object instead of peremptorily taking it from another person's hand.

The claim that gaze alternation, repair of failed messages, and ritualization of instrumental gestures index an emerging ability to engage in intentional communication is supported by a variety of additional studies. Sugarman-Bell (1978) pointed out that gaze alternation enables an infant to integrate intentional behavior toward an object (topic) with intentional behavior directed toward a social partner (comment). With respect to the repair of failed gestural messages, Golinkoff (1983) was able to show that such attempts became increasingly sophisticated, even during the last months of the first year. Initially, message repetitions were the most common technique of message repair, whereas message augmentations and signal substitutions became more common during the later preverbal stage.

Studies of mother-infant play also describe behaviors fulfilling the three criteria indicative of communicative intent. Trevarthen and Hubley (1979) reported that infants under 9 months of age could not yet coordinate person and object attention (reminiscent of Sugarman-Bell's 1978 findings regarding gestural requests). A dramatic shift occurred at 9 months, when infants began to look up from object to mother during joint play and to invite mothers' participation by offering and giving objects. What is more, the infants began to understand the instructive intent of maternal behavior. For example, when the mother pointed from a peg to the hole into which it fitted, 9-month-olds did not slavishly imitate her incomplete demonstration. Instead, they displayed their understanding of mother's instructive intent by placing the peg in the hole. Furthermore, studies of infant-adult play have documented infants' attempts at repairing failed messages. Ross and Kay (1980) found that, in turn-taking games with an unfamiliar adult companion, 12-month-olds employed a variety of strategies for reviving interrupted reciprocal games. In the Ross and Kay paradigm, the adult stopped "playing the game" for 10 seconds after smooth turntaking had been established. Infants responded to this by looking back and forth from adult to toy, by partially or fully retaking their own turn and then waiting, or by holding up their hands to invite a turn from the adult (in object exchange games). These signals occurred almost exclusively during game interruptions. The infants also watched the adult play-mate's face more during interruptions, whereas they looked more at her hands and at game-related objects during the normal phases of the game. Inspection of the data provided by Ross (1980) revealed that all infants had several of these strategies at their disposal. Ross concluded that the infants knew that it was now the partner's turn to act and that they understood the structure that controlled the interaction. In view of the fact that the infants were able use a variety of communicative behaviors to reinstitute interrupted games, it also seems plausible to assume that the infants expected the partner to understand their signals.

The following two examples furnish an especially vivid illustration of intentional communicative acts in preverbal infants. In the first, an infant aged 14 months uses gaze alternation as well as two ritualized behaviors (vestigial crying and lipsmacking) to communicate with each of two adults in turn (from Lock, 1980):

Mother enters the room holding a cup of tea. Paul turns from his playpen in her direction and obviously sees it. (i) He cries vestigially and so attracts his mother's attention; immediately he points toward her and smacks his lips concurrently (Paul's way of asking for food or drink).

Mother: No, you can't have this one, it's Andy's.

Mother gives me (the observer) the cup of tea, and I put it on the mantelpiece to cool. Paul crawls across to me and grasps my knees. (ii) I turn to look at him; he *looks toward the mantelpiece and points, turns back to me, continues to point, and smacks his lips* (pp. 95-96; clarification in parentheses and italics added).

This communicative interchange can be interpreted as follows: The child first indicated a desire by producing ritual emotion signals directed toward the partner. Only then did he focus the partner's attention on the object of his desire (by lipsmacking and pointing). When the addressee refused the child's request, passing the desired tea to someone else, the child turned to that person. He attracted the attention of the new "owner" of the cup of tea and attempted to request it from him (pointing, gaze alternation, lipsmacking). He was able to do so despite the fact that the tea was now resting on the mantelpiece, at a distance from both adult conversants. Note the precise timing and directionality of the communicative signals as well as the ritualization of consummatory and emotional behaviors in the service of conveying an intentional message.

The second example illustrates the successful negotiation of an initially ambiguous message between a 14-month-old preverbal infant and his mother at lunchtime (from Golinkoff, 1983):

1. Jordan: Vocalizes repeatedly until his mother turns around.
2. Mother: Turns around to look at him.
3. Jordan: points to one of the objects on the counter.
4. Mother: "Do you want this?" (Holds up milk container).
5. Jordan shakes his head "no", continues to point.
6. Mother: "Do you want this?" (Holds up jelly jar).
7. Jordan: Shakes his head "no", continues to point.
8., 9., 10., 11., Two more offer-rejection pairs.
12. Mother: "This?" (Picks up sponge).
13. Jordan: Leans back in highchair, puts arm down, tension leaves body.
14. Mother: Hands Jordan sponge. (pp. 58-59).

The mother interpreted the infant's initial pointing as a request, but she was uncertain of the desired object's identity. By holding up a series of possible targets, she was actually helping the child to repair the failed message, but the child was an equally active participant by continuing to give the required feedback. The process worked only because the mother assumed that the child was communicating about a specific goal and because the child appeared to assume that the mother was attempting to discover his goal.

Why use fancy terms like *intersubjectivity* or *interfacing of minds* when it might be more parsimonious to credit the infant with intentionality, pure and simple (see Shatz, 1983)? After all, the acquisition of intentional gestures seems to coincide with an emerging understanding of physical means-end relations and physical causality (see Bates et al., 1975; Bates et al., 1979; Harding & Golinkoff, 1979). My objection to an explanation couched purely in terms of understanding physical relations is that it fails to take into account the infant's budding ability to *specify messages for the addressee*. The communicative gestures just described look like deliberate efforts to attract and direct the addressee's attention to topics of mutual interest. Especially interesting, in this regard, are efforts to repair failed messages, as well as the timing of attention-getting and attention-directing gestures. I suggest that the most parsimonious explanation of these phenomena is that, by the end of the first year, infants have acquired a rudimentary ability to impute mental states to self and other (what Premack & Woodruff, 1978, called a theory of mind) and, further, that they have begun to understand that one mind can be interfaced with another through conventional or mutually comprehensible signals (Bretherton & Bates, 1979; Bretherton & Beeghly, 1982; Bretherton, McNew, & Beeghly-Smith, 1981).

Other evidence favors this interpretation. For example, during the period when infants acquire the ability to engage in intentional communication, they become able to reverse roles in social games (Ratner & Bruner, 1978), to engage in deliberate imitation of another person's facial movements (Piaget, 1962), and somewhat later to take the maternal role in play with dolls or live partners (Miller & Garvey, 1984; Nicolich, 1977; Wolf, 1982) and to comfort distressed adults or children (Zahn-Waxler, Radke-Yarrow, & King, 1979).

Let me add some qualifications at this point. I do not mean to suggest that 1-year-old infants can reflect on their own theory of mind; nor do I presume to claim that 1-year-olds are mind-body dualists who make a clear distinction between inner states and outward behavior. What I do argue is that infants from about 9 months onward seem to operate with an implicit theory of mind, in the same way that 3-year-olds operate with grammatical rules that they are unable to state verbally. With respect to mind-body dualism, I propose that, before humans can understand that outward expressions do not always reflect inner feelings and goals, they must discover that a person's inner states and expressive behaviors are, for the most part, concordant and therefore interpretable (Bretherton, Fritz, Zahn-Waxler, & Ridgeway, 1986).

INTERFACING OF MINDS
DURING THE ONE-WORD STAGE

With the mastery of first words at around the end of the first year, evidence for infants' theory of interfacible minds becomes even stronger, because some referents of infant communications can now be explicitly labeled. Nevertheless, the attention-getting and -directing signals from the preverbal stage continue to play a crucial role in message construction (Bretherton, 1988). Infants' one-word utterances are comprehensible to adult partners only because some of the referents are at least potentially visible to both partners and because the child is skillful at obtaining and then directing the partner's attention through gestures. Take, for example, the following description from Greenfield (1980) about a child whose mother was unable to attend to him immediately because she was in charge of a swimming class:

> The child goes towards his mother, whining "shoes, shoes" (he only has socks on). He comes back towards me and gets his blue sandals. I try to help him while standing up, but cannot do it. So I sit down with one shoe, put him on my lap, and put his shoe on. Then I put him down, not saying

anything. He walks straight to his other shoe, picks it up and comes back to me. I put him on my lap and put his other shoe on. He then runs towards his mother still talking, saying "shoe, shoe" in an excited voice. He lifts his foot to show her. When she attends, he points to me. She understands, saying something like "The lady put your shoes on". Both are very excited. (p. 275)

This message is primarily carried by precisely timed and well-directed gestures. After naming the desired topic of attention, the child holds up his foot until mother does attend. Only at that moment does he point to the person who helped him put on his shoes. Although the mention of shoes initially helps to clarify the topic, his message could have been transmitted through nonverbal signals alone. The following example, also from Greenfield (1980), illustrates the negotiation of an unclear message in one-word speech. Note the similarity between this anecdote and the earlier gestural example that was cited from Golinkoff (1983):

(Matthew's sister Lauren had gone out of the room)
Matthew: Lara (Lauren)
Mother: Yeah. Lauren. What happened to Lauren?
Matthew: Oh (or ou, two transcribers disagreed)
Mother: Oh?
Matthew: No
Mother: Hoe?
Matthew: Ou
Mother: Out?
Matthew: Yeah, Yaya (Lauren). (Greenfield, 1980, p. 271)

Like Jordan in Golinkoff's (1983) report, Matthew repeated his message with slight variations until the mother had guessed the correct answer. Without patience on her part, his communication could not have succeeded, but, conversely, without Matthew's patient feedback, his mother could not have been certain that she had hit on the correct (desired) object.

Topic-Comment Constructions

As toddlers' vocabulary grows, it becomes important to distinguish between the acquisition nouns and relational words (e.g., Bloom, 1973). Relational words include such terms as "allgone," "up," "no," and "uh-oh," which (in contrast to nouns) do not make reference to specific objects or particular actions. They take on meaning only in the context of relationships among agents, objects, and actions that are either present, presupposed, or established through naming or pointing. Bloom (1973) argued that one-word utterances consisting of relational words are often more readily interpretable by an adult partner than one-word utterances formed with names or nouns, because the intended relationships among objects and agents may be more difficult to infer from gestures and context than the objects to which the relationships apply. For example, if mother and child are emptying containers filled with blocks, the utterance "allgone" as the child looks into the container is relatively unambiguous. The utterance "block" in the same context is more difficult to interpret. We know that the topic is block, but we do not know what the child is trying to say about the block.

In a detailed case study, Bloom (1973) reported that her daughter Allison used relational words in a variety of situations that had to do with notions of appearance, disappearance, absence, and recurrence of objects and actions. Allison said "gone" when looking into an empty container, while her mother was drinking juice from a cup, as a soap bubble popped, and while she was searching for a missing object. She used "more," initially, to request more food, more tickling, and more reading of a book. Somewhat later, "more" served to point out several instances of the same category. Allison began to use "uh-oh" when she dropped or spilled something; later, she commented with "uh-oh" when her mother caused a mishap. Finally, she seemed to be teasing her mother by announcing "uh-oh" before she inverted an almost empty cup to spill some more liquid on the floor. McCune-Nicolich (1980) corroborated and amplified Bloom's (1973) findings. In both studies (Bloom, 1973; McCune-Nicolich, 1981), the children appeared to expect their mothers to make use of the shared context in order to understand the relationships about which they were commenting. The children's mothers, conversely, seemed to be able to live up to these expectations. Both partners relied on their experience of a shared here-and-now reality to effectively convey and understand meanings.

In terms of toddlers' understanding of mind, Bloom's (1973) distinction between relational words and nouns during the single- word stage becomes even more intriguing, once a variety of words in both classes have been mastered. We can now examine whether and under which conditions a toddler chooses one word class over the other. For example, in their detailed longitudinal case study, Greenfield and Smith (1976) noticed that when their subjects, Matthew and Nicky, communicated about an object (topic) that was already the focus of joint attention, they chose to comment on the action component of the situation with a relational word. By contrast, when the focus of attention was uncertain, the children would verbally establish the topic rather than comment on it with a relational word. Hence, the object was frequently named in issuing a demand, but the relational word "no" was generally used in refusals where the joint topic was already known or obvious. For example, in drawing attention to events, one of the children always mentioned the record player (topic) before commenting that it was "ong." The other child named toy cars he was not holding or cars that were passing by outside, but mentioned the action of a toy (allgone), if he had just been manipulating it. Likewise, when the mother established the topic of conversation by asking what the car outside was doing, the child answered with the comment "bye-bye." On reanalyzing utterances in their own and in Bloom's (1973) case studies, Greenfield and Smith (1976) discovered that, in almost every relevant instance, the child referred first to the object if a joint topic of attention with the partner had not yet been established, and mentioned an activity first if the topic of conversation was already clear.

Greenfield (Greenfield & Smith, 1976; Greenfield, 1979) used the concept of informativeness (relative certainty) to explain toddlers' choices of object words versus relational words. An object in the child's hands was said to be relatively certain, whereas an object not in the child's possession was said to be relatively uncertain. The child's tendency is to mention the uncertain aspect of the situation. But who is experiencing uncertainty? Greenfield (1979) claimed that the child was labeling the most informative (most uncertain or unclear) aspect of the situation for himself or herself, but this seems unlikely, because the child presumably knew what he or she was communicating about. An explanation in terms of perspective taking seems much more plausible. The problem for Greenfield was that this was supposedly beyond a toddler's capacity. But is it? Granted that even 1-year-olds can understand, establish, and communicate about topics of joint attention through pointing, looking, and other intentional gestures, it seems reasonable to assume that young children in the one-word stage know that establishment of a joint topic through word or gesture is a prerequisite for further verbal comment about the topic (see also Ninio & Snow, 1984). Moreover, the data (including findings by Scollon, 1979), support this assumption.

Scollon coined the term *vertical construction* for topic-comment propositions that are continued across several speaker turns (as opposed to horizontal constructions, in which topic and comment are contained in the same speaker turn). In constructing such a vertical proposition, the child establishes the topic during one turn, the mother acknowledges what the child is proposing, and the child then comments on the now-shared topic during a later turn. The earliest vertical constructions contained many repetitions, as illustrated by the following example (Scollon, 1979):

Brenda: "[feī], [fǽ] ".
Mother: "Hm?"
Brenda: "[fǽ]".
Mother: "Bathroom?"
Brenda: "[fanī], [faī]."
Mother: "Fan. Yeah."
Brenda: "kʰu."
Mother: "Cool, yeah. Fan makes you cool." (p. 217)

As children's phonology improves, the need for repetitions declines, making the adult partner's acknowledgment no longer necessary. Finally, children learn to comment on topics provided by a parent—the beginning of true discourse. For example, in a game format (playing at eating toes), Matthew's father said, "toe, toe," and Matthew commented "eat" (Greenfield & Smith, 1976). The father's previously established topic of "toe" is presupposed in Matthew's subsequent reply.

Note that, in order to make reliable inferences about a child's communicative intentions, it is crucial that the transcriptions take into account all aspects of the communicative situation: the timing and directedness of child's gestures, emotional expressions, and words, as well as the responses of the partner. An example from Atkinson (1979) illustrates the power of such contextual analyses especially well:

> . . . consider the following situation which I have observed with my own son. His mother has been out for several minutes, and he approaches me saying *mummy* with no signs of distress or special intonation to indicate that he might be asking a question. It is clearly difficult to gloss his utterance as a statement. *That's mummy* and similar candidates just do not make sense, and what happened next is interesting. My response to the child was *Mummy?* using marked question intonation to which the child immediately responds with gone. . . . for the moment I merely want to suggest that a plausible candidate for the function of the initial *mummy* is that of drawing the father's attention to that individual, and only when the child gets some feedback to indicate that his addressee is suitably attending does he go on and predicate something of mummy. (pp. 235–236)

Atkinson's anecdote is an instance of Scollon's (1979) vertical topic-comment construction with adult help, clarified here by the addition of vital contextual information about timing: the child proceeds to elaborate on the topic only once the father has signalled its uptake. On the basis of this and other detailed examples, Atkinson suggested that adult inattentiveness (in addition to phonological problems) may often be the reason for the topic repetitions noted by Scollon (1979). Such findings *lend further support to the hypothesis that children who are still in the one-word stage attempt to use their limited linguistic capacity so as to guide the adult's understanding.*

In the course of further communicative development during the second year, children begin to engage in lengthier conversations about absent topics. Take, for example, the following instructive conversation recorded by Bloom (1973), when her daughter Allison was almost 21 months old and just beginning to use topic-comment constructions in successive single-word utterances. Mother and child are playing together in a laboratory playroom; the child mentions a bathtub:

> Mother: "Bathtub? I don't see a bathtub."
> Allison (turns, pointing but not looking): "Home."
> Mother: "Home. Home."
> Allison: "Home."
> Mother: "What do we do in the bathtub?"
> Allison: "bath/bath."
> Mother: "We take a bath."
> Allison: "Mommy/shower."
> Mother: "Mommy shower. Mommy takes a shower."
> Allison: "Nudie."
> Mother: "Nudie. Yes."
> Allison (touching her head): "Hat/on."
> Mother: "With a hat on, yes." (shower cap). (p.227)

I suggest that, without their shared life history and, hence, an extensive shared knowledge base, such adult-child conversations would be impossible, because the child still lacks much expertise in establishing shared meaning through language. Yet a few judicious words can go a long way when so much can be jointly presupposed or taken for granted.

EXPLICIT COMMUNICATION ABOUT INTERNAL STATES

In light of the fact that significant psychological understanding is implied in the way toddlers manage communicative situations during the single-word phase of language development, it is, perhaps, not surprising that, by 18 months, some begin to use verbal labels for internal states in appropriate contexts. This ability, along with the acquisition of the shifting pronouns (you and I), burgeons rapidly during the third year (Bretherton & Beeghly, 1982; Dunn, 1988; Dunn, Bretherton, & Munn, 1987; Kagan, 1981) as part of the more general ability to communicate in sentences (Bates, Bretherton, & Snyder, 1988). Concurrent developments are the capacity to express empathy toward distressed others (e.g., Zahn-Waxler et al., 1979; for a review, see Thompson, 1987), to use dolls as active partners in symbolic play (Bretherton, O'Connell, Shore, & Bates, 1984; Wolf, Rygh, & Altshuler, 1984), and to recognize the self in a mirror (Lewis & Brooks-Gunn, 1979). From now on, we can rely on the content, not just the process, of communications in order to make inferences about toddlers' "theory of interfacible minds."

Classical diary studies summarized by Stern and Stern (1928) suggested that even infants who are still in the one-word stage occasionally produce appropriate labels for some feeling states. Using these diaries as a basis, Bretherton et al., (1981) conducted a study with a larger sample of children ($N = 30$). Their mothers were instructed to record child utterances about internal states in everyday contexts (Bretherton et al., 1981; Bretherton & Beeghly, 1982), and to note the context in which the utterance occurred (note that the resulting findings were subsequently corroborated through direct observation of family conversations in the home; Dunn, Bretherton, & Munn, 1987).

Bretherton et al., (1981) found that *some* 20-month-olds already made appropriate reference to hunger, pain, disgust, ability, volition, and moral approval (see also Dunn et al., 1987). It was noteworthy that these children did not use these labels only to refer to their own experiences. Some even labeled the assumed feelings of people in picture books. By 28 months, a majority of the children had acquired a fairly rich vocabulary with which to discuss internal states (Bretherton & Beeghly, 1982). Almost all talked about perceptions, sensations, physiological states, and volition/ability. About two thirds of the sample labeled at least some of the basic emotions (happy, mad, sad, scared). With respect to moral judgment, a majority used "good" and "bad" as terms of moral approval and disapproval, but terms referring to moral obligation (supposed to, should, must, and so forth) were still somewhat rare. Utterances about cognitive processes (remembering, forgetting, thinking and so forth) were even less frequent at 28 months, although these tend to become more common after 30 months (Shatz, Wellman, & Silber, 1983). There was a tendency for the 28-month-olds to attribute internal states to themselves before they imputed them to others, but the lag was slight. In addition, many of the children were able to converse about past or anticipated states ("I not sad anymore," "Santa will be happy when I pee in the potty").

Perhaps most intriguing, in terms of understanding others as psychological beings, was the finding that many 28-month-old toddlers made causal statements about internal states (see Table 4.l).

TABLE 4.1
Causal Utterances Containing Internal-State Lebels
(from Bretherton & Beeghly, 1982)

1a. Alleviation of uncomfortable or undesirable experiences (48 statements)

CAN'T SEE	I'm going to be a cloud in the sky so you can't see me. (1)
HOT	I'm hot. Coat off. (5)
COLD, FREEZING	You better get shirt, so you won't freeze. (6)
HUNGRY, STARVING	I hungry. Make breakfast. (5)
THIRSTY	Me thirsty. Please water. (5)
TIRED	I tirod. Let's go to bed. (2)
SICK	I sick. I need vitamin. (2)
FEEL BAD	I feeld bad. I want aspirin. (1)
NOT FEEL GOOD	Stop it. Doesn't feel good. (2)
SCARED	I scared of the shark. Close my eyes. (2)
CRY	I cry. Lady pick me up and hold me. (5)
DIRTY, MESSY	Wash my hands. They're messy. (4)
WANT, NEED	It's cold. I want my gloves. (6)
HARD	It's hard. Mommy do it. (1)
HAVE TO	Jimmy help me. I have to pick up the toys. (1)

1b. Attainment or continuation of comfortable of desirable state (17 statements)

WARM	Take bubblebath, Mom, to get warm. (4)
FULL	I'm full for (meaning because of) breakfast. (1)
ASLEEP	Baby is alseep. Don't wake her up. (1)
HAPPY	I give a hug. Baby be happy. (3)
GOOD TIME	Mommy exercise. Mommy having good time. (1)
MAKE BETTER	Doctor made me better. I spill(ed) (hot) coffee. (1)
NICE	I nice? I get to ride the horse again? (1)
NO CRY	No cry, Mamma. It will be all right (1)
GOOD	If I'm good, Santa will bring toys. (3)
LAUGH	Maybe Gregg would laugh when he saw Beth do that. (1)

2. Antecedent of or reason for experience or judgment (53 statements)

HOT	The fire's hot. We hot too? (1)
THIRSTY	Me ski. Thirsty. (1)
HURT	If I do X, I will hurt myself. (5)
SICK	If I eat poison, it will make me sick. (1)
HURT FEELINGS	I'm hurting your feelings, 'cause I was mean to you. (1)
HURT	Bobby hurt me. (5)
MAD	Grandma mad. I wrote on wall. (3)
MAD AT (person, but no action specified)	Mommmy's mad at you. (9)
SCARED, AFRAID	It's dark. I'm scared. (fear of dark, 3)
	The firecracker scared me. (fear of noises, 1)
	I afraid of the Hulk (fear of monsters, 2)
	I see tiger. That too scary. (fear of animals, 3)
	Bad dreams scare me. (fear of nightmares, 1)
	Bobby scare me. (fear of people's behavior, 9)
SAD	You sad, Mommy. What Daddy do? (2)

(Continued)

TABLE 4.1 (continued)

CRY	Me fall down. Me cry. (3)
BAD/NAUGHTY	I bad girl. I wet my pants. (7)
HAS TO	Her turn. She has to. (1)

3. Explanation of one experience in terms of a physical symptom, an affect expression, or another psychological state (16 statements)

HOT	I'm too hot. I'm sweating. (1)
SICK	Dickie sick. Throw up. (1)
NOT HUNGRY, SICK	Not hungry, Mommy. Me sick. (1)
SICK, HURT	Sick. Arm hurts. (2)
FEEL BAD, HURT	I feel bad. My tummy hurts. (1)
LAUGH, FUNNY	I laugh at funny man. (1)
HAPPY, CRY	I not cry now, I happy. (1)
NOT HAPPY, SAD	I not cry now, I happy. (1)
NOT HAPPY, SAD	Katie not happy face. Katie sad. (3)
HARD, CANNOT	Too hard. Can't do it. (3)
CAN, GOOD	Me can do it. Me good girl (1)
NOT NICE, BAD	Lisa not nice to me. Lisa bad. (1)

Note.   Because laugh and cry appeared to be used to indicate affect, causal utterances cotaining these terms are included. The numbers in parentheses indicate the number of children who made utterances of this type. We did not count similar utterances made by the same child. On the other hand, a few utterances were double classified, although most of the expressions containing two internal state labels are listed only once under Category 4. The total number of utterances here is thus 139, not 142 (the total reported by the mothers).

The word "causal" in this context does not imply that the utterances invariably contained causal connectives like "so," "because," or "if," but that they referred to internal states in causally related sequences ("Grandma mad [because] I wrote on wall."). Hood and Bloom (1979) provided detailed justification for interpreting such utterances as causal. Three types of causal statements about internal states occurred: (a) utterances about the events or actions that precede or cause a particular state, (b) utterances about negative states as motivators or causes of subsequent behavior, and (c) utterances explaining an emotion in terms of a related mental state or in terms of behavioral/expressive correlates (e.g., "Katie not happy face, Katie sad."). The underlying causal notion in the latter type of utterance is the logical inference, "Katie looks unhappy. This makes me think she must be sad." Data from a project by Radke-Yarrow and Zahn- Waxler (1973) corroborate and extend these findings (for details see Bretherton et al., 1986; for a review on young children's understanding of psychological causality, see Miller & Aloise, 1989).

Analyses of mother-child conversations in the home (Dunn et al., 1987) corroborated the findings obtained through maternal report (Dunn et al., 1987). Between 18 and 24 months, the children studied by Dunn and her colleagues not only came to label a wider range of feeling states but had begun to use the labels to influence or guide a partner's behavior or to make causal statements about feelings rather than just to comment on their own or someone else's feeling states. It is also worth noting that many conversations about feeling states between young siblings (when the target child was 24 months old) took place in the context of social pretend play with mothers and siblings. Internal state labeling has also been observed in play with small human and animal figures (Wolf, Rygh, & Altshuler, 1984), but its onset is somewhat later in this context than in social pretense with mother or sibling.

FURTHER DEVELOPMENTS:
EXPERIMENTAL STUDIES

As previously noted, some investigators (e.g., Shatz, 1983; Johnson, 1988) have questioned whether it is advisable to use the term *theory of mind* to characterize infants' intentional communication and even toddlers' speech about internal states. Leslie (1987) proposed that the advent of shared pretense at around 18 months offers sufficient grounds but failed to consider infants' communicative achievements at the end of the first year. One problem is that there are disagreements on what is denoted by the term *theory of mind* and whether one can speak of a theory when its "postulates" are only held implicitly and not reflectively.

Wellman (1988) has recently proposed that, even when the term *theory of mind* is defined more formally than by Premack and Woodruff (1978), a case can be made for $2\frac{1}{2}$-year-olds. Premack and Woodruff (1978) defined theory of mind as the ability to impute internal states to self and others (which includes implicitly held theories). Wellman required more. He proposed that three criteria must be met before one may claim that someone has a theory of mind. First, the individual must have basic constructs or categories for defining reality. Second, these basic constructs or categories must be organized into a coherent system of interrelationships; and third, the individual must have developed a causal-attributional framework of human behavior. Obviously, infants' implicit theory of mind at the end of the first year does not fulfill Wellman's more explicit criteria, but semantic difficulties aside, it is interesting to ask when young children acquire a theory of mind in this more stringent sense.

Wellman's criteria are, I suggest, met by some of the 28-month-olds in the Bretherton and Beeghly (1982) study. For example, a few of the children distinguished real from nonreal ("Is that monster real?"; "It's only pretend."), some defined one mental state in terms of another (looking unhappy = sadness), and many talked about causes and consequences of such mental states as emotions (sad, happy, scared, mad) and physiological states (e.g., hunger, thirst, and disgust). Furthermore, in a study of mental verb acquisition, Shatz, Wellman, and Silber (1983) were able to demonstrate that utterances in which an explicit distinction between reality and internal states is drawn become quite frequent during the second half of the third year. Nevertheless, during the third year these abilities tend to be somewhat fragile, in the sense that they do not withstand rigorous questioning.

By 36 months, however, more formal questioning techniques can be attempted. For example, in interviewing 3-year-olds, Wellman discovered that requests to explain the distinction between reality and thought posed no special problems. The children claimed that a real cookie could be touched, whereas a "thought" cookie could not (or could only be touched "with my dream hands"). When asked about absent objects as opposed to "pictures in your head" (Estes, Wellman, & Wooley, in press), children aged 3, 4, and 5 years gave different reasons for their inability to touch a real, absent object ("because it's not there") and a thought object ("it's not real"). These findings demonstrate that young children have categories for distinguishing mental from nonmental phenomena, hence satisfying Wellman's first criterion for a theory of mind. In addition, Wellman's 3-year-olds defined mental states by recourse to other mental states ("it's like dreaming"; "People can't see my imagination"), satisfying his second criterion. With respect to the third criterion, a causal explanatory framework, Wellman directs our attention to social cognitive studies of intentionality and emotional understanding. For example, Shultz (1980) reported that 3-year-olds are quite expert at distinguishing acts that a person meant to perform from mistakes, reflexes, and passive movements. What is more, the children seemed to understand intentions as causes of behavior. In terms of a causal understanding of emotions, Trabasso, Stein, and Johnson (1981) have shown that children as young as 3 years of age can produce plausible antecedents and consequences of positive and negative emotions in response to being presented with simple emotion labels (see also Farber & Moely, 1979). Based on this and similar evidence, Wellman (1988) reasoned that 3-year-olds seem to be engaged in the same interpretive enterprise as older children and adults. In other words, not only do young children not seem to hold a stimulus-response or mechanistic theory of human behavior, but by 3 years of age, they can say so explicitly. They thus differ from 9-month-olds, who can only use their theory of mind, but not reflect on it. They also differ from 4-year-olds, who have acquired a much firmer grasp on more complex mental phenomena, such as false beliefs (see Astington, this volume for a review). Nevertheless, by 3 years of age, a fairly sophisticated framework is already place.

INTERFACING OF MINDS: SIMILARITIES
BETWEEN INFANT AND ADULT COMMUNICATION

In his writings on the architecture of intersubjectivity in adulthood, Rommetveit (1971, 1972, 1979a, 1979b) contended that intentional communication crucially depends on the partners' ability to establish a common spatial, temporal, and intersubjective framework. That is, the conversants (you and I) must agree on what constitutes here and now (versus the there and then) in the present dialogue. Hence, the primary problem of communication is *what is made known and how it is made known in a shared social reality* (Rommetveit, 1971). Grammatically incomplete utterances (ellipses; see Holzman, 1971) are the norm under conditions of trust and a shared social world. Only what is new needs to be explicitly stated; the rest is based on shared representations. Hence, when an adult speaker encodes a message, he or she is intuitively monitoring it from the listener's perspective (anticipatory decoding), taking note of what can and what cannot be taken as jointly known. The listener's task is to reconstruct the intended message from the verbal and nonverbal message components. Where much is shared, much less needs to be explicitly conveyed. Take, for example, the utterance "magnificent" after the last bars of a rousing symphony performance. It makes sense to the addressee because of the timing and context of the utterance. Out of context this statement would be completely ambiguous, but complemented by a shared social framework, its meaning is quite transparent (Rommetveit, 1979a).

It is interesting to note that, when adults employ "rich interpretation" (Bloom, 1970; Brown, 1973; Greenfield & Smith, 1976) to decode an infant's intentional gestures and one-word utterances, they are doing exactly what Rommetveit described. They use the timing and directedness of infant signals in conjunction with shared presuppositions to make sense of what the infant is trying to convey. What Greenfield and Smith (1976) did not point out, however, is that during the last few months of the first year, infants, too, come to apply "rich interpretation" to messages addressed to them by adults. In other words, rich interpretation is not a technique used by skilled adults to comprehend the messages of young and inexperienced communicators, it is the sine qua non for all intentional communicative acts, whatever the age and skill of the communicator. What emerges at around 9 months, then, is a basic intuitive understanding that intentional communication or interfacing of minds can be achieved through minimal signals when a shared social reality can be assumed. Throughout the life span, this ability is further elaborated. New abilities in the use of language lead to more sophisticated shared representations, which, in turn, facilitate more complex communication.

Nevertheless, it is impressive that, beginning around 9 months of age, infants are already able to set up intersubjective coordinates through pointing, gaze direction, and other gestures and that, at the same time, they begin to understand intersubjective coordinates set up by adult partners. Whereas they do not always succeed in making themselves understood, when they do not, they frequently help their conversational partners by well-timed gestures, and by repeating, augmenting, or substituting another signal when the partner indicates that the message has not been understood (repair of failed messages). This specification of messages for the addressee could not be achieved without the infant's assumption of a shared mental world and without some primitive ability to take the role of the other (Mead, 1934). Even 10-month olds make an attempt at constructing communicative acts with some attention to listener needs, and they assume that a partner can convey important information about the environment to them.

Around the end of the first year, children begin to notice and acquire complex conventional meaning-exchange systems used by other people in their environment (verbal or manual languages). We still do not know all the factors that contribute to this developmental shift, but the available evidence suggests that it is not only the acquisition of sensorimotor notions of objects, means-end relations, and causality that makes the interfacing of minds possible. The realization that persons can share understandings (that minds can be interfaced) does not follow after, but is a prerequisite for, learning to engage in deliberate meaning exchange. A creature without the potential for developing a theory of interfacible minds could not acquire and would not be motivated to learn the complex message- making strategies involved in speech. To quote Rommetveit (1979b) again, "We must naively and unreflectingly take the possibility of perfect intersubjectivity for granted in order to achieve partial intersubjectivity in real life discourse with our fellow men" (p. 161).

It appears that this naive and unreflecting assumption emerges at around 9 months, inducing a developmental shift of enormous significance. A second shift occurs at around 12 months, when language is added to the infant's message-making capacities, although gestures continue to be important. Later, during the single- word stage, differential use of relational words and nouns indicates that infants can take listener needs into account. If a common topic has not been set up, they tend to do so with a noun, but if the joint topic has already been established, they tend to comment on it with a relational word, such as "allgone."

By 18 to 20 months, we need no longer limit ourselves to an analysis of the process of communication to infer something about children's understanding of mind. Once toddlers begin to talk about a limited range of inner states (amongst them hunger, thirst, and disgust), we can begin to rely on the *content* of their communications to gain access to their "theory of mind." During the third year, the ability to converse about inner states grows by leaps and bounds and is used in attempts to influence, persuade, and cajole others. By the age of 3 years, there is evidence of yet a fourth shift. This involves children's ability to discuss their reflections about emotions, intentions, desires and thoughts at a more abstract level in the context of formal interviews (see Astington, this volume, for a detailed discussion of these later developments).

Should we be surprised that an ability to understand, communicate about and then reflect on feelings, intentions, desires and beliefs emerges so early and rapidly in human development? Not really. As Johnson-Laird (1983) and more recently Dunn (1988) have noted, if organisms are going to regulate their social interactions through highly complex systems of communication, it is to their advantage to understand and learn to talk to each other (truthfully and sometimes not) about those matters that *govern* and *motivate* their behavior, rather than to limit their interest to the outward forms of behavior.

ACKNOWLEDGMENT

While writing this chapter, I received support from the John D. and Catherine T. MacArthur Foundation Network for the Transition from Infancy to Early Childhood.

REFERENCES

Atkinson, M. (1979). Prerequisites for reference. In E. Ochs & B. B. Schieffelin (Eds.), *Developmental pragmatics* (pp. 215–247). New York: Academic Press.

Baldwin, J. M. (1884). *Mental development of the child and the race: Methods and processes.* New York: Macmillan.

Baldwin, J. M. (1906). *Social and ethical interpretations in mental development* (4th ed.). London: The Macmillan.

Bates, E. (1979). Intentions, conventions and symbols. In E. Bates, L. Benigni, I. Bretherton, L. Camaioni, & V. Volterra, *The emergence of symbols* (pp. 33–42). New York: Academic Press.

Bates, E., Benigni, L., Bretherton, I., Camaioni, L., & Volterra, V. (1979). Cognition and communication from 9–13 months: Correlational findings. In E. Bates, L. Benigni, I. Bretherton, L. Camaioni, & V. Volterra, *The emergence of symbols* (pp. 69–140). New York: Academic Press.

Bates, E., Bretherton, I., & Synder, L. (1988). *From first words to grammar.* New York: Cambridge University Press.

Bates, E., Camaioni, L., & Volterra, V. (1975). The acquisition of performatives prior to speech. *Merrill-Palmer Quarterly, 21,* 205–226.

Bloom, L. (1970). *Language development: Form and function in emerging grammars.* Cambridge, MA: MIT Press.

Bloom, L. (1973). *One word at a time.* The Hague: Mouton.

Bretherton, I. (1988). How to do things with one word: The ontogenesis of intentional message making in infancy. In J. Lock & M. Smith (Eds.), *The emergent lexicon* (pp. 225–260). Orlando, FL: Academic Press.

Bretherton, I., & Bates, E. (1979). The emergence of intentional communication. In I. Uzgiris (Ed.), *New directions for child development* (Vol. 4, pp. 81–100). San Francisco: Jossey-Bass.

Bretherton, I., & Beeghly, M. (1982). Talking about internal states: The acquisition of an explicit theory of mind. *Developmental Psychology, 18,* 906–921.

Bretherton, I., Fritz, J., Zahn-Waxler, C., & Ridgeway, D. (1986). Learning to talk about emotions: A functionalist perspective. *Child Development, 57,* 529–548.

Bretherton, I., McNew, S., & Beeghly-Smith, M. (1981). Early person knowledge as expressed in gestural and verbal communication: When do infants acquire a "theory of mind"? In M. E. Lamb & L. R. Sherrod (Eds.), *Infant social cognition* (pp. 333–373). Hillsdale, NJ: Lawrence Erlbaum Associates.

Bretherton, I., O'Connell, B., Shore, C., & Bates, E. (1984). The effect of contextual variation on symbolic play: Development from 20 to 30 months. In I. Bretherton (Ed.), *Symbolic play: The development of social understanding* (pp. 271–298). New York: Academic Press.

Brown, R. (1973). *A first language: The early stages.* Cambridge, MA: Harvard University Press.

Bruner, J. (1975). The ontogenesis of speech acts. *Journal of Child Language, 2,* 1–19.

Bruner, J. (1980). Afterword. In D. R. Olson (Ed.), *The social foundations of language and thought* (pp. 376–386). New York: Norton.

Butterworth, G. (1979, September). *What minds have in common is space: A perceptual mechanisms for joint reference in infancy.* Paper presented to the Developmental Section, British Psychological Society, Southampton, England.

Campos, J. J. (1983). The importance of affective communication in social referencing: A commentary on Feinman. *Merrill-Palmer Quarterly, 28,* 445–470.

Campos, J. J., & Stenberg, C. R. (1981). Perception, appraisal and emotion: The onset of social referencing. In M. E. Lamb & L R. Sherrod (Eds.), *Infant social cognition* (pp. 273–314). Hillsdale, NJ: Lawrence Erlbaum Associates.

Charlesworth, W. R., & Kreutzer, M. A. (1973). An ethological approach to research on facial expressions. In P. Ekman (Ed.), *Darwin and facial expressions* (pp. 317–334). New York: Academic Press.

Condon, W. (1979). Neonatal entrainment and enculturation. In M. Bullowa (Ed.), *Before speech: The beginning of interpersonal communication* (pp. 131–148). Cambridge, England: Cambridge University Press.

Dunn, J. (1988). *The beginnings of social understanding*. Cambridge, MA: Harvard University Press.

Dunn, J., Bretherton, I., & Munn., P. (1987). Conversations about feeling states between mothers and their young children. *Developmental Psychology, 23,* 132–139.

Estes, D., Wellman, H. M., & Wooley, J. D. (in press). Children's understanding of mental phenomena. In H. Reese (Ed.), *Advances in child development and behavior.* New York: Academic Press.

Farber, E. A., & Moely, B. E. (1979, March). *Inferring others' affective states: The use of interpersonal, vocal and facial cues by children of three age levels.* Paper presented at the biennial meeting of the Society for Research in Child Development, San Francisco.

Feinman, S. (1982). Social referencing in infancy. *Merrill-Palmer Quarterly, 28,* 445–470.

Feinman, S., & Lewis, M. (1983). Social referencing at 10 months: A second-order effect on infants' responses to strangers. *Child Development, 54,* 878–887.

Flavell, J., Botkin, P., Fry, C., Wright, J., & Jarvis, P. (1968). *The development of role-taking and communication skills in children.* New York: Wiley.

Garvey, C. (1975). Requests and responses in children's speech. *Journal of Child Language, 2,* 41–63.

Golinkoff, R. M. (1983). The preverbal negotiation of failed messages. In R. M. Golinkoff (Ed.), *The transition from prelinguistic to linguistic communication* (pp. 57–78). Hillsdale, NJ: Lawrence Erlbaum Associates.

Greenfield, P. M. (1979). Informativeness, presupposition, and semantic choice in single-word utterances. In E. Ochs & B. B. Schieffelin (Eds.), *Developmental pragmatics* (pp. 159–166). New York: Academic Press.

Greenfield, P. M. (1980). Toward an operational and logical analysis of intentionality: The use of discourse in early child language. In D. R. Olson (Ed.), *The social foundations of language and thought* (pp. 254–279). New York: Norton.

Greenfield, P. M., & Smith, J. (1976). *The structure of communication in early language development.* New York: Academic Press.

Harding, C. G., & Golinkoff, R. M. (1979). The origins of intentional vocalizations in prelinguistic infants. *Child Development, 50,* 33–40.

Holzman, M. S. (1971). Ellipsis in discourse: Implications for linguistic analysis by computer, the child's acquisition of language, and semantic theory. *Language and Speech, 14,* 86–98.

Hood, L., & Bloom, L. (1979). What, when, and how about why: A longitudinal study of early expressions of causality. *Monographs of the Society for Research in Child Development, 44,* (Serial No. 181).

Johnson, C. N. (1988). Theory of mind and the structure of conscious experience. In J. Astington, P. Harris, & D. Olson (Eds.), *Developing theories of mind* (pp. 47–63). New York: Cambridge University Press.

Johnson-Laird, P. N. (1983). *Mental models.* Cambridge, MA: Harvard University Press.

Kagan, J. (1981). *The second year.* Cambridge, MA: Harvard University Press.

Klinnert, M., Campos, J., Sorce, J., Emde, R., & Svejda, M. (1983). Emotions as behavior regulators: Social referencing in infancy. In R. Plutchik & H. Kellerman (Eds.), *Emotions in early development: Vol. 2. The emotions* (pp. 57–86). New York: Academic Press.

Leslie, A. M. (1987). Pretense and representation: The origins of "theory of mind." *Psychological Review, 94,* 412–426.

Lewis, M., & Brooks-Gunn, J. (1979). *Social cognition and the acquisition of self.* New York: Plenum.

Lock, A. (1980). *The guided reinvention of language.* New York: Academic Press.

Maratsos, M. P. (1973). Nonegocentric communication abilities in preschool children. *Child Development, 44,* 697–700.

McCune-Nicolich, L. (1981). The cognitive bases of relational words in the single word period. *Journal of Child Language, 8,* 15–34.

Mead, G. H. (1934). *Mind, self and society.* Chicago: University of Chicago Press.

Meltzoff, A., & Moore, M. (1977). Imitation of facial and manual gestures by human neonates. *Science, 198,* 75–78.

Miller, P., & Garvey, C. (1984). Mother-baby role-play: Its origin in social support. In I. Bretherton (Ed.), *Symbolic play: The development of social understanding* (pp. 101–130). New York: Academic Press.

Miller, P. H., & Aloise, P. A. (1989). Young children's understanding of the psychological causes of behavior: A review. *Child Development, 60,* 257–285.

Murphy, D. J., & Messer, D. J. (1977). Mothers, infants and pointing: A study of a gesture. In R. H. Schaffer (Ed.), *Studies in mother-infant interaction* (pp. 323–354). New York: Academic Press.

Nicolich, L. (1977). Beyond sensorimotor intelligence: Assessment of symbolic maturity through analysis of pretend play. *Merrill-Palmer Quarterly, 23,* 88–99.

Ninio, A., & Snow, C. (1984). *Language acquisition through language use.* Unpublished Manuscript, Hebrew University, Israel.

Piaget, J. (1959). *The language and thought of the child.* London: Routledge & Kegan Paul.

Piaget, J. (1962). *Play, dreams and imitation in childhood.* New York: Norton.

Premack, D., & Woodruff, G. (1978). Does the chimpanzee have a theory of mind? *The Behavioral and Brain Sciences, 4,* 515–526.

Preyer, W. (1888/1889). *The mind of the child* (2 vols.). New York: Appleton.

Radke-Yarrow, M., & Zahn-Waxler, C. (1973). *Developmental studies of altruism.* NIMH Protocol, Clinical Project No. 73-M-02, J00.111.

Ratner, N., & Bruner, J. (1978). Games, social exchange, and the acquisition of language. *Journal of Child Language, 5,* 391–401.

Rommetveit, R. (1971). Words, context and verbal message transmission. In A. E. Carswell & R. Rommetveit (Eds.), *Social context of messages* (pp. 13–26). New York: Academic Press.

Rommetveit, R. (1972). Language games, syntactic structures and hermeneutics. In J. Israel & H. Tajfel (Eds.), The context of social psychology (pp. 212–267). New York: Academic Press.

Rommetveit, R. (1979a). On the architecture of intersubjectivity. In R. Rommetveit & R. M. Blakar (Eds.), *Studies of language, thought and verbal communication* (pp. 93–107). New York: Academic Press.

Rommetveit, R. (1979b). On negative rationalism in scholarly studies of verbal communication and dynamic residuals in the construction of human intersubjectivity. In R. Rommetveit & R. M. Blakar (Eds.), *Studies of language, thought and verbal communication* (pp. 147–161). New York: Academic Press.

Ross, H. S. (1980, April). Infants' use of turn alternation signals in games. Paper presented at the International Conference on Infant Studies, New Haven, CT.

Ross, H. S., & Kay, D. A. (1980). The origins of social games. In K. Rubin (Ed.), *Children's play* (pp. 17–32). San Francisco: Jossey-Bass.

Scaife, M., & Bruner, J. (1975) The capacity for joint visual attention in the infant. *Nature, 253,* 265–266.

Scollon, R. (1979). An unzippered condensation of a dissertation on child language. In E. Ochs & B. B. Schieffelin (Eds.), *Developmental pragmatics* (pp. 215–227). New York: Academic Press.

Shatz, M. (1983). Communication. In J. H. Flavell & E. M. Markman (Eds.), *Handbook of child psychology: Vol. 3. Cognitive development* (pp. 841–889). New York: Wiley.

Shatz, M., Wellman, H. M., & Silber, S. (1983). The acquisition of mental verbs: A systematic investigation of the first reference to mental state. *Cognition, 14,* 301–321.

Shultz, T. R. (1980). The development of the concept of intention. In A. Collins, (Ed.), *Minnesota symposium on child psychology* (Vol. 13, pp. 131–164). Hillsdale, NJ: Lawrence Erlbaum Associates.

Stern, C., & Stern, W. (1928). *Die Kindersprache: Eine psychologische und sprachtheoretische Untersuchung* (4th ed.). Leipzig: Barth.

Stern, D. (1985). *The interpersonal world of the infant.* New York: Basic Books.

Stern, D., Jaffe, J., Beebe, B., & Bennett, S. K. (1975). Vocalizing in unison and alternation: Two modes of communication within the mother-infant dyad. In D. Aaronson & R. W. Rieber (Eds.). *Developmental psycholinguistics and communication disorders* (pp. 89–100). New York: New York Academy of Sciences.

Stern, W. (1914). *Die Psychologie der fruehen Kindheit bis zum sechsten Lebensjahr.* Leipzig: Quelle & Meyer.

Sugarman-Bell, S. (1978). Some organized aspects of preverbal communication. In I. Markova (Ed.), *The social context of language* (pp.49–66). London: Wiley.

Thompson, R. A. (1987). Empathy and emotional understanding: The early development of empathy. In N. Eisenberg & J. Strayer (Eds.), *Empathy and its development* (pp. 119–145). Cambridge: Cambridge University Press.

Trabasso, T., Stein, N. L., & Johnson, L. R. (1981). Children's knowledge of events: A causal analysis of knowledge structure. *The psychology of learning and motivation* (Vol. 15, 237–282). New York: Academic Press.

Trevarthen, C. (1979). Communication and cooperation in early infancy: A description of primary intersubjectivity. In M. Bullowa (Ed.), *Before speech: The beginning of interpersonal communication* (pp. 321–347). Cambridge, England: Cambridge University Press.

Trevarthen, C., & Hubley, P. (1979). Secondary intersubjectivity: Confidence, confiding, and acts of meaning in the first year. In A. Lock (Ed.), *Action, gesture and symbol* (pp. 183–229). New York: Academic Press.

Tronick, E., Als, H., & Adamson, L. (1979). Structure of early face-to-face communicative interactions. In M. Bullowa (Ed.), *Before speech* (pp. 349–372). New York: Cambridge University Press.

Watson, J. B. (1928). *Psychological care of infant and child.* New York: Norton.

Wellman, H. M. (1988). First steps in the child's theorizing about the mind. In J. Astington, P. Harris, & D. Olson (Eds.), *Developing theories of mind* (pp. 64–92). New York: Cambridge University Press.

Wolf, D. (1982). Understanding others: A longitudinal case study of the concept of independent agency. In G. Forman (Ed.), *Action and thought: From sensorimotor schemes to symbol use* (pp. 297–327). New York: Academic Press.

Wolf, D. P., Rygh, J., & Altshuler, J. (1984). Agency and experience: Actions and states in play narratives. In I. Bretherton (Eds.), *Symbolic play: The development of social understanding* (pp. 195–217). New York: Academic Press.

Zahn-Waxler, C., Radke-Yarrow, M., & King, R. (1979). Childrearing and children's prosocial initiations towards victims of distress. *Child Development, 50,* 319–330.

CHAPTER 5

The Language of Emotion, the Emotions, and Nominalist Bootstrapping

Richard T. Beckwith
Princeton University

When comparing the literature on children's theories of mind with that on children's use of language about mind, one is struck by an apparent contradiction. On the one hand, the performance of preschool children on a variety of tasks demonstrates that they have a good deal to learn about mental states (Gopnik & Astington, 1988; Perner, this volume); on the other hand, research into the language of preschool children seems to indicate that they do learn a vocabulary that allows them to refer to states of mind (Bloom, Rispoli, Gartner, & Hafitz, 1989; Bloom, Tackeff, & Lahey, 1984; Hood & Bloom, 1979; Moore & Furrow, this volume).[1] Thus, children seem to learn the terms that refer to mental states before they learn about the referents. The goal of this chapter is to demonstrate that this contradiction is only apparent. In so doing, I address the influence of children's nascent theories of mind on the way they learn language and the impact this has on the language of emotion and emotions themselves. A further goal is to describe a likely path that children take to move beyond their early theories of mind. In general, I am concerned with how children learn terms with abstract reference.

---

[1] Although terms that refer to mental states are earlier than theories of mind, they are by no means early (Bloom & Beckwith, 1989).

Specifically, I am concerned with how children learn emotion words, a special case of abstract reference.

THE PROBLEM: ABSTRACT REFERENCE

An emotion is abstract in the sense that the emotion of one person cannot be directly perceived by another. We can, of course, see a smile on a friend we are greeting, see a child hugging a favorite toy, or hear the crying of one who mourns. What we cannot see or hear is the emotion that we assume lies beneath or causes these behaviors.

Abstract objects present an interesting problem for learning, because abstract objects cannot, strictly speaking, be perceived by the learner. To learn a word, one must, at the minimum, have a representation of the meaning, which requires a representation of the referent. However, because perception cannot cause the representation of an abstract object, names for abstract objects would appear to be unlearnable. As adults, we might follow Bentham (on a well-worn trail behind Russell and Quine) and claim that terms that refer to abstract entities actually refer to phrases or propositions (Ogden, 1932; Hookway, 1988). On Bentham's analysis, one might imagine that *sadness* is a second-order referring term and that lying behind it is a noun phrase something like *the behavior of a person immediately following the loss of something valued.* The problem here is that very young children, new to the language banquet, would not be able to make use of this noun phrase even if it were to be served up to them. In general, children are not able to comprehend reference to nonpresent objects (but see Engle, 1986, and Sachs, 1983, for the types of displaced reference that children may be able to appreciate). I do, however, offer an explanation that differs only slightly from Bentham's. The representation of an emotion is not a sentence or noun phrase, but rather, a nonlinguistic, script-like representation (Abelson, 1973; Nelson & Gruendel, 1981) called a paradigm scenario (de Sousa, 1980, 1987), which is described in the section "A Characterization of Emotion." This explanation, like Bentham's, emphasizes nominalist assumptions.

The theoretical framework within which this is spelled out is called *nominalist bootstrapping* (Beckwith, 1988b). Nominalist bootstrapping is, essentially, the conjunction of the meaning of the two words. Nominalist theories hold that only objects with causal efficacy exist, that is, that abstract objects do not really exist (Field, 1980). Bootstrapping is the notion that the development of knowledge in a domain proceeds by means of knowledge of some part of that domain. The position presented in this chapter is that knowledge of emotions is bootstrapped by nominalistically statable categories.

NOMINALIST BOOTSTRAPPING

Nominalist theories hold that abstract objects do not exist. These theories can be profitably contrasted with conceptualist theories, such as Chomsky's linguistic theory, which hold that abstract objects exist as (typically innate) properties of the mind, and to Platonist theories, such as Katz's linguistic theory, which hold that abstract objects exist independently of minds (Katz, 1981). From a developmental perspective, both the conceptualist and platonist alternatives to nominalism are psychologically untenable or incomplete, because, under them, representations—the stuff of psychology—are not something that we can hope to study. Under the conceptualist approach, we have to take on faith that abstract objects exist, because they are not representations proper, that is, they are only mental, and there is no thing outside the mind that they represent (see Danto, 1983, for an exposition of this notion of representation as "representation of"). Under the Platonist approach, abstract objects exist in the world, but the benefits of this "reality" are mitigated by the fact that Platonists offer no mechanism that will cause the representation of an abstract object.[2] For conceptualists, abstract objects are in the mind and never had to get there, whereas for Platonists, abstract objects exist in the world, but there is no claim that they wend their way into the mind. Thus, conceptualism and Platonism are both shackled with the problem of unverifiability.

Nominalist bootstrapping avoids the problem of unverifiability, because it claims that representations should be considered an effect of experience and, to the extent possible, developmental explanations should postulate primitives that are representations of perceptable entities. It stands to reason that abstract entities themselves cannot be primitives in development, because such entities have no empirical reality for the child. The ontology of primitives—which follows from the rejection of abstractness—distinguishes nominalism from other perspectives. This is not to say that the child develops no representation of

---

[2]Platonists have not offered a mechanism for representation, because they have no specific interest in mental representation or language as it is known. Any set of mechanisms for the representation of language (including those presented in this chapter) are likely to be acceptable within a Platonist account.

abstract objects, but simply that representations of abstract objects should be considered to follow from representations formed on the basis of experience.

Nominalist bootstrapping also leads to a more parsimonious theory. To see why this is the case, we can defer to the father of parsimony, William of Ockham, who was a nominalist (Moody, 1975). Ockham is best known for his razor and for having said (in various ways), "What can be done with fewer, it is vain to do with more." One of Ockham's concerns was science, where the criteria for something being a science included that science is an investigation of some domain, and in this investigation some truth can be found. He believed that if it is possible to explain some phenomenon on the basis of concrete entities, it is unparsimonious to introduce abstract entities into the ontology. Ockham acknowledged that a restriction to concrete phenomena worked best for such sciences as physics, where the terms of the theory designate phenomena that can be observed. For "nonempirical" sciences, which include abstract objects, he believed that abstract objects could be reduced to analyses of sets of concrete objects.[3] Under Ockham's analysis, the most parsimonious account will reduce the abstract terms of logic and similar (nonempirical) sciences to complexes of concrete terms.

There is some suggestion that nominalism offers the correct characterization of children's representations because concrete categories predate the abstract in several domains. Nominalist bootstrapping accounts for findings in the literature on children's performance in object perception, the reversal shift, and the acquisition of grammatical functions, such as subject or object, by assuming that learners form mental representations of concrete objects and build paradigms out of these representations (Beckwith, 1988b). Nominalist bootstrapping also offers explanations for data from the literature on children's theories of mind. Gopnik and Astington (1988) have argued that it may be "easier to construct metarepresentations of representations that are more perceptually based than those that are more abstract" (p. 34). Nominalist bootstrapping suggests that this would be the case, because abstract representations are metarepresentations of previously formed represen-

---

[3]Ockham claimed that such nonempirical sciences as logic are, in essence, analyses of the propositions of physics and that the abstract terms of logic referred to the concrete observations of physics (Moody, 1975). Ockham called the concrete terms of empirical sciences "terms of the first intention." The abstract terms of nonempirical sciences Ockham dubbed "terms of the second intention." Developmentalists will note that this is identical to Piaget's first-degree operations that deal with real objects and events and second-degree operations that deal with propositions or statements based on the first-degree, concrete ones (Piaget & Inhelder, 1964).

tations (typically of concrete objects), and those of abstract objects must come later. Emotion terms and cognitive terms are learned relatively late (Bloom & Beckwith, 1989; Bretherton & Beeghly, 1982). Bretherton and Beeghly suggested that cognitive terms appear relatively late because they lack clear, external correlates. Nominalist bootstrapping would account for the late appearance of cognitive terms by claiming that children must build paradigms of the appropriate external correlates. Thus, nominalist bootstrapping accounts for the types of children's concepts and words that children use relevant to their theories of mind. We turn next to a discussion of implications for emotions more generally and the target language.

A CHARACTERIZATION OF EMOTION

Up to this point, I have discussed emotion as abstract but have withheld any characterization of what sort of abstract thing an emotion might be. This section offers an analysis of what an emotion is. This analysis borrows heavily from de Sousa (1987), and the interested reader is referred there.

De Sousa presents a critique of a number of standard theories of emotion (all inadequate), which are echoed here and expanded to address the particular problems of word learning. The first to consider are *feeling theories*, which are quite close to the folk theory of emotion. They hold that emotion is a kind of sensation. The problem with feeling theories as theories of emotion is that they offer no criteria for deciding whether something is an emotion or not. For example, what distinguishes a vibration from an emotion? Certainly, both are feelings, and no one would claim that a feeling of vibration is an emotion. Simply claiming that the emotions are feelings will not allow us to distinguish between the two. Thus, despite the closeness of feeling theories to our folk theory, much more is needed. With respect to acquisition, we should note that if feeling theories were correct, the ability of a child to learn the term would be diminished by the fact that the child would be able to learn the referring term only when (a) the child was experiencing a particular feeling, (b) an adult realized that the child was experiencing this particular feeling, (c) the adult named the feeling, and (d) the child took the name to be a label for the feeling. The child would not be able to ascertain the reference in any application of the label to other people's feelings and it is difficult to see how another person would know that the assertability conditions were fulfilled in the child (outside of behavior) for the naming to take place.

Second, we have *cognitive theories* of emotion. These theories hold emotion to be a kind of cognitive state. On analogy with feeling theories, we have the unresolved analytic problem here of how to distinguish emotions from other cognitive states and no change in our acquisition problem. Children will be no more able to learn a term with abstract reference simply because its referent has been assimilated to the cognitive class. In fact, the mental referring capacity of cognitive terms must likewise be difficult to acquire. Thus, although some species of cognitive theory is undoubtedly correct (as is some species of feeling theory), something more is required because the child is still saddled with an acquisition problem.

In a related, more internally directed analysis of emotions, the eliminative materialists have argued that in a future neuroscience, emotion terms will be replaced by reference to brain states. That is, rather than saying (in the folk psychological jargon), "I am angry," we will (more correctly) say, "My amygdala is firing in pattern 451," or "Neurons 1984 and 2001 are firing again," where these locations are distinctly not neural longhand for the emotion term *angry*. Presumably, neural activity in these regions is thought to be a better indication of the presence of an emotion than is personal reflection. It is obvious that it would be difficult to learn a term that refers to a brain state. It should be equally obvious that neural firings are not the semantic target of emotion terms. This is simply because many emotions are directed toward objects. Kenny (1963), in his discussion of objects of emotion, said, "The sense of 'object' [of emotion] which I have hitherto employed and wish now to discuss is one which derives from the grammatical notion of the object of a transitive verb. The object of fear is what is feared, the object of love is what is loved, the object of cutting is what is cut, the object of heating is what is heated" (pp. 187-188). Such directedness requires representation proper, that is, representation of some external object, and such representation can never be sufficiently accounted for by reference to only the representational media—in this case, the neural substrate (Danto, 1983).

A third potential theory of emotion is one that is offered within behaviorism. Within behaviorism, an emotion is just a set of behaviors. Behaviorists look to behavior as both data and explanation for one reason: behaviors are observable. The problem here is that most of us believe that mental states, not behaviors, distinguish between emotions. For example, most people would believe that an event in which someone bravely stands his or her ground in the face of the enemy is different from an event in which someone is paralyzed with fear in the face of the enemy, although in both cases the behavior and situation appear to be identical. That the events (based on the descriptions offered) are clearly different is hardly the case. The ability to determine what it is that makes these situations different is not among the abilities of the behaviorist, and, for this reason, behaviorism is an inadequate theory of emotion. Nevertheless, a child could make some use of canonical relations between some behaviors and some state names, whether the behaviors are necessarily present or not. Thus, behaviorism presents to us our first potential referent.

Several other theories of the emotions and considerable argumentation later, de Sousa settled on a relational theory of emotions centering around what he called "paradigm scenarios." Paradigm scenarios are, essentially, scripts containing such concrete phenomena as a subject (the holder of the emotion) and a target (that thing toward which the emotion is directed). The paradigm scenarios of specific emotions also have their typical "feel" (as in the feeling theories), the subject's evaluation of a goal-directed situation (as in many of the cognitive theories), and co-occurrent behaviors (as in behaviorism). Together these various aspects of a paradigm scenario constitute the emotion.

Given nominalist bootstrapping, children would be predisposed to construct paradigm scenarios of emotions. Nominalist bootstrapping assumes that the acquisition of terms referring to abstract objects is grounded in perceptable correlates of the "object." The nominalist foundation upon which children build their emotional constructs is well suited to a paradigm scenario analysis, because children are laboring under the misconception that emotion terms refer to nominalistically stable eliciting conditions, typical behaviors and interventions, and the like, which will come to be incorporated into the paradigm scenario. Under the assumptions of nominalist bootstrapping, all the child needs to do is add frequently occurring perceptual features to the scenarios associated with particular words. Thus, paradigm scenarios are not only consistent with, but also are explicable given, nominalist bootstrapping of emotions. We turn now to a more detailed description of the acquisition of abstract reference.

ABSTRACT REFERENCE AND THE EMOTIONS

In the acquisition of mental ascription terms under nominalist bootstrapping, children would be something of *logical positivists* (or behaviorists). Logical positivists, as described by Putnam (1975), hold that mental ascription terms referred to "public events involving 'observable things' and 'observation predicates'" (p. 445). The theories of mind held by young positivists (and determining the semantics of their mental ascription utterances) would not require that the children "establish . . . the existence of entities which are altogether unobservable" (Ayer, 1948, p. 131) but would rather have mental ascriptions about others defined "in terms of empirical manifestations . . . and ultimately in terms of sense-contents" (Ayer, 1948, p. 130).

For children, "more concrete words . . . appear easier to map onto sensory elements than ones which refer to internal, more subjective experience" (Gardner, 1974, p. 89). However, it seems that not only do children learn concrete terms more quickly than they do abstract terms; children actually learn terms of abstract reference as if they refer to concrete phenomena.

Children use mental ascription terms, when first acquired, to refer to physical stimuli and not feelings. For example, Shatz, Wellman, and Silber (1983) found that the children in their study first used mental verbs to direct interaction, that is, without making "specific reference to the listener's or speaker's knowledge state" (p. 302). Furthermore, there are data in the literature that suggest that children believe that emotion terms refer to physical attributes. Wolman, Lewis, and King (1972) found that young children tend to describe emotions as "external" features, and, as children grow older they begin to assign body zones to particular emotions until, eventually, children locate emotions in their heads.

Children have good reason to believe that emotion words refer to external phenomena. Dunn, Bretherton, and Munn (1987) and Capatides (1990) found that when mothers talked to children about feeling states—although it was most likely to be the children's feelings under discussion—the function of these utterances was not to comment on feeling states but rather to guide behavior, that is, to suggest emotion-relevant interventions or to explain and clarify the causes or consequences of the feelings, thereby focusing on external dimensions. Nevertheless, when we use an emotion term, we believe that we are referring not to the behavioral manifestation of the emotion but rather to the abstract mental correlate of the behavior (Putnam, 1975). The rest of this chapter addresses formulating an explanation of children's behavior and exploring some of the implications of the nominalist bootstrapping explanation.

WORD LEARNING

To explain how children learn emotion terms, we must consider how children learn words in general. For this, I look to ostension, a name-learning mechanism with some currency in the philosophical and developmental literature (Beckwith, 1988a; Bruner, 1983; Devitt, 1981; Kripke, 1980). Names are either learned through ostension (called designation) or through definition (called denotation) (Devitt, 1981). In an instance of designation, reference to some object is nonlinguistically fixed, and then that object is named. For example, a mother enters a room, the child's attention is fixed on the mother, and the father says "Mommy." In this situation, the child can learn that "Mommy" refers to the mother. When ostension is not possible, the learner must rely on denotation. In an instance of denotation, reference to the object is fixed using language (e.g., a definition), and then the object is named. For example, someone might say, "The woman who goes out of the front door every morning with a briefcase is Mommy." If one can understand the noun phrase, "the woman who goes out the front door every morning with a briefcase," and knows the person picked out by the noun phrase, then one can learn that "Mommy" refers to that person described by the noun phrase. In order to avoid circularity, the defining terms must ultimately be reducible to designation.

Most of young children's lexical items almost certainly must be learned under conditions of ostension rather than definition, that is, children will assume that the term designates some present concrete instance.[4] Most of the time when caregivers talk to children, the language is just this sort of coding of cotemporaneous events (Bloom, 1973; Snow, 1977). This line of reasoning suggests a method for learning terms of mental ascription. A young child's first encounters with words putatively making mental ascription, if they are to be learnable at all, are most likely to be considered (by the child) as terms that designate. Consequently, I am assuming that emotion terms are learned through designation rather than through definition.

Of course, ostensive learning, as a special case of reference, cannot be properly considered successful unless the speaker and listener have the same object in mind. There can be no successful reference given a nominalist listener and a speaker making reference to categories that have no causal efficacy—for example, abstract objects such as that referred to by mental ascriptions. However, if the speaker refers to an abstract object (e.g., happiness), and the listener believes that the reference is to some concrete correlate of the abstract object (e.g., a smile) we can then have what might be considered semisuccessful reference. This is what I assume here.

What aspect of the situation might the child consider the emotion

---

[4]This offers an easy explanation for the early predominance of nouns reported by Bloom (1973) and Gentner (1982).

term to be designating and what implications might this have? The use of ostension to pick out the emotional-state referent of, say, anger is relatively difficult to imagine. In fact, it's much easier to imagine a solution to what is being designated if one is a logical positivist. For the logical positivist, knowing the reference of an emotion term involves knowing what kinds of behavior (e.g., a frown) would hold in the contexts in which that term could apply, and the frown would be the target of the designation. It was mentioned earlier that children use emotion terms as though they referred to external dimensions; that is, the attested use of these terms is consistent with the input (Dunn et al., 1987; Capatides, 1990) and with nominalist bootstrapping. Nominalist bootstrapping also has implications for not only the course of acquisition of emotion terms but also a characterization of the emotions themselves and the syntax and semantics of the target language.

NOMINALIST BOOTSTRAPPING AND THE STRUCTURE OF LANGUAGE

It is commonplace to argue that the structure of language is strongly affected by the fact that it must be learned by children (Andersen, 1973). I now move on to some data that suggests that nominalist bootstrapping of emotional reference influences the structure of the language both lexically, in terms of polysemy, and syntactically, in terms of argument structure.

Emotion and Polysemy

Words can have one or many senses. If a word has more than one sense, it is called polysemous. For example, the word *eye* can be used to refer to the organ of sight or a part of a potato, or the word *tree* can be used to refer to a form of plant life or a graph of the syntactic relations in a sentence. Many words used to refer to emotions have more than one sense. If we look at the senses of terms referring to emotions, we find that certain relations hold between the different senses. As an example, consider the following quote from Senator Robert Dole of Kansas on the occasion of having lost a primary election. Dole said, "I've been beaten before and no doubt will again, but I've never been defeated and never will be." When Dole said this, he was using the word *beaten* to refer to a possible eliciting condition of an emotion and the word *defeated* to refer to an emotional state but these can easily be turned around so that *beaten* refers to the emotion and *defeated* refers to the eliciting conditions. So, for example, we can imagine having heard Congressman Joe Biden saying, on the occasion of his withdrawal from the presidential race, "I've been defeated before and no doubt will again, but I've never been beaten and never will be."

We can see from the preceding examples that one of the meaning relations that holds between different senses of polysemous emotion terms is that the term might be used to refer to either eliciting conditions of emotions or the emotions themselves. Terms that have both of these senses include *gratification, amusement, perturbation, infuriation,* and *discouragement.* Another relation that might hold between senses is that of an act accompanying the emotion or the emotion itself. Terms that have both these senses include *admiration, scorn, enjoyment, contrition,* and *disapproval.*

Polysemous emotion terms include a sense that refers to a concrete action either on the part of an experiencer or with the experiencer as the affected object. Such a pattern of polysemy would be predicted if children were to learn emotion terms as if they referred to observables or, better, were to learn that these actions were included in the emotional constructs that are the targets of emotion terms. In fact, polysemy and acquisition do seem to be related. The more polysemous a word is, the easier it is for a child to acquire it (Hayes, 1988). Hayes has claimed that this is because the resemblance between word senses allows the child to use existing knowledge to assist in the acquisition of a new sense. Here, we see that, sometimes, the child's ontology and semisuccessful reference can support the development and maintenance of polysemous relations in the target lexicon. Thus, the semantics of the emotion lexicon supports the acquisition of one sense under nominalist assumptions, thereby allowing the child to learn the term more easily.

Psych Verbs and Argument Structure

The problem of language apparently preceding cognition takes a new turn when we consider the acquisition of "psych verbs" and children's conceptual repertoires and cognitive abilities. Psych verbs are called psych verbs because they assign the thematic role *experiencer* to one of their arguments. Verbs of emotion are psych verbs because one of the referents of one of the arguments of the verb experiences the emotion described by the verb. This type of verb has received considerable attention recently in the linguistics literature (Belletti & Rizzi, 1988; Grimshaw, in press). The problem addressed in the linguistic research

AGENT → EXPERIENCER → GOAL/SOURCE/LOCATION → THEME
SUBJECT   DIRECT OBJECT   INDIRECT OBJECT

FIG. 5.1.   The thematic hierarchy.

on psych verbs has to do with their semantics, argument structure, and the notion of basic verb or basic sentence (these are discussed later).[5] Specifically, the problem is that a class of nonbasic verb—a marked case—is found across languages as a type of psych verb. These psych verbs are marked because, unlike basic verbs, the role prominence of their arguments on the thematic hierarchy (the upper tier of Fig. 5.1) does not predict syntactic category. I next discuss Grimshaw's (in press) solution to the psych verb problem and then propose an alternative that is based on the assumptions of nominalist bootstrapping.

The way to read Fig. 5.1 is to think of terms in the upper row as roles that objects play in some situation. The words in a sentence might refer to objects filling any of these roles. The roles on the left are more "prominent" than those on the right. For example, *agent* is more prominent than *experiencer,* and experiencer is more prominent than *theme.* In basic sentences, prominence determines the grammatical function (e.g., subject or object) of a verb's arguments. In a basic sentence (that is a sentence that is nonpassivized, etc.), the most prominent role becomes the subject, the next most prominent role becomes the direct object, and finally, if there is another argument, it becomes the indirect object. Theme is the least likely of all the roles in this hierarchy to become the subject;[6] however, in one class of psych verb, the theme is the subject despite the fact that *experiencer,* a more prominent role, is present.

The top row on Fig. 5.1 might look familiar from the child language literature. At least since 1970, it has been known that young children's grammars can be described using such categories as *agent* and *goal* (Beckwith, 1988a; Bloom, 1970; Bloom, Lightbown, & Hood, 1975; Pinker, 1984; Rispoli & Bloom, 1988). The frequency with which these roles appear in descriptions of children's language suggests that children may be predisposed to attend to something like thematic roles. Thus, it is especially problematic that there is an exception to this semantically driven rule that occurs across languages. It will help to see exactly what the exception is.

---

[5]Basic sentences are significant within a recent model of language acquisition—semantic bootstrapping—in which the primary data of the language learner consists only of basic sentences (Pinker, 1984). Nominalist bootstrapping can be seen as a nominalist reduction of semantic bootstrapping.

[6]There are at least two thematic hierarchies in the linguistics literature. The differences between the two are irrelevant to this discussion.

John fears lightning

EXPERIENCER   THEME

FIG. 5.2. The Fear Class

In the sentence in Fig. 5.2, "John fears lightning," *John*—the experiencer—is the subject, and *lightning*—identified by Grimshaw as the theme—is the direct object. The argument structure of *fear* is exactly as the hierarchy would predict.

In Fig. 5.3, the problem with the *frighten* class verbs is apparent. *John* is still the experiencer, but is now the direct object. The *lightning* is still the theme, but is now the subject.

The grammar normally assigns such grammatical functions as subject and object to the arguments of a verb on the basis of prominence; the most prominent role is assigned subject and so on. Verbs such as *frighten* are marked because the prominent but preassociated experiencer is passed over in syntactic category assignment, and the theme is made subject. Grimshaw's analysis (in press) hinges on the assumption that, with such verbs as *frighten*, the argument that refers to the experiencer is preassociated with accusative case and, because of this, is assigned to direct object. The preassociation argument suggests that *frighten* verbs simply violate case assignment rules.

This is a problem with respect to acquisition. A child cannot know that an argument is preassociated with a syntactic category, and there is no property of the input, other than the argument structure of the verb, that could cause the child to learn this. *Frighten*, because it is a marked case, would simply need to be learned brute force. However, recent work that I've done in collaboration with Erin Tinker indicates that young children make correct thematic category assignments with the verb *frighten*, which is the marked case, and incorrect category assignments with the verb *fear*, the acquisition of which is supposed to be easier because it is unmarked.

In that study, we presented children with a pronoun resolution task. Children were shown a scene with small plastic animals. In the scene, one animal snuck up behind another animal and made a noise. The second animal ran away screaming, and the child was asked, "Who *frightened/feared* whom?". The child's task was to fill in the animals' names in the sentence. That is, the children were asked to use the same verb and replace *who* and *whom* with the names of the animals.

Lightning frightens John

THEME   EXPERIENCER

FIG. 5.3. The Frighten Class

The children resolved the pronouns in 16 sentences. Eight of the sentences used the verbs *frighten* and *fear*. Of the four sentences for each verb, two sentences involved an interaction between two nonthreatening animals (e.g., Bugs Bunny and Gumby), and two sentences involved a monster (i.e., The Tasmanian Devil) and a nonthreatening animal, with roles reversed between the two sentences (i.e., the monster doing the scaring in one and being scared in the other). This counterbalancing was to determine whether scariness had a role in determining argument structure. Of the seven 4-year-old children who did the task, all seven resolved the pronouns correctly with four instances of *frighten*, and none of the seven got any of the four instances of *fear* correct (p < .01). Thus, the children's performance was the opposite of the prediction based on argument structure markedness.

If we assume that the child is learning emotions and emotion terms according to nominalist bootstrapping, we can account for the problem with psych verbs. Given the previous arguments, we can see that children's understanding of the semantics underlying sentences with psych verbs is not capable of supporting the thematic hierarchy that the preassociation theory assumes. That is, the young child's analysis of *frighten* events would not be that *John* is the experiencer and the *lightning* is the theme. The child's thematic hierarchy, if such a thing exists, would not have room for the experiencer role at all, because the child could not assign that role until a concept of other minds was acquired. However, under the present analysis, *John* is the entity that the *lightning* caused to behave in a particular way. Therefore, rather than the experiencer, *John* would be the theme. The *lightning* would not be the theme. If children try to assimilate the scene to a paradigm scenario, the *lightning* can be properly considered to have caused *John* to fear, which our child is assuming means to cause *John* to behave in a particular way. *Lightning* is more like an agent and the child would expect the agent to be the subject. This accounts for why the unmarked verb—*fear*—is difficult to acquire. The agent is the direct object of the verb, and this is in violation of the child's rules. The seeming ease of learning *frighten* is due to the child learning its argument structure in a way that the marked form (for adults) is most consistent with their grammar.

A POTENTIAL PATH OUT OF
LOGICAL POSITIVIST SEMANTICS

So far, we have claimed that the nominalist analysis has allowed us to say something about why emotions should be considered to contain behaviors and interventions in addition to feelings, why patterns of polysemy look like they do, and why there's a cross-linguistically present violation of standard case assignment rules. However, we know equally well that children quickly come to believe that emotion terms refer to mental states of people. The problem with the logical positivist analysis is that, most would agree, if there is anything analytic (i.e., necessarily true) about the meaning of emotion terms, it is not the behaviors, causes, and consequences frequently associated with emotion terms use but rather the internal states.

I am proposing that children's movement to adult conceptions of other minds requires some reasoning on the children's part. Reasoning is difficult for children, and they use various sorts of strategies to make it easier. Analogical reasoning is a simplification strategy used by children (Gentner, 1988), adults (Gick & Holyoak, 1983), and even scientists (Thagard, 1988). Analogy fits in well with this framework for two reasons. First, analogy suggests the "induction of a general schema from concrete analogs" (Gick & Holyoak, 1983, p. 1). Thus, it is compatible with the nominalist bootstrapping movement from the concrete to the abstract (although in the analogy case the movement is more toward genericity than abstractness). Second, analogy figures into the standard argument for other minds which holds that, "I know that I have a mind because of my experiences, but, since I do not have any experiences of your experiences, how do I know that you also have a mind? The standard argument from analogy is that you are like me in having a body and behaving in certain ways; so by analogy I can infer that you are also similar in having a mind" (Thagard, 1988, p. 116).

How might this work for children? Although adults have a strong bias toward using causal or implicational relations in determining the appropriateness of an analogy, young children are more likely to focus on attributes of the reasoned-about objects (Gentner, 1988). The similarity of attributes is "among the earliest determinants of ease of analogical mapping" (Gentner & Toupin, 1986, p. 297). The kinds of attribute that children of this age are most likely to use for establishing similarity include movement (Dent, 1984), perceptual, or functional similarity and completeness of mapping (Holyoak, Junn, & Billman, 1984). Perceptual and functional features, such as behaviors, interventions, and consequences, are central to children's paradigm scenarios of emotion. These features of instances of emotion will allow the child to map his or her own subjectivity onto others.

Experimental evidence supports the suggestion that children use the analogical solution to the other minds problem. Inagaki and Hatano (1987) have found that kindergarten-age children use "personification," an analogical reasoning strategy wherein the target object is assimilated to the model of a person. Personification is used by children when they need to generate predictions about the presence of unobservable attributes (including emotions) in nonhuman objects. However, these children did have constraints on their use of such analogizing. If an action or movement would be predicted and the child knew that the object was incapable of action or movement, then the personification strategy was blocked.[7] This means that until some knowledge of the attributes of particular physical objects is acquired, there will be little distinction between animate and inanimate entities—between, say, lightning and a dog.

Based on children's performance on analogical reasoning in general, the standard analogical argument for other minds would be available to children at about age 4 (Holyoak et al., 1984). Four is a significant age, because this is the age at which it appears that children are forming a theory of mind that includes internal representations in others (Perner, this volume). I have argued that children have already formed paradigm scenarios including perceptual and functional features, which are the component attributes that are best for mapping between discrete objects (Dent, 1984; Holyoak, et al., 1984). Because the children will be aware of their own phenomenology and the relations of emotions to their own plans, they can project these attributes of feeling and cognitive theories of the emotions onto others. Because others are capable of the same behaviors as the child, there is no reason to block the analogy, and it will be considered valid.

SUMMARY

To summarize, I can first return to the apparent contradiction with which we began. How would it be that children learn the language of emotions before they learn about minds? The response was that children do not learn the referring term before they learn the abstract referent. To understand this, the notion of semisuccessful reference was introduced, and it was claimed that children learn the concrete aspects of emotions as the referents of the emotion terms. The terms may then help them to organize emotional concepts or the emotion lexicon (see Johnson-Laird & Oatley, 1988, for a possible organization of the emotion lexicon).

In developing this response, a developmental perspective was introduced: nominalist bootstrapping. This allowed learning of emotion

---

[7]When known properties of objects did not conflict with the personification strategy, young children were willing to attribute properties of themselves to get a heuristic search space that was then pruned to remove predictions inconsistent with their knowledge base. With rocks and other objects that are not capable of locomotion, such a pruning means that the child will not assume that the object will, for example, run in the presence of danger. (This suggests that children will be more likely to attribute emotions that are low on the activity dimension to nonlocomoting objects.)

terms to be subsumed under standard ostension. Nominalist bootstrapping can account for, and was initially motivated by, the fact that children first use emotion terms to refer to concrete phenomena. However, nominalist bootstrapping does more than account for the way that children use emotion terms. There seem to be echoes of nominalist bootstrapping in the adult's model of emotions and in the language itself. With respect to the emotions, nominalist bootstrapping suggests an ontology of the emotions (i.e., de Sousa's paradigm scenarios) and an explanation of the genesis of the script-like quality of emotions. With respect to language, nominalist bootstrapping first (through paradigm scenarios) explains patterns of polysemy in the lexicon; specifically, it claims that the relation of eliciting conditions and co-occurrent behaviors to emotions is a natural one for language learners to see or even impose. Second, nominalist bootstrapping (by making the assumption that children's models of emotions do not need to include an experiencer) also accounts for both the linguistic problem with psych verbs and experimental results.

I have argued that nominalist bootstrapping offers both a parsimonious account of the emotions and language learning, because it has no abstract primitives, and a verifiable one, because it predicts that the environment has effects on development. Finally, I pointed to a potential path that the child could take to move beyond nominalism. In fact, this entailed little more than the standard analogical solution to the other minds problem. Thus, children can bootstrap emotion terms and emotions nominalistically, and it appears that they do.

ACKNOWLEDGMENTS

This research was supported by the James S. McDonnell Foundation. I thank Erin Tinker for her collaboration on the study reported here. For their comments on drafts of this chapter, I thank the lexigangsters (Christiane Fellbaum, Ute Fischer, Derek Gross, Judy Kegl, George Miller, Kitty Miller, and Paul Thagard), Lois Bloom, Chris Moore, and Erin Tinker. I also thank the children and parents of Our Lady of Pompeii Nursery Center in New York City for their involvement in the study reported here and especially Linda Jones, the Director, and Fabrizia Carrigan for their support and insight.

REFERENCES

Abelson, R. P. (1973). The structure of belief systems. In R. C. Schank & K. M. Colby (Eds.), *Computer models of thought and language* (pp. 287–339). San Francisco: W. H. Freeman.

Andersen, H. (1973). Abductive and deductive change. *Language, 49,* 765–793.

Ayer, A. J. (1948). *Language, truth, and logic.* London: Gollancz.

Beckwith, R. (1988a). *Learnability and psychological constraints.* Unpublished doctoral dissertation, Teachers College, Columbia University.

Beckwith, R. (1988b). *Nominalist bootstrapping or wielding Ockham's razor as he would have it wielded.* Unpublished manuscript.

Belletti, A., & Rizzi, L. (1988). Psych verbs and theta theory. *Natural Language and Linguistic Theory, 6,* 291–352.

Bloom, L. (1970). *Language development: Form and function in emerging grammars.* Cambridge, MA: MIT Press.

Bloom, L. (1973). *One word at a time.* The Hague: Mouton.

Bloom, L., & Beckwith, R. (1989). Talking with feeling: Integrating affective and linguistic expression in early language development. *Cognition and Emotion, 3,* 313–342.

Bloom, L., Lightbown, P., & Hood, L. (1975). Structure and variation in child language. *Monographs of the Society for Research in Child Development, 40,* (2, Serial No. 160). Bloom, L., Rispoli, M., Gartner, B., & Hafitz, J. (1989). Acquisition of complementation. *Journal of Child Language, 16,* 101–120.

Bloom, L., Tackeff, J., & Lahey, M. (1984). Learning *to* in complement constructions. *Journal of Child Language, 11,* 391–406.

Bretherton, I., & Beeghly, M. (1982). Talking about internal states: The acquisition of an explicit theory of mind. *Developmental Psychology, 18,* 906–921.

Bruner, J. (1983). *Child's talk: Learning to use language.* New York: Norton.

Capatides, J. (1990). *Mother's socialization of their children's expression and experience of emotion.* Unpublished doctoral dissertation, Teachers College, Columbia University.

Danto, A. (1983). Toward a retentive materialism. In L. Cauman, I. Levi, C. Parsons, & R. Schwartz (Eds.), *How many questions?: Essays in honor of Sidney Morgenbesser* (pp. 243–255). Indianapolis: Hackett.

Dent, C. H. (1984). The developmental importance of motion information in perceiving and describing metaphoric similarity. *Child Development, 55,* 1607–1613

de Sousa, R. (1980). The rationality of emotions. In A. Rorty (Ed.), *Explaining emotions* (pp. 127–151). Berkeley: University of California Press.

de Sousa, R. (1987). *The rationality of emotion.* Cambridge, MA: MIT Press.

Devitt, M. (1981). *Designation.* New York: Columbia University Press.

Dunn, J., Bretherton, I., & Munn, P. (1987). Conversations about feeling states between mothers and their young children. *Developmental Psychology, 23,* 132–139.

Engle, S. (1986, May). *Remembering together.* Paper presented at the New York Child Language Conference, New York, NY.

Field, H. H. (1980). *Science without numbers: A defence of nominalism.* Princeton: Princeton University Press.

Gardner, H. (1974). Metaphors and modalities: How children project polar adjectives onto diverse domains. *Child Development, 45,* 84–91.

Gentner, D. (1982). Why nouns are learned before verbs: Linguistic relativity vs. natural partitioning. In S. A. Kuczaj (Ed.), *Language Development, Vol. 2: Language, thought, and culture* (pp. 301–334). Hillsdale, NJ: Lawrence Erlbaum Associates.

Gentner, D. (1988). Metaphor as structure mapping: The relational shift. *Child Development, 59,* 47–59.

Gentner, D., & Toupin, C. (1986). Systematicity and surface similarity in the development of analogy. *Cognitive Science, 10,* 277–300.

Gick, M. L., & Holyoak, K. J. (1983). Schema induction and analogical transfer. *Cognitive Psychology, 15,* 1–38.

Gopnik, A., & Astington, J. (1988). Children's understanding of representational change and its relation to the understanding of false-belief and the appearance-reality distinction. *Child Development, 59,* 26–37.

Grimshaw, J. (in press). *Argument structure.* Cambridge, MA: MIT Press. [Paper circulated as Psych Verbs and the Structure of Argument structure.]

Hayes, D. P. (1988). *Word polysemy, children's lexical ecology and the acquisition of word knowledge* (Tech. Rep. No. 88–3). Ithaca, NY: Cornell University.

Holyoak, K., Junn, E., & Billman, D. (1984). Development of analogical problem-solving skill. *Child Development, 55,* 2042–2056.

Hood, L., & Bloom, L. (1979). What, when, and how about why: A longitudinal study of early expressions of causality. *Monographs of the Society for Research in Child Development, 44,* (6, Serial No. 160).

Hookway, C. (1988). *Quine: Language, experience, and reality.* Cambridge, England: Polity.

Inagaki, K., & Hatano, G. (1987). Young children's spontaneous personification as analogy. *Child Development, 58,* 1013–1020.

Johnson-Laird, P., & Oatley, K. (1988). *The language of emotions: An analysis of a semantic field.* (Rep. No. 33). Princeton, NJ: Princeton University Cognitive Science Laboratory.

Katz, J. J. (1981). *Language and other abstract objects.* Totowa, NJ: Rowman and Littlefield.

Kenny, A. (1963). *Action, emotion, and will.* New York: Humanities Press.

Kripke, S. (1980). *Naming and necessity.* Cambridge, MA: Harvard University Press.

Moody, E. A. (1975). *Studies in medieval philosophy, science, and logic: Collected papers 1933–1969.* Berkeley: University of California Press.

Nelson, K., & Gruendel, J. (1981). Generalized event representations: Basic building blocks of cognitive development. In A. Brown & M. Lamb (Eds.), *Advances in developmental psychology (Vol. 1, pp. 131–158).* Hillsdale, NJ: *Lawrence Erlbaum Associates.*

Ogden, C. K. (1932). *Bentham's theory of fictions.* New York: Harcourt, Brace and Company.

Piaget, J., & Inhelder, B. (1964). *The early growth of logic in the child: Classification and seriation.* London: Routledge and Kegan Paul.

Pinker, S. (1984). *Language learnability and language development.* Cambridge, MA: MIT Press.

Putnam, H. (1975). *Mind, language, and reality.* Cambridge, England: Cambridge University Press.

Rispoli, M., & Bloom, L. (1988). *The conceptual origins of the transitive/intransitive distinction.* In Papers and Reports of the Child Language Research Forum. Stanford, CA: Stanford University Department of Linguistics.

Sachs, J. (1983). Talking about the there and then: The emergence of displaced reference in parent-child discourse. In K. E. Nelson (ed.), *Children's language* (Vol. 4, pp. 1–28). New York: Gardner Press.

Shatz, M., Wellman, H., & Silber, S. (1983). The acquisition of mental verbs: A systematic investigation of the first reference to mental state. *Cognition, 14,* 301–321.

Snow, C. E. (1977). Mother's speech research: From input to interaction. In C. E. Snow & C. A. Ferguson (Eds.), *Talking to children: Language input and acquisition* (pp. 31–49). Cambridge, England: Cambridge University Press.

Thagard, P. (1988). Dimensions of analogy. In D. H. Helman (Ed.), *Analogical reasoning: Perspectives of artificial intelligence, cognitive science, and philosophy* (pp. 105–124). Dordecht: Kluwer Academic Publishers.

Wolman, R., Lewis, W., & King, M. (1972). The development of the language of emotions: I Theoretical and methodological introduction. *The Journal of Genetic Psychology, 120,* 167–176.

CHAPTER 6

Young Children's Understanding of Other People: Evidence from Observations Within the Family

Judy Dunn

Pennsylvania State University

In infancy, babies are apparently both interested in and responsive to the emotions and behavior of other people. They are born predisposed to attend to stimuli with the characteristics of the human face and voice, and they develop quickly "remarkable abilities to perceive the actions and expressions of other people" (Spelke & Cortelyou, 1981). They learn rapidly about stimuli that change in a manner that is contingent upon their own behavior—as does the behavior of other people interacting with them. By 2 months old, they respond differently to a person who intends to speak to them and one who speaks to someone else (Trevarthen, 1977). By the second half of their first year, they have begun to share a common communicative framework with other family members, and, as we have learned from the elegant experimental studies of *social referencing* (Klinnert, Campos, Sorce, Emde, & Svejda, 1983), in situations of uncertainty, they monitor the emotional expressions of their mothers and change their behavior appropriately in response to those expressions. As the work of those studying early language has shown particularly clearly, their comprehension of social procedures is surprisingly subtle. Bruner, for example, has persuasively argued that children have mastered the culturally appropriate use of requests, invitations, and reference well before they are correctly using the conventional linguistic forms (Bruner, 1983).

It seems, in common-sense terms, highly adaptive for babies to develop early in life some grasp of the intentions, feelings, and actions

97

of the all-important members of their family world. However, this growing sophistication about the social world, documented in babies who have hardly begun to talk, stands in notable contrast to the limitations in much older children's understanding of other minds, which have been revealed by experimental research focused on the "metarepresentational" level of reflection on others (see Perner, this volume; Astington, this volume). This experimental work underlines the deficiencies in 3- and 4-year-olds' ability to conceptualize how others think and perceive the world. The discrepancy between the emphasis on infants' social sensitivities and these limitations in older children's understanding of other minds—at least when faced with questions about hypothetical others—raises several serious questions. If preschool children are so limited in their ability to understand others, how do they manage to function effectively in the complex world of the family? Is it possible that there are differences between children's understanding of others (at least their practical, "ready-to-hand" understanding [Packer, 1986]) in their intimate emotional family world, on the one hand, and their ability to reflect on and talk about the minds and actions of the hypothetical others that are the focus of most experimental studies on the other hand? Does the ability to recognize others' emotional states develop well in advance of the ability to conceptualize others' thoughts? In this chapter, I consider the nature of children's understanding of familiar others during the transition from infancy to childhood, with a discussion of evidence from naturalistic observations of children within their families.

With these naturalistic data, we cannot, obviously, make such clear-cut inferences about details of children's problems in understanding others as is possible with the experimental research reported elsewhere in this volume. However, such naturalistic observations do have three important a priori advantages. First, we are able to study children in social settings that have real emotional significance for them. It is now well documented that very young children's abilities can be gravely underestimated if the children are studied in task settings that do not make "human sense" to them (Donaldson, 1978). Second, with unstructured observation, we are able to monitor and study the comments and inquiries about other people that are generated by the children themselves—rather than those that are imposed by the adult psychologist. Thus, we gain a window on what the child finds interesting or puzzling about others. And third, by studying the context in which children perform at their most mature, we may be able to generate hypotheses about the key processes that contribute to developmental change in the domain of interest.

The findings that I discuss (described fully in Dunn, 1988) are drawn from three longitudinal studies of secondborn children in their second and third years: six children followed at 2-month intervals through the second year, six followed similarly through their third year, and 43 families studied when the secondborn children were 18, 24, and 36 months old. The families were middle- and working-class families living in and around Cambridge in England, and all the observations, which were unstructured, were made while the children were at home, playing, fighting, and talking with their mothers and siblings. Examples are also cited from an ongoing study of children in Pennsylvania. Our strategy was to examine a number of different features of the children's behavior within their families. It would clearly be foolish to attempt to draw general inferences about children's social understanding from a focus on just one feature of their behavior; rather, we studied the children within a range of social situations, with different social partners, and in very different emotional contexts. The following domains were systematically studied: disputes, prosocial behavior, response to distress in others, cooperation and play, jokes, and conversations about others.

Two issues that are pertinent to the theme of this book stand out from these studies. The first is the evidence for the children's growing ability, over the second and third years, to understand the feeling states, intentions, and behavior of others. The second is that the results give some useful indications of which processes may be important in these developments. Two, in particular, are discussed in the second section of the chapter: the role of discourse about others' feelings and intentions and the significance of affective experience in such developments. More generally, the implications of the way in which children's growing understanding is used in their family relationships is considered.

CHILDREN'S UNDERSTANDING OF OTHERS IN THE SECOND AND THIRD YEAR

Disputes

Within each domain that we studied—disputes, jokes, empathetic and prosocial behavior, cooperation, pretend play, and conversations about other people—we found evidence for children's growing grasp of the feelings of others, of their intended actions, and of how social rules applied to other people and to themselves. In disputes, for example, the children showed a growing sophistication in teasing—actions that demonstrated a practical grasp of what would upset or annoy a particular person. Early in the second year, acts that we categorized as teasing were pretty simple; for example, children in disputes with their older siblings often seized or removed their siblings' transitional object or most special toys, or attempted to destroy something that had special significance for the sibling. In the course of the second year such teasing acts became more frequent and more elaborate. One 24-month-old, for instance, whose older sister had three imaginary friends called Lily, Allelujah, and Peepee, would, in the course of disputes with this sister, announce that *she* was Allelujah. It was an act that was reliably followed by anger or distress on her sister's part, and it was also an act of notable sophistication for a 24-month-old, because it involved both some grasp of what would upset her sister and a transformation of her own identity.

Our analysis of disputes between the siblings showed, too, that early in the second year the children's attempts to enlist the aid of their mothers on their own behalf differed sharply according to whether the siblings had acted in an aggressive or hostile fashion first or whether they themselves had done so. The probability that the children would appeal to their mothers was high (66%) if the sibling had been the first to act in an aggressive or teasing manner. In contrast, they rarely appealed to their mothers for help in incidents when they *themselves* had acted in such way: In only 4% of such incidents did they do so. Such a distinction in the children's behavior, and indeed the evasive actions that second-year children take to avoid future punishment (see Dunn, 1988), indicate some anticipation of the mothers' actions, although, of course, they imply no elaborate understanding of the mothers' *minds*. This grasp of how other people can be expected to behave in relation to social rules becomes strikingly evident during the third year, when children's language abilities increase. Our analysis of disputes showed, for example, that *blaming* the sibling for incidents in which the child might be in trouble, and drawing the attention of the mother to the sibling rather than the self, are both common by 36 months— demonstrating a ready anticipation of how the mother will respond to another's transgression. The children's justifications showed, then, that notions of responsibility and of blame are well in place by 36 months and that these were used frequently by the children, revealing an effective grasp of how their mothers would react to cultural breach.

Particularly illuminating were the *excuses* that the children used in their attempts to avoid disapprobation. The nature of the excuses that the children used in disputes showed an increasingly elaborate grasp of how social rules applied to different people in different contexts and of how these rules could be questioned. For our present purposes, it is excuses of intent that are of special interest. In our culture, we see as crucial the distinction between acts that are intended to harm others or transgress rules of conduct and acts that have similar consequences but are accidental (Darley & Zanna, 1982). The question of when children begin to make this distinction is, however, a matter of some dispute. Piaget (1965) considered that there was "some reason to doubt whether a child of 6-7 could really distinguish an involuntary error from an intentional lie . . . the distinction is, at the best, in the process of formation" (p.145). In contrast to this view, Shultz (1980) reported observations that children as young as 3 may make such a distinction. The children in our studies made the excuse that they "didn't mean to" rather infrequently, during the observations. However, among the incidents when they did refer to intentions were some that involved children as young as 26 months:

Example 1: Child aged 26 months (Study 3)

Child climbs on Mother to investigate light switch:

M: You're hurting me!

C: Sorry. Sorry. I don't mean to.

This example could be interpreted as a "rote-learned" strategy for getting out of trouble, rather than evidence that the child really understood the significance of his intentions for his mother. For several of the earliest examples of the references to intentions, such explanations in terms of the child having learned to repeat phrases without understanding their meaning can be offered (cf. Astington, this volume). However, the wide variety of situations and the appropriateness with which these phrases are used should be borne in mind: It should be noted that there is not one example of such a phrase being used inappropriately. The children in both the Cambridge and Pennsylvania studies very clearly understood the significance of the phrase that an act (either against them or by them) had been done *on purpose*, and they used this in their attempts to obtain comfort or help, to good effect. The following example comes from an observation of a 33-month-old girl in the Pennsylvania study, who came crying to her mother after her brother had deliberately bitten her on the forehead:

Example 2: Child 33 months (Pennsylvania study)

C: Look what Philip did!

He bited me!

[crying]

M: He bit you on the head?

C: Yes.

M to Sib: Philip is that true?

S: No.

C to M: Yes!

        On purpose!

M to C: He did it on purpose?

C: Yes!

M to Sib: Come on over Philip.

Sib to M: I didn't do it on purpose Mom.

C to M: Yes he did.

In the course of the third year the children's references to intentions — usually but not always their own — were more clearly expressed and are not easily explained simply in terms of the children having learned a "formula" that works without any grasp of the significance of the reference to intention. In the example that follows, the 33-month-old is resisting his mother's attempts to get him down off the settee by referring to his own honorable intentions (cleaning the TV set):

Example 3: Child 33 months (Study 3)

M: Get off!

C (sits down on the settee still): Look. I'm not — (stands up). Mummy. I'm not — I'm not standing on there. I'm trying to get a paint off (rubs TV).

M: —-

C: I going try and get a paint off. All I'm trying to do is — there.

This child's repeated attempts to get out of trouble by mentioning his good intentions surely reflects some notion that his mother's view of the action will differ according to the nature of those intentions. His "creative" use of his own worthy goal (getting the paint off) as a justification for employing particular means (staying on the settee) is very unlikely to have been learned as a rote formula, and with this reference to a goal as justification for means we have the necessary elements of an understanding of intention as set out by Frye (this volume).

The same general point is supported by the finding that children sometimes made excuses that a transgression was made in *pretend*. They also commonly made excuses on grounds of *lack of control*, or *incapacity*. In their claims to be too tired to pick up their toys or their refusal to help their mothers on the grounds that they have a headache or—quite simply—are still "a baby," we see that they have begun to understand that their mothers will apply rules differently according to the intention, incapacity, or lack of control of the transgressor.

Two further points concerning these excuses and attempts to blame others should be noted. The first is that the children made reference to the needs and intentions of others as well as themselves in their attempts to get their way. In the next example, for instance, the boy refers to his mother's needs in an attempt to blame his sister and exclude her from the football game he was enjoying with his mother:

Example 4: Child 36 months (Study 2)

Child and Mother are playing with soccer ball. Sibling attempts to join game by kicking ball when it comes near her.

C to Sib: No! It's Mummy's go again. No! It was Mummy's go again.

M: Chrissie (sib) did it for me.

C: I'll put this ball away. I'm going to put it away if Chrissie's going to spoil it for Mummy.

Martin, the 36-month-old boy in this example, refers to a principle of justice and to his mother's enjoyment—all in the service of his own interest.

This matter of the importance of the child's interests brings us to the second point raised by these early discussions of rights, intentions, and the behavior of others. This is that the children's grasp of these issues of how people respond to rule violations, blame, and responsibility appears to be a very practical one. This is not a trivial point. Their understanding is of how excuses and justifications can be used to reach their own ends in the complex world of the family. They apply this understanding differently in different relationships, according to the nature of that relationship and their needs within that relationship. This differentiation of their behavior according to whether it is their father, mother, or sibling with whom they are interacting was apparent in each of the domains we examined—whether disputes, cooperative play, prosocial behavior, or propositional discussion; and it underlines the point that children's understanding of those other family members— what will annoy or please them, what will enlist their aid or attention, how they will react to excuses and justifications, under what circumstances they can be expected to cooperate or punish—is an increasingly differentiated understanding. This matter of the practical use to which the children put their understanding of others—and the adaptive importance of that understanding within the family—is one we return to later, when we consider the developmental processes that may contribute to these developments.

Cooperative Pretend Play

The analysis of children's behavior in cooperative play, in response to others' distress, as humorists, and in conversation about others, provides further evidence on the nature of their understanding of the other people in their world. During the third year, children's participation in joint pretend play, for example, changed dramatically. Between 18 and 24 months, they joined their older siblings' pretend play as compliant participants who obeyed (usually) the managerial—and often dictatorial—instructions of their siblings (Dunn & Dale, 1984). In the course of the third year, their cooperation became a far more active affair, in which they were innovative actors who not only anticipated the goals and intentions of their partner in play, but who, in their own original contributions, demonstrated some understanding of the intentions and feelings of the pretend "other" whose role they were enacting. In the example that follows, the 30-month-old girl was playing a game of mothers and babies with her older sister. The game began with a command from the older sister to "pretend you're a baby or my mummy." The sequence was not unusual in its length or complexity: It lasted for 140 conversational turns, and Annie, the younger sister made a number of contributions to the play narrative—relevant to her role as baby. She also acted both compliantly and noncompliantly:

Example 5: Child 30 months (Study 3)

Child's innovations in the joint pretend play, for her role as Baby:

Makes babbling noises.

Crawls.

Says she can't put slippers on: "I'm baby."

Designates "baby bed."

Asks for porridge.

Plays guitar in a way she designates as "a babby way . . . Me babby."

Addresses sibling as "Mummy."

Acts naughty with the guitar.

Pretends to get lost.

Snores.

In answer to sibling enquiring why she is crying ("What's wrong babbu?") replies "Me can't get to sleep."

Instructs sibling on what she should say, as Mummy.

Child's disputes and noncompliance with sibling over course of pretend play:

When told to babble and not to cry, cries.

Criticizes sibling's action in terms of role: "No you not a baby."

Denies that they are both tired in the game.

Refuses to go on "Mummy's" knee.

Child's compliance with sibling's actions or suggestions in the game:

Sibling says go to sleep: Child pretends to sleep.

Sibling gives "drink": Child pretends to drink.

Sibling gives "food": Child pretends to eat it.

Such innovations in joint pretend became increasingly evident from the middle of the third year. The ability to imagine being another person with intentions and feelings that are different from one's own is surely important evidence for children's growing understanding of others—evidence that parallels the signs of children's ability to deceive. Now, it has been plausibly argued that there is a major change in children's ability to reflect on others' minds and behavior during the third year (Wellman, 1988). It has been shown, for instance, that children first begin to talk about mental states in themselves and others—about knowing, remembering, forgetting—during the second half of the third year (Shatz, Wellman, & Silber, 1983; Wellman, 1988). It has been argued by Wellman, on the basis of experimental and naturalistic studies, that after $2\frac{1}{2}$ years, children begin to have an understanding of mind that is a coherent and interconnected set of concepts—that make a distinction between mental and physical entities (Wellman, 1988). The evidence from these pretend episodes supports the argument that such capacities indeed develop markedly during the third year. (It should be noted, however, that close study of the six individual children in our study does not support the idea that there is a sudden shift in understanding at 28-30 months; rather, the changes appear gradually, and there are marked individual differences in the timing of their development.) Further support for the idea that there is a major change in children's understanding of other minds around the middle of the third year comes from two other sources: first, our analyses of the children's conversations about other people and, second, the analysis of children's interventions in conversations between other family members.

Conversations About Others

From the transcripts of the observations of the six children observed at 2-month intervals during their third year, we examined all the children's questions about other people, categorizing such inquiries according to whether they were about the whereabouts, actions, or inner states of the people concerned or about the application of social rules to those others. Figure 6.1 shows that inquiries about inner states and social rules were absent during the first months of the third year but showed a sharp increase in the second half of that year.

A similar analysis of the 43 children in the larger study as 36-month-olds provided an encouraging replication of these findings, with very similar proportions of questions about the inner states and feelings of others. What is particularly notable about such conversations, for our present concern, is that a relatively high proportion of the conversations included discussion of the cause or consequence of the feelings or inner state of the person discussed (Dunn, Brown, & Beardsall, 1990). The rise

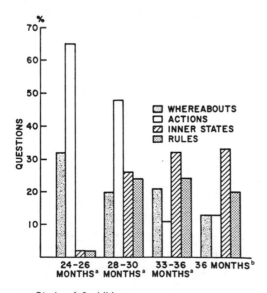

a: Study of 6 children
b: Study of 43 children

FIG. 6.1. Percentage of questions about other people.

of questions about others at this time and our analysis of the pragmatic context of such questions indicate that, as their ability to reflect on other minds develops, there is a growth of "disinterested" curiosity about others. It seems that as children's ideas about others become more elaborate, there are more issues for them to clarify with questions.

A strikingly parallel set of findings, again highlighting children's interest in the inner states of others during the second half of the third year, came from an analysis of the children's narratives about other people during the third year. As with the questions about others, narratives about other people became increasingly focused on inner states and social rules during the second half of that year (Fig. 6.2).

The results from our study of children's interventions in conversations also provide relevant evidence—in this case evidence for children's growing ability to understand the focus of others' interests. Much of the talk in families with small children is not directed to the children; the ability to participate effectively in such conversations is a developmental achievement of major importance. Analyses of the children's interventions in talk between their mothers and siblings in the third year show that the children attempted to join the conversations between others from early in the third year; however, such interventions were frequently not relevant to the topic of the others' talk, and although the children often *interrupted* the others' talk, they did not make a contribution of new or relevant information to that previous conversation. But, in the course of the third year, their interventions became increasingly relevant and contributed new information to the topic of the previous interlocutors' talk (Dunn & Shatz, 1989). The results highlighted both the salience of the conversation between other family members for

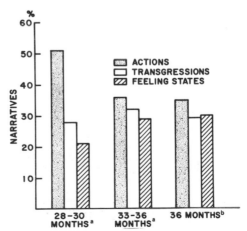

FIG. 6.2. Percentage of narratives about actions, transgressions, and feelings.

a: Study of 6 children
b: Study of 43 children

young children, their increasing skill at joining such conversations in a relevant fashion, and their adeptness at turning the focus of such talk to their favorite subject—themselves.

Jokes

A further instance of the children's sensitivity to the interests and feelings of the different people in their social world was provided by an analysis of the children's humor. Even before they are using many words, children find the behavior of others in their world a source of amusement, and of jokes that can be pointed out to and shared with others. Sharing a joke implies, at some level, an expectation that another person will also find this distortion of the expected absurd or comic. What our examination of the children's jokes showed was that children made different jokes to their siblings than to their mothers or the observer. With parents, play with naming jokes, true-false assertions, transgressions of social rules, and with the emotional dynamics of their relationships stood out:

Example 6: Child 24 months (Study 1)

M: Do you like your Mummy, John?

C: No yes! (smiles)

M: No yes? No yes?

C: No yes!

With their siblings, the children enjoyed and developed ritual insults, scatalogical jokes, and word play on forbidden topics. The results strongly suggest that, by 36 months, children already have a considerable and differentiated understanding of what familiar others will find funny or offensive.

THE DEVELOPMENTAL COURSE OF CHILDREN'S UNDERSTANDING OF OTHERS IN THE SECOND AND THIRD YEAR

In summary, the results of these observations within the family suggest the following course of development: Children's understanding of others' feelings grows early in the second year from an "affective tuning" to the distress or amusement of others (see Stern, 1985) to a grasp of how certain actions lead to disapproval or anger in others, how certain actions can comfort other family members (see Yarrow, Zahn-Waxler, & Chapman, 1983), and what actions can be a shared source of amusement with others. They respond empathetically to others' distress early in the second year, and they show in both their nonverbal and verbal behavior much interest in the feeling states of others. With increasing explicitness, they show curiosity about and understanding of the causes of pain, anger, distress, pleasure, dislike, fear, comfort in others. They play with and joke about these feelings in others and tell stories about them.

They also, during the second year, show increasing sensitivity to the goals and intentions of others—understanding that is evident in their disputes, pretend, narratives, and questions. Understanding of mental states, as opposed to emotional states and intended actions, appears to develop somewhat later, during the second half of the third year.

Of course, the limitations of this early understanding of others' emotions, intentions, and mental activity are notable. We have little evidence for the ability to recognize the nuances of the "social" emotions (embarrassment, shame or guilt), and experimental studies show that children of this age do not grasp the idea that people can experience combinations of emotions (Harris, 1989). It is obvious that children in their third year could have only a rudimentary understanding of the causes of adult emotions and that their grasp of the intentions of others will be limited to the intentions of others in familiar contexts. And, as Wellman has cogently argued, although they understand that human action is governed by wishes, beliefs, and attitudes, they do not have a concept of mind as an interpreting processor of information (Johnson & Wellman, 1982; Wellman, 1988). What remains particularly unclear is the extent to which their early understanding of mental states is dependent on the familiarity of the person and context. This matter of the family context, in which the earliest signs of understanding others are observed, brings us to the issue of what processes may be involved in the development of such abilities. I have discussed elsewhere (Dunn, 1988) several themes that stand out as important contributors; here, given space constraints I discuss just two, the emotional context of family interactions and the significance of family discourse.

The Possible Importance of the Emotional Context. In considering the ways in which family interactions might play a special role in fostering the development of social understanding, it is surely important to examine the possible role of affective experience. One provocative set of findings here came from our analysis of the disputes between children and their mothers and siblings (Dunn & Munn, 1987). We were interested in the relations between the emotions that the children expressed during the disputes, the topic of these disputes, and the likelihood that they would *reason,* rather than behave in a less mature way (such as resorting to hit or howl). The results showed that as 18-month-olds they were most likely to be angry or distressed in disputes over the topic of rights and interests (usually their own!). The emotional significance of these disputes might lead one to predict that as 3-year-olds they would be most likely to regress to hitting and howling, rather than to reason in mature fashion when frustrated in conflict over these issues.

But the results told a very different story. Eighteen months later, when the children were 36 months old, it was in these disputes over rights and interests that they showed their most "mature" behavior, by marshalling justifications and excuses for their actions. The children, that is, showed their most mature behavior over the issues that their earlier emotional behavior had suggested they cared most about. One inference from these findings might be that children use their intelligence on what matters most to them emotionally. Another, which is not incompatible with the first, is that the experience of mild distress and anger during these family conflicts may actually contribute to the children's learning—that the arousal they experience may heighten their vigilance and attentive powers. (See Arsenio & Ford, 1985 and Masters, Barden, & Ford, 1979 for parallel arguments based on experimental studies.)

Yet another possibility is that the mothers' behavior during these conflicts was an important influence: Our analyses showed that mothers were indeed more likely to reason with children in conflicts in which the younger child was distressed or angry than in incidents in which the child was not upset. They were, too, more likely to use reasoning in conflicts over rights than in disputes over other topics. It could be, therefore, that what the children are learning is that it is more appropriate and practically successful to use reasoning and justification in certain kinds of dispute than in others. We cannot, on the basis of our observations, assess separately the plausibility of these different possibilities; yet, the observations make clear that, in real life, the emotional state of the child, the salience of the topic, and the mothers' articulation of reasons and excuses are closely linked in the children's experience (see also Miller & Sperry, 1987). It could well be that it is this combination of a powerful cognitive and affective experience that contributes to the children's developing grasp of the way social rules and others' behavior are linked.

The general point is that the distress, anger and amusement that the children show highlight the importance of the frustration of goals and the pleasure in shared positive experience for children, and our findings suggest that these emotions may contribute to the learning that takes place. This is not to argue that the development of understanding takes place only in such contexts. It is evident that in older children passages of intellectual search often occur in calm, reflective exchanges between children and adults (Tizard & Hughes, 1984). Nevertheless, there may well be special significance in the emotion-laden exchanges in the family—exchanges in which it is clearly of great importance for the child to learn how others will behave and think. Because these are settings that are rarely studied by psychologists, they are unlikely to be given prominence in accounts of cognitive development. A further general point is that the new understanding of others' mental states and intentions has great significance for their strategies in conflict and in situations where their own goals are frustrated (Dunn, 1988). The adaptive importance of their new capability to understand other people is highlighted in these findings on the links between emotion, conflict and justification.

The Possible Significance of Family Discourse.   The second theme that should be highlighted in any consideration of the processes that are important in the developments in understanding of others is the contribution of family discourse about others. The evidence from studies in both the United States and Britain show that young children in our cultures grow up in a world in which there is much conversation within families about the feelings and behavior of others and about their motives, intentions, and the permissibility of their actions. Messages— implicit and increasingly explicit—about such matters are conveyed to them each day in a wide variety of ways (see also Shweder, Mahapatra, & Miller, 1987). Children are participants in conversations about such matters from a very early age; they monitor, comment on, and join in such discussions between others, and they question, joke about, and argue as to the causes and consequences of the feelings and behavior of others. It appears very likely that children's differentiated under- standing of other minds is influenced by such discourse. Here, the analysis of individual differences supports such a contention. Differ- ences between families in the frequency and extent of discussion of others' feelings, motives, and behavior are striking; in our studies in Cambridge, correlations were found between such differences in the first 3 years of children's lives and in a variety of "outcome' measures, such as the child's own participation in conversation about inner states (Dunn, Bretherton, & Munn, 1987), their friendly behavior towards their younger siblings (Dunn & Kendrick, 1982), and, most strikingly, their performance 3 to 4 years later on affective-perspective taking tasks (Dunn, Brown, & Beardsall, 1990).

CONCLUSION

In conclusion let us return to the questions raised at the outset. The first question concerned how, if their ability to understand others is as limited as was formerly supposed, preschool children relate to others and manage their lives within the complex social world of the family. Here, the results of our observations are unequivocal. By 36 months of age, the children "managed" their family lives very effectively: They anticipated and manipulated the reactions of others, "read" their emotions, used others to reach their own ends, and influenced the feeling states of others intentionally and practically by teasing, comforting, and joking. They questioned and disputed the application of social rules to themselves and others and they successfully redirected blame onto others.

The second question concerned the possible differences in children's abilities within the family, as well as their capacities in more formal and less familiar settings. The direct comparisons that would allow us to answer the question have not yet been made. However, the very early ages at which children can recognize and respond to the feeling states and intentions of other family members lead one to predict that such comparison would show the children more capable within the familiar and emotionally significant context of the family. It appears, indeed, that the more carefully the experimental setting is designed to be relevant to the children's emotional interest, the better their understanding and performance is in such settings (Donaldson, 1978). It should be noted, however, that the abilities that we have documented and discussed here concern primarily the children's abilities to understand and inquire about others' feelings, behavior, and intentions, rather than their cognitive processes. Our third question concerned the issue of whether the ability to recognize and reflect on *emotional states* develops well before the ability to understand and reflect on *other minds*. It appears, from the evidence of children within their families, that this is probably so. This conclusion is, perhaps, unsurprising given the accessibility of peoples' emotional expression and behavior and—even more significantly—given the adaptive importance of understanding the emotional state of others with whom one shares a family world and upon whom, as a small child, one is emotionally dependent.

ACKNOWLEDGMENTS

The research discussed in this chapter was supported by the Medical Research Council of Great Britain and by a grant from the National Institute of Health (HD23158-03).

REFERENCES

Arsenio, W. F., & Ford, M. E. (1985). The role of affective information in social-cognitive development: Children's differentiation of moral and conventional events. *Merrill-Palmer Quarterly, 31,* 1–17.

Bruner, J. (1983). *Child's talk.* New York: Norton.

Darley, J. M., & Zanna, M. P. (1982). Making moral judgements. *American Scientist, 70,* 515–521.

Donaldson, M. (1978). *Children's minds.* London: Fontana.

Dunn, J. (1988). *The beginnings of social understanding.* Cambridge, MA: Harvard University Press.

Dunn, J., Bretherton, I., & Munn, P. (1987). Conversations about feeling states between mothers and their young children. *Developmental Psychology, 23,* 132–139.

Dunn, J., Brown, J., & Beardsall, L. (in press). Family talk about feeling states, and children's later understanding of others' emotions. *Developmental Psychology.*

Dunn, J., & Dale, N. (1984). I a Daddy: Two-year-olds' collaboration in joint pretend with mothers' and siblings. In I. Bretherton (Ed.), *Symbolic play: The development of social understanding* (pp. 131–158). New York: Academic Press.

Dunn, J., & Kendrick, C. (1982). *Siblings: Love, envy and understanding.* Cambridge, MA: Harvard University Press.

Dunn, J., & Munn, P. (1987). The development of justification in disputes with mother and with sibling. *Developmental Psychology, 23,* 791–798.

Dunn, J., & Shatz, M. (1989). Becoming a conversationalist despite (or because of) having a sibling. *Child Development, 60,* 399–410.

Harris, P. L. (1989). *Children and emotion.* Oxford: Blackwells.

Johnson, C. N., & Wellman, H. M. (1982). Children's developing conceptions of the mind and brain. *Child Development, 53,* 222–234.

Klinnert, M. D., Campos, J. J., Sorce, J. F., Emde, R. N., & Svejda, M. (1983). Emotions as behavior regulators: Social referencing in infancy. In R. Plutchik & H. Kellerman (Eds.), *Emotion: Theory, research and experience* (Vol. 2, pp 57–86). New York: Academic Press.

Miller, P., & Sperry, L. L. (1987). The socialization of anger and aggression. *Merrill-Palmer Quarterly, 33,* 1–32.

Masters, J.C., Barden, R.C., & Ford, M. E. (1979). Affective states, expressive behavior, and learning in children. *Journal of Personality and Social Psychology, 37,* 380–390.

Packer, M. J. (1986, January). *Social interaction as practical activity: Implications for social and moral development.* Proceedings of the conference on social process and moral development, Miami, FL.

Piaget, J. (1965). *The moral judgement of the child.* New York: Free Press.

Shatz, M., Wellman, H.M., & Silber, S. (1983). The acquisition of mental verbs: A systematic investigation of the first reference to mental state. *Cognition, 14,* 301–322.

Shultz, T. R. (1980). The development of the concept of intention. In A.Collins, (Ed.), *Minnesota symposium on child psychology* (Vol. 13, pp. 131–164). Hillsdale, NJ: Lawrence Erlbaum Associates.

Shweder, R. A., Mahapatra, M., & Miller, J. G. (1987). Culture and moral development. In J.Kagan & S. Lamb (Eds.), *The emergence of moral concepts in young children* (pp. 1–83). Chicago: Chicago University Press.

Spelke, E. S., & Cortelyou, A. (1981). Perceptual aspects of social knowing: Looking and listening in infancy. In M. E. Lamb & L. R. Sherrod, (Eds.) *Infant social cognition* (pp. 61–84). Hillsdale, NJ: Lawrence Erlbaum Associates.

Stern, D. (1985). *The interpersonal world of the infant.* New York: Basic Books.

Tizard, B., & Hughes, M. (1984). *Young children learning.* London: Fontana.

Trevarthen, C. (1977). Descriptive analyses of infant communicative behaviour. In H. R. Schaffer, (Ed.), *Studies in mother-infant interaction* (pp. 227–270). London: Academic Press.

Wellman, H.M. (1988). First steps in the child's theorizing about the mind. In J. W. Astington, P. L. Harris, & D. R. Olson, (Eds.), *Developing theories of mind* (pp. 64–92). Cambridge, England: Cambridge University Press.

Yarrow, M. R., Zahn-Waxler, C., & Chapman, M. (1983). Prosocial behavior. In P. H. Mussen (Ed.), *Handbook of child psychology: Volume 4. Socialization, personality and social development* (pp. 469–545). New York: Wiley.

CHAPTER 7

A Meeting of Minds in Infancy: Imitation and Desire

Dale F. Hay
Carol A. Stimson
Jennifer Castle
Institute of Psychiatry, London

If 4-year-old children can be said to hold theories about the minds of others (e.g., Astington, this volume; Perner, this volume), how do they build and test their theories? Is there, as in some theories set forth by adult scientists, an initial data collection phase, followed by the generating of hypotheses and the construction of explanatory models? Furthermore, what developmental processes underlie this theory-building exercise? Can one account for the development of a theory of mind in terms of general maturational and learning processes, or does one need to invoke special explanatory principles? Put the other way round, how do general learning processes, such as reinforcement and observational learning, contribute to the development of social understanding? Do infants and young children explicitly learn that other people have minds?

The purpose of this chapter is to examine one particular social learning process, imitation, with respect to its contribution to the young child's emerging conceptions of the minds and hearts of other people. A consideration of this topic requires that we examine what imitation in early life is all about. In particular, should imitation itself be viewed as mindless mimicry, and are developmental attainments made through the process of observing others therefore devoid of meaning?

In contrast to such views of imitation as a rote learning process, we view the infant's tendency to copy the actions of others quite differently. In particular, we propose that imitation in early life is selective, sociable, and creative but, for all that, relatively ineffective. These propositions about the nature of early imitation derive from a series of experimental and controlled observational studies of children in the first and second years of life. After reviewing this evidence about the nature and functions of imitation in very early childhood, we then return to the question of its contribution to the development of the child's theory of mind by examining an additional study of the mother's modelling and the 1-year old's associated use of mental state terms. Thus, in this chapter, we are asking two complementary questions: Does an infant's act of imitating a model require some understanding of that model's mental life? And, does the information acquired by observing others and imitating their actions directly contribute to the young child's emerging conceptions of other people's minds?

SOME DEFINITIONS

The words *imitation* and *modelling* have various connotations, and so, in this chapter, we use the following terminology consistently: *Imitation* refers to an observer's copying the action of another person; *modelling* refers to the model's original demonstration of that action, whether or not it was deliberately enacted for the observer's benefit; and *observational learning* is the general developmental process whereby a model's actions influence the observer's behavior and development.

By applying the concept of observational learning to the problem of determining how children develop theories of mind, we are, in essence, working at the ragged interface of the behaviorist and cognitivist traditions. As such, we are following in the interactionist footsteps of the major social learning theorists, who, by exploring the concepts of imitation and modelling, have long tried to bridge the world views of learning theorists, psychoanalysts, and cognitive scientists (see, e.g., Bandura, 1977; Sears, Maccoby, & Levin, 1957). Nevertheless, we soon have found ourselves in murky waters, discomfited by the need to use such terms as *meaning* and *mind*. In this chapter, we argue that imitative actions are meaningful and reflect understanding of another's meaning, that imitation is mindful activity and promotes the emergence of a concept of mind.

Proper usage of the concept of mind has been vigorously debated (Searle, 1980), and there is some thought that an understanding of meaning can only be attained through humanistic interpretation of evidence, not scientific observation (Home, 1966). Thus, we use these terms with some trepidation and have tried not to stray too far from their common usage, as set forth in dictionary definitions. But the dictionary itself alerts us to the conceptual issues surrounding our argument. *Mind* is defined as "the seat of consciousness, thoughts, volitions, and feelings; also, the incorporeal subject of the psychical faculties" (Shorter Oxford English Dictionary, 1973); thus, the denotative use of the term *mind* stresses the breadth of mental phenomena beyond the strictly cognitive and the importance of personal agency in our conceptions of mental life.

Agency and subjectivity are also, perhaps surprisingly, invoked in the dictionary's presentation of the term *meaning*, which is permeated with the concept of intent. The archaic use of the term is, in fact, "intention, purpose," and the contemporary use subsumes both the mental and the observable: "That which is intended to be or actually is expressed or indicated; the significance, sense, import; the intended sense of a person's words" (Shorter Oxford English Dictionary, 1973). Thus, by using everyday definitions of terms like *meaning* and *mind*, we soon arrived at the problem of volition. In exploring the link between imitation and the understanding of another's mental life, a concern with volition has ultimately led us to examine the relationship between imitation and desire. We must begin, however, with a look at some of the factors that promote observational learning in very early childhood.

STUDIES OF EARLY IMITATION AS A SOCIAL AND DEVELOPMENTAL PROCESS

Our interest in the topic of imitation in infancy derives from a common criticism applied to our previous studies of prosocial behavior in the first years of life. When we and our colleagues presented evidence documenting that very young children share objects with others (Rheingold, Hay, & West, 1976), cooperate with them (Hay, 1979), or help adults perform household tasks (Rheingold, 1982), we were frequently asked, "But isn't it only imitation?". That question implies that developmental achievements based on watching what others do are somehow devoid of meaning. Presumably, young children do observe their companions share, help, and cooperate, but does this necessarily imply that their own attempts to do so are reflexive and mindless? In addition, the question raises an important issue for theories of development: We are quite ready to invoke observational learning as an explanation of young children's behavior, but how much do we actually know about the role of observational learning in early development? Given that the capacity to imitate may be available in the first days of life (Meltzoff & Moore,

1983), how does that capacity facilitate development, and how important is it?

Most of the previous studies of children's imitation have fallen into one of two basic categories: social learning analyses of older children's tendencies to copy particular types of models in experimental simulations of socializing experiences (for a review, see Bandura, 1977) or cognitive developmental analyses of the early development of the ability to imitate anything at all (e.g., Meltzoff & Moore, 1983; Piaget, 1962). The latter set of studies do not take up the issue of whether the developing capacity to imitate can be invoked as an explanation of other attainments; the former set of studies focused on imitation as a socializing process but typically did not study children during the early years when social skills and dispositions are first emerging. Thus, it is not easy to synthesize the two domains of research.

In contrast, we wished to examine imitation in infancy and very early childhood not simply as a cognitive attainment but as a social process and developmental mechanism. That is, we asked, firstly, what are the social determinants and functions of infants' tendencies to copy the actions of others? Under what circumstances are infants likely to choose to imitate their companions? And, secondly, how does observational learning compare with other social processes as an influence on development? Is modelling more or less effective than other ways of getting infants to do particular things?

To address these questions, we have examined imitation in infancy by means of three different experimental paradigms: (a) tasks that require place learning; (b) social facilitation of familiar activities; and (c) observational learning of new social behaviors. Each particular study was undertaken with respect to a particular set of questions. We shall thus describe each study in some detail and sketch out its general findings before evaluating the general evidence for our characterization of early imitation as selective, sociable, and creative, but relatively ineffective.

Place Learning

One of the earliest manifestations of observational learning in human life is the tendency of infants to follow other people around the environment. Learning by following a leader has been demonstrated for adult rats (Church, 1957), young pigeons (Neuringer & Neuringer, 1974), and kittens (Berry, 1908) and has been implicated in the acquisition of food preferences by young mammals (Galef & Clark, 1971; Rosenblatt & Schneirla, 1962); however, human infants' following of their mothers has been viewed primarily as a manifestation of attachment to the mother, not as an opportunity to learn about the environment (see Hay, 1981). The purpose of our study (Hay, 1977) was to examine infants' following as an instance of observational learning, asking what leaders infants are likely to follow and what information they are thereby likely to acquire.

Three experiments were conducted. The first demonstrated that infants did not always reflexly choose to follow a leader, and, furthermore, when they did so, the leader followed was not necessarily a familiar caregiver. Sixteen infants were presented with the opportunity to follow either their mothers or an unfamiliar woman; neither leader was followed reliably more often than the other. The infants were then given the choice between following the mother and a novel, nonhuman leader, a moving toy. All but one of the infants crept or toddled away after the toy.

The next two experiments investigated whether, when infants did follow familiar leaders, the experience facilitated their subsequent independent exploration of new environments. In the second experiment, a new sample of 16 infants were randomly assigned to one of two groups; either they were given the opportunity to follow their mothers to a toy hidden behind a barrier in an adjoining room (the modelling condition), or they were simply permitted to engage in independent exploration, their mothers remaining stationary in one location (the control condition). Mothers who led their infants to the hidden toy were encouraged to exhort their infants to follow them, and so all of their infants entered the testing room, explored behind the barrier, and discovered the hidden toy. In contrast, only two infants in the control condition entered the testing room, and only one found the toy.

Of special concern, however, was whether this experience of following the mother facilitated infants' subsequent independent exploration. In two further trials, all mothers remained stationary in one location while their infants were free to move about. In the first of these test trials, the environment was as before; the door to the testing room was open and the infants were free to enter and explore behind the barrier. However, most of the infants in both groups confined themselves to the starting room, and differences between the groups in the number who explored the testing room were not reliable. Effects of the initial modelling experience were discerned on behavior in a third trial, when the environment was slightly altered. The door to the original testing room was closed; what the infants saw instead was a door open to a new, yet identical, room in which a new toy was located, hidden behind a similar barrier. Infants who had followed their mothers to the first toy were now reliably more likely than those in the control condition to explore behind the barrier in the new room. Thus, the infants' imitation of the adult model's exploration in the first trial facilitated their own exploration; they had learned how to learn about new environments.

The third experiment sought to determine which feature of the modelling experience facilitated infants' independent exploration. Was it simply the fact that, by following their mothers, infants had been informed of the existence of a toy behind the barrier in the first room, or was their own self-produced imitative action critical? To address this question, another sample of infants who followed their mothers was compared with a group who were carried by their mothers to the hidden toy. Infants who had followed their mothers originally were reliably more likely than those who had been carried to explore behind a new barrier in a similar testing room, a finding that suggested that the opportunity for active imitation was, indeed, important. Unexpectedly, however, the two groups also differed in the extent of information about the environment that was provided them; as if to compensate for their infants' immobility, mothers who carried their infants were more likely than those who led them to provide a great deal of supplementary information about properties of the environment in which they traveled.

Social Facilitation of a Communicative Gesture

The previous experiments demonstrated one role played by observational learning in the first year of life. We next focused more specifically on the contribution of observational learning to social development, by asking whether modelling facilitates infants' performance of social actions (Hay & Murray, 1982).

We began with the assumption that the basic unit of social life is the dyad, not the individual (e.g., Cairns, 1979), with the corollary that social development is best measured in terms of an emerging capacity for social relations, not the acquisition of discrete classes of behavior. Social learning processes must operate within a stream of actions and reactions. So how effective is modelling, as compared with other interactive processes, in teaching infants how to relate to others?

Consider, for example, the case where an infant might produce a particular action, X. What could induce the infant to do so? An adult's modelling of X is one possibility. Alternatively, if X is frequently preceded in the course of ordinary social interaction by a complementary behavior, Y, the infant might also be likely to produce X in response to the adult's modelling of Y. The latter event provides an interactive slot into which the infant can slip the desired action; in Gibsonian terms, it is a *social affordance*. In a sense, then, the probability that X occurs might be increased by modelling X or by modelling something else, its complement.

We made this comparison with respect to a target social action, the offering of objects to another person. Infants begin to offer objects to their companions towards the end of the first year (Hay, 1979). Here, we asked whether modelling facilitates performance of this action. We compared the effectiveness of modelling the target action with the effectiveness of modelling its complement, that is, requesting objects with an outstretched hand.

Thirty-two 12-month-olds were observed in three trials. In the first trial, which was 3 minutes in duration, the infant sat on his or her mother's lap, across a table from an adult experimenter. A set of small toys was displayed on the surface of the table. The infants were randomly assigned to four groups, in which the experimenter either offered objects to the infant, requested them from the infants, both offered and requested objects (i.e., played the conventional game of "give and take"), or simply chatted pleasantly with mother and infant. The frequency of the infant's own offers of toys to the experimenter and to the mother was recorded.

Modelling the target action alone was ineffective; infants who observed the model offer objects to them were no more likely than those in the control condition to offer objects in turn. In contrast, the model's requesting objects and playing give-and-take facilitated offers to the experimenter, relative to infants in the control condition. Offers to the mother were infrequent in this trial and were unaffected by the experimental treatment.

All infants were then observed in two test trials, in the absence of further modelling. In the first of these trials, again 3 minutes in duration, the infant again sat on the mother's lap across the table from the experimenter, who chatted with them but refrained from either offering or requesting objects. A new set of small toys was provided. No effects of the experimental treatment persisted into this trial.

The testing environment was then modified for the final trial. The table was removed, some new toys were distributed on the floor, and the infant was provided with the opportunity to explore the room for 10 minutes while the mother and experimenter sat on cushions on the floor and chatted. What emerged was an effect of the experimental conditions on the infants' tendency to offer toys to their own mothers in this transfer trial. Infants who had played give-and-take with the experimenter in the first trial (i.e., had seen both the target action and its complement modelled) were now reliably more likely to offer objects to their mothers than were infants in the control condition. In other words, the give-and-take experience appears to have facilitated a familiar response that was now available for use in interaction with a familiar partner in a different situation.

The experimental conditions did not, in contrast, influence offers to the experimenter during the transfer trial. This was largely due to an unexpected sex difference. Girls were reliably more likely than boys to offer objects to the experimenter in the transfer trial. A floor effect for the boys prevented any signs of the experimental treatments on the sample as a whole.

Acquisition of New Social Behaviors

In the study just discussed, we assumed that infants were not learning to offer objects to other people for the first time under our eyes, but rather that the experimental procedures were facilitating an action that was already firmly in their repertoires. To determine whether infants actually learn new things by observing other people, it is important to model actions that they are not likely to perform on their own. Thus, in the next study, infants watched adults use familiar objects in unfamiliar ways (Hay, Murray, Cecire, & Nash, 1985). All of the modelled actions were social ones, insofar as they were directed explicitly to particular recipients. We asked what factors might induce an infant to attempt to copy a novel social act, and what factors influence the infant's choice of recipient for that act? Two experiments were conducted.

The major question asked in the first experiment was whether infants would be more likely to imitate novel social actions directed to themselves than those directed to other persons. In the typical experiment on imitation in infancy (e.g., Meltzoff & Moore, 1983), models direct actions explicitly to infants themselves. It is not clear whether infants pay much attention at all to interactions taking place between other individuals, and so we tested their tendency to do so in this experiment.

We reasoned, however, that the effectiveness of modelling an action directly to the infant as recipient might be tempered by the familiarity of the model and the intrusiveness of the action. Thus, we examined infants' imitation of novel actions directed to themselves and to an unfamiliar adult when the mother or another adult served as model and when the actions themselves were performed at a distance or impinged directly on the infant. All of the modelled actions entailed using familiar objects socially but in novel ways; using a paper party hat as if it were a horn or as if it were a shoe, using a string of plastic beads as if they were a telephone or as if they were a comb.

Sixty-four 18-month-old infants were observed in three trials. During the first trial, the child, the mother, and two adults (designated the experimenter and the experimenter's assistant) were present, seated on the floor in a small room furnished with distractor toys. In an attempt to simulate a real-world situation, the target actions were modelled in the course of much extraneous interaction among the adults, when there were a number of other things that the child might do. The experimenter and her assistant conversed with the mother and interacted freely with the child, thus modelling many actions other than the target ones. Half the children observed the experimenter demonstrate each target action twice, and the others observed their mothers do so. For half the children in each condition, the actions were directed towards themselves as recipients, whereas for the others, the actions were directed to the experimenter's assistant, who expressed pleasure in being the recipient of each action. The child's own reaction to the modelled event was rated on a 3-point scale. The child's performance of each action was ascertained during the modelling trial and in two subsequent test trials, the first in an unaltered environment and the second in the presence of novel distractor toys.

In this study, modelling was quite effective, in that 72% of the children imitated at least one novel social action at least once. The experimental manipulations did not reliably affect the overall likelihood of imitation, but they did influence its social functions, that is, the child's choice of recipient. Children who had observed either their mothers or the experimenter direct the novel actions to the experimenter's assistant were more likely than other children similarly to direct their imitative actions to that person. They were somewhat less likely to direct imitative actions to themselves. In other words, children who observed actions directed to others were more likely to preserve the social character of the modelled actions by similarly using them to serve a social function.

Although delayed imitation was relatively infrequent, this effect of the identity of the recipient of modelling persisted into both test trials. It seems that what these children learned was as much about the recipient's role and personal preferences as about the novel action itself. For example, they may have noted that the assistant quite liked having her hair combed with a string of beads, hats placed on her feet, and so on, and thus they were encouraged to direct such bizarre acts to that person.

If, as we have just speculated, the children were sensitive to the recipient's affective response to modelling, did their own affective reactions influence their tendency to imitate? The children in general, as might be expected, reacted more positively to the acts modelled at a distance than to the more intrusive experiences of having "shoes" placed on their feet or having their hair "combed." They also exhibited more pleasure when their mothers, as opposed to the experimenter, performed these odd feats, but only in the case of the distal actions. Children whose mothers served as models were, in fact, quite likely to try to get the mother to perform the odd actions again (what we termed child-guided modelling) rather than imitating the behavior themselves.

Despite the overall trend for children to respond more favorably to distal actions, the affect ratings reliably predicted the children's imitation of the distal acts, not the proximal ones. Informal observations indicated that, even when the child seemed to find the intrusive event quite obnoxious, imitation was likely to occur. Indeed, the modelling of the proximal acts may have produced learning even in the absence of overt imitation. For example, one child, who actively resisted having her hair combed with the beads, and never imitated that action, was, at the end of the session, asked by her mother to find the "comb"; she immediately retrieved the beads.

This emphasis on the recipient's affective reaction to modelling indicates that what is learned in the observational learning paradigm is more than motor responding; rather, modelled events are themselves meaningful, for the model and for the recipient. In the second experiment, we asked whether the children would be as likely to imitate the unconventional uses of familiar objects if they were not quite clear what the model was doing. Forty additional children were tested. The model in all cases was an adult experimenter, who directed a single target action (placing the party hat on a recipient's foot) to the child as recipient or to a second unfamiliar adult. For half of the children, the model explained what she was doing by labelling the pretend action, that is , by saying, for example, "Oh, look! What a pretty shoe!." For the other children, the model merely drew attention to the stimulus properties of the object: "Oh, look! What pretty colors." In the latter case, the hat was not redesignated as a shoe.

In addition, the second experiment was designed to provide a more stringent test of the findings of the first. The models did not call attention to their actions at all, thus simulating the natural performance of particular actions in the context of all other interaction. Furthermore, the conclusion that the experimental procedures were leading to the acquisition of novel actions, not the facilitation of existing ones, was evaluated by including a control condition in which no modelling occurred.

The children were observed during a 10-minute modelling trial, a 5-minute test trial with new distractor objects, and then a 5-minute transfer trial, in which the environment was altered. During the transfer trial, the paper party hat and distractor objects were removed and replaced by cloth hats, real slippers, and large plastic cones (soccer endline markers). A new potential recipient of imitative actions was also provided, that being a large toy rabbit with prominent feet.

No child in the control group ever produced the target action (placing the party hat on someone's foot as if it were a shoe), confirming our assumption that the children who did so were learning something new. Children in the control and experimental conditions were, however, equally likely to use the hat properly as a hat. The basic finding of the first experiment was reproduced in the second: Children who had observed the target action directed to an unfamiliar adult were reliably more likely than the others to place the hat on that person's foot. In contrast, the children who had observed the model place the hat on his or her own foot were reliably more likely than the others to do so as well.

The model's explanation of her action also influenced the likelihood of self-directed imitation. None of the children ever placed the party hat on their own feet if the model had not told them that the hat was being used as a shoe. (This finding was primarily accounted for by the performance of boys, not girls, the latter engaging in relatively little self-directed imitation.)

Delayed imitation of the target act was virtually absent; however, the impact of the experimental procedures was seen once again in the transfer trial, when the children were presented with real hats, real shoes, and unfamiliar cone-shaped objects. When confronted with the ambiguous objects, children in the experimental groups were reliably more likely than those in the control condition to use the cones as shoes, but they were reliably less likely than the control children to use them as if they were hats. Furthermore, all those children who pretended the cones were shoes in the third trial had been told by the model that the original party hat was a shoe; if the model had not explained her action, no generalized imitation occurred in the third trial. The experimental and control conditions did not differ with respect to the use of real hats and real shoes, suggesting again that what had been learned was not a particular action (putting something on one's foot) but rather the idea that one could pretend an object was something else.

Modelling Versus Instruction

The next study, a doctoral thesis conducted by Patricia Murray (1986), derives directly from the two preceding ones. The experiment on infants' offers to adults had indicated that asking an infant to do something might be as effective as, or more effective than, modelling the desired action, at least when the action was a social gesture already in the infant's repertoire. The study just described had further underscored the importance of language as a supplement to modelling, in terms of the facilitatory effect of the model's explaining her action to the child. In her thesis, Murray asked whether verbal instruction alone was ever as effective as modelling, with respect to the facilitation of a familiar response and the acquisition of a novel one. In addition, she evaluated the contribution of competencies and dispositions that the child brought to the modelling situation, by examining the extent to which the child's chronological age, mental age, and general helpfulness mediated the effects of the experimental manipulations.

Seventy-two children between the ages of 15 and 21 months of age were observed (a broader age range was chosen in this study in an effort to assess the effect of chronological and mental age). The Cattell-Binet Short Form was used to assess mental age. The child's tendency to respond positively to requests was assessed by instructing the mother to ask the child to help put away the toys at the end of the first trial.

The children were observed during a 10-minute modelling trial, a 5-minute transfer trial, and a 5-minute delayed test trial. During the first trial, the experimenter either modelled or instructed the child to perform two target actions, one with a conventional object and the second with an unconventional object. Two sets of objects were used, so that, for half the children, the tasks were to pretend to drink from a cup and to place a hat on the foot as a shoe; for the others, the tasks were to place the hat on the head as a hat and to place a cup on the foot as a shoe.

For a third of the children in each condition, no supplementary linguistic information was supplied; both the modelling and the "instruction" were conveyed entirely by nonverbal means. For example, to instruct the child to drink from a cup, the experimenter first pointed to the cup and then to the child's mouth. For another third of each group, some linguistic information was provided, but the object itself was not given a name; it was merely referred to as "this." For the remaining children in each group, full information was provided, in that both the action that was being modelled or requested was described and the object that was to be used was named. In the case of the unconventional actions, the pretend name, not the actual name, was used. For example, the experimenter picked up the hat and either placed it on the child's foot (modelling condition) or handed it to the child (instruction condition), saying, "See the shoe. Let's put this shoe on your foot," in the former case, and "See this shoe. Put this shoe on your foot," in the latter case. As in the previous study, modelling and instruction again took place against the background of ongoing interaction and in the presence of distractor toys.

The effect of the experimental manipulations was ascertained with respect to response facilitation (performance of the conventional action) and response acquisition (performance of the unconventional action). With respect to response facilitation, which was shown by 46% of the sample, modelling was more effective than instruction only in the absence of any verbal information. If the experimenter spoke at all, instruction was as effective as modelling in getting the child to perform the familiar action. If complete information was provided, that is, the object to be used was named, then instruction was somewhat more effective (a nonsignificant trend). These findings parallel those obtained in the experiment on infants' offers to adults (Hay & Murray, 1982).

Perhaps because of the restricted number of actions modelled, but also the greater range of ages tested, only 22% of the sample performed the unconventional actions, and thus findings with respect to the experimental manipulations must be viewed with caution. Again, modelling was reliably more effective than instruction in inducing the performance of the new action, but only in the absence of supplementary speech. Furthermore, a reliable interaction with the child's sex indicated that boys found modelling more effective, whereas girls were more likely to profit from instruction. The completeness of the explanation offered did not reliably affect the child's performance of the target actions, in contrast to our earlier finding (Hay et al., 1985). Because the procedures, including the choice of age range, did not afford a true replication of the earlier ones, it is impossible to say when precisely a model's explanation facilitates the child's learning of novel actions and when it does not. In this study, too few children showed generalized or delayed performance to assess the persisting effects of the information provided.

In contrast to our earlier studies, Murray's thesis provided the opportunity to explore some dispositional sources of the great individual differences in performance. All three individual difference variables — chronological age, mental age, and helpfulness in response to mother's requests — were themselves reliably interrelated, but none predicted the children's performance of the target actions. In other words, none of these dispositional variables were as potent as the manipulations made in the social setting, that is, the type of social influence being used (modelling vs. instruction) and the use of language.

Summary: Some Propositions About Early Imitation

Some common themes emerged from all of the foregoing studies, which have led to the following four propositions about the nature of early imitation.

Proposition 1: Imitation Is Selective. The wide range of individual differences in all these studies leads to the proposition that imitation is not an automatic reflex action. Rather, infants choose to copy some actions and not others, and they sometimes choose not to imitate at all. For example, in the place-learning experiments (Hay, 1977), some infants chose not to follow either their mothers or the unfamiliar woman. In the study of social facilitation of infants' offers to adults (Hay & Murray, 1982), the experimenter modelled two classes of behavior, offering objects and requesting objects with an outstretched hand. The latter action prompted offers but was never itself imitated. Thus, infants select certain things to imitate from the vast array of potential models in their natural environments.

Proposition 2: Imitation Is Sociable. Our studies also confirm the fact that imitation is, in essence, a social process. Infants' tendency to imitate others is influenced by social factors and serves social functions, in that it is a means of interacting with, and forming relationships with, other persons. For example, in the study of the acquisition of new social actions (Hay et al., 1985), when the recipient of the modelled actions was an unfamiliar person, the infants' own imitation was more likely to be directed to that person; the modelling experience provided information about that person's preferences that then gave the infant some ideas about how to relate to a new acquaintance.

Proposition 3: Imitation Is Creative. Given that imitation is used as a vehicle for interacting with others, it is important to note that it is used creatively. An unexpected finding of all the studies is that the effects of a modelling experience may be more clearly discerned in a slightly different situation, rather than in a repeat of the original situation. Frequently when infants are tested again in the same setting, they go on to do other things than what they had been induced to do before. The effects of what they learned are then apparent in a transfer trial.

For example, infants who followed their mothers to a hidden toy were not more likely than infants in the control condition to return to that toy, but they were more likely to venture behind a similar barrier in a different room (Hay, 1977). Infants who played give-and-take with an unfamiliar woman were not necessarily more likely to offer objects to her in a second trial in the same setting, but they were more likely than infants in the control condition to offer objects to their mothers in a transfer trial. Infants who had observed a paper party hat as if it were a shoe in one setting were likely to use ambiguous cone-shaped objects as shoes at a later opportunity (Hay et al., 1985); they were not particularly likely to repeat the use of the original hat as a shoe in a delayed test trial (Murray, 1986). All of these findings indicate that imitation is not a mere matter of repeating some trick learned in the past, but rather applying a new idea to a new situation.

Proposition 4: Imitation Is Not Always That Effective. Some of the findings from our studies confirm the effectiveness of observational learning as a means of acquiring new information and new skills; for example, infants who followed their mothers were much more likely than those who ventured forth independently to discover hidden properties of a novel environment. Almost three quarters of the 18-month-olds who observed models demonstrating the unconventional uses of familiar objects were able to see those possibilities in the objects, whereas the children in a control condition never did (Hay et al., 1985); in this case, modelling seemed to be accelerating an ability that would appear a month or two later in development.

On the other hand, the studies also indicated that modelling alone is not always the most effective way of promoting learning. Of particular note is the fact that language is often a necessary supplement, or a more effective technique, even when the infants themselves are not yet verbally fluent. For example, if one wants infants to offer a toy, it is more effective simply to ask for it than to model the desired behavior (Hay & Murray, 1982). The modelling of a pretend action is only more effective than simply instructing the child to perform the action if the instruction itself is nonverbal, that is, has to be carried out with ambiguous hand signals; if language is used at all, instruction is as effective as modelling (Murray, 1986). There are also some indications that, at least in some situations, explanations are required if infants are to imitate strange actions (Hay et al., 1985).

Given this evidence for the effectiveness of language versus modelling, it is interesting to note that, in the place-learning experiment, when infants were prevented from immediately imitating what they had observed (i.e., when they were carried by their mothers and thus could not move freely themselves), the mothers spontaneously chose to supplement this more passive modelling experience with rich verbal descriptions of the environment (Hay, 1977). Thus, even in the earliest years of life, modelling and imitation are not strictly behavioral; modelling provides information, and sometimes the mere provision of that information through symbolic and verbal means is more effective.

MODELLING AND IMITATION IN THE REALM OF THOUGHT AND FEELING

In reviewing our previous studies of imitation in infancy, we have been at pains to stress that modelling and imitation entail an exchange of ideas, or what we have termed in our title a "meeting of minds." The next question to be asked then is what very young children learn about their own minds and the minds of others through this form of exchange. Theorists of various persuasions have invoked imitation as a process in the development of awareness of self and others. For example, Baldwin (1906) contended that, by imitating, the child gains awareness of the self and the other in tandem: "The growth of the individual's self-thought, upon which his social development depends, is secured all the way through by a two fold exercise of the imitative function. He reaches his subjective understanding of the social copy by imitation, and then he confirms his interpretations by another imitative act by which he ejectively leads his self-thought into the persons of others" (p. 527, cited in Kohlberg, 1982).

Furthermore, empirical analyses of very young children's early discussions of mental states raise the possibility of modelling influences; for example, children who mention feeling states frequently at the age of 28 months tend to have mothers and siblings who mentioned feeling states frequently months earlier (Dunn, Bretherton, & Munn, 1987). We sought to explore this topic further by seeking associations in mothers' and 1-year olds' use of mental state terms .

Before drawing any conclusions about the role of observational learning in the development of "theories of mind," some preliminary questions need to be asked. First of all, what kinds of models of thinking about the minds of others are provided by caregivers and others? Secondly, what associations exist between caregivers' and children's references to mental states?

A positive correlation between caregivers' and children's use of such terms would not necessarily document the causal role of the modelling provided by caregivers. The caregivers' comments could be responsive to the child's own emerging concerns about mental life. Nor should we necessarily expect whatever correspondence exists between the caregiver's and the child's awareness of mental states to be a precise, quantitative one: There might be qualitative links between the ways in which caregivers talk about mental life and the ways in which children themselves come to experience mental life that do not reduce to correlations based on raw frequencies. Nonetheless, that is one place to start to identify such correspondences, and it is the path that we have pursued to date.

Some Preliminary Findings

Our analyses are derived from a small, limited study of mother-child interaction in a laboratory playroom (Hay et al., in preparation), and thus the possibilities for generalization from these findings are correspondingly limited. The sample consisted of twenty-four 20- to 24-month-old children, balanced with respect to sex and birth order. The children were observed in the presence of their mothers and six novel toys (selected by the mothers on the basis of their relative novelty from a pool of ten possibilities displayed in photographs). The mothers had been instructed first to encourage their children to play independently while the mothers themselves read magazines; then to join into the child's activities; and then to again withdraw to one side and read magazines. We reasoned that this procedure simulates the usual state of affairs when a mother has 10 minutes or so to play with her toddler in the midst of household work and other activities.

Of particular concern was the mother's and the child's use of three classes of mental state terms: terms referring to cognition (thought, knowledge, memory, and inference), preference (liking and loving) and desire (want). All three classes contain an element of intentionality and therefore qualify as "mental" by Brentano's criterion (see Perner, this volume). In this way, our analysis on this limited sample bridges part of the gap between Dunn et al.'s (1987) analysis of feeling states in general and the more experimental studies of children's maturing awareness of desire and belief (Astington, this volume Perner, this volume; Wellman & Woolley, 1988).

We recorded the frequency with which mothers and children used each class of mental state term, with reference to themselves and the other, in the form of declarative and interrogative statements. We focused on the mother's use of the terms only during the trial in which she was encouraged to interact with her child, insofar as individual differences among mothers in the other trials probably only represent differential responsiveness to our instructions. We tabulated the child's use of the terms throughout all three trials.

All of the mothers and 58% of the children used one of the three classes of mental state terms (cognition, preference, or desire) at least once in the experimental session. An example of a dialogue between mother and child in which such terms are used is presented in Table 7.1. The majority of references to mental states fell into the category of desire. Only one child ever used a cognitive term, and only two children ever referred to liking or loving. The majority of the mothers' references to mental states also pertained to desire. In general, both mothers and children were talking about what the children might want in this situation; thus a mother's use of the term most frequently took the form of inquiries about the child. Only four mothers ever referred to their own desires. (Mothers were more likely to talk about their own cognitions, i.e., remarking "I know," "I think," and the like.)

TABLE 7.1
An Illustrative Dialogue in which Mental State Terms
Are Used

MOTHER:	What's this one?
CHILD:	Blue.
MOTHER:	No, this one. This one's blue. What's this one?
CHILD:	Blue.
MOTHER:	This one's red.
CHILD:	Red.
MOTHER:	Red, like a red light. Is that the only toy you **like**, Alex? See the dolly?
CHILD:	Yeah.
MOTHER:	Give the dolly a kiss. Give the dolly a kiss. Oh, nice dolly. That's Raggedy Ann. That's Raggedy Ann. See it's got red hair. It's got red hair.
CHILD:	(Laughs).
MOTHER:	You didn't **know** it did that, huh?

What, then, was the nature of associations between the mothers' use and the children's use of these mental state terms? When we considered all three categories together, a nonsignificant positive association between the frequencies with which mothers and children mentioned mental states was obtained ($r = .39$, $p < .10$). Given, however, that the majority of mentions pertain to the category of desire, is this association explicable purely in terms of that category? This proved not to be the case. The mother's use of the term *want* was not reliably associated with the child's use of *want*. Unexpectedly, what did predict the child's use of the term *want* was the mother's use of the cognitive terms (think, know, remember, forget, and guess), $r = .54$, $p < .01$.

There seem to be two possible interpretations of this association between the mother's references to thought and knowledge and the child's references to desire, and they are not necessarily incompatible. Firstly, the correlation describes a Vygotskian situation, in which mothers are operating in the "zone of proximal development"; children who are demonstrating a particular developmental accomplishment (talking about one mental state, desire) have mothers who are modelling the next step in this developmental sequence. This finding is in line with Dunn et al.'s (1987) home observations of correlations among mothers', siblings', and second-born children's references to feeling states. It raises the general issue of anticipatory social influences in development.

There is, however, a second and equally plausible interpretation of the association between mothers' thoughts and children's desires. As we noted earlier, in the province of desire, mothers and children alike are primarily focusing on what the child, not the mother, wants. In the case of the mother's use of the cognitive terms, she is sometimes referring to her own thoughts and knowledge and other times to the child's cognitions. Perhaps at a more general level of analysis, the correlation expresses an association between the mother's and the child's references to personal mental states.

This possibility was partially tested by comparing the mother's reference to her own thoughts and her reference to the child's thoughts as predictors of the child's expression of desires. The mother's expression of her own thoughts reliably predicted the child's use of the term *want*, $r = .64$, $p < .01$, whereas the mother's allusions to the child's own cognitions are positively but not reliably predictive, $r = .38$, $p < .10$. In other words, self-conscious women appear to have self-conscious children.

In the absence of experimentation, it is impossible to rule out one of these two possible interpretations of the association between maternal cognition and child desire; perhaps both are correct, and Baldwin's "dialectic of personal growth" takes place within Vygotsky's "zone of proximal development." Is there, however, a more parsimonious interpretation? Are we simply talking about verbally fluent women whose children are acquiring a particular vocabulary word sooner than children of less verbal mothers?

On the basis of the analyses we have undertaken to date, it is impossible to rule out this interpretation. One finding that casts some doubt on it, however, is that the mother's use of the three categories of mental state terms does not resemble a set of converging measures of a single construct, verbal fluency; the mother's references to desire are unrelated to her use of the preference terms (liking and loving) and negatively associated with her references to thoughts, knowledge, and memory.

In general, then, our preliminary findings raise the possibility of explicit maternal influences on the child's emerging understanding of intentional mental states. The fact that the mother's influence is seen first in the realm of desire is consonant with Wellman's claim that the 2-year-old is a desire psychologist before becoming a belief-and-desire psychologist (Wellman & Woolley, 1988). It is important to note that the mother's influence does not take the form of the child's parroting of particular vocabulary words modelled by their mothers. Once again, the child's imitation, now in the realm of mental life, qualifies as selective, sociable, and creative.

CONCLUSIONS

We return now to the question with which we began this essay: Does the process of observational learning contribute to the child's development of a "theory of mind"? A partial answer to that question lies in the fact that we now think it appropriate to raise a complementary question, namely, does the infant's and very young child's emerging theory of mind contribute to the capacity to profit from observational learning? In other words, must the infant have at least a primitive understanding of the mental lives of others to imitate their actions? Do the nature and functions of imitation at a given point in development both reflect the child's current level of social understanding and derive from it?

Throughout the first years of life, there seem to be clear parallels between infants' general attention and responsiveness to the feelings, desires, and ideas of others and the infants' attempts to match or reproduce those psychological states. With the exception of the newborn infant's inexplicable fascination with an adult's protruded tongue (Abravanel & Sigafoos, 1984; Meltzoff & Moore, 1983), much imitation in the earliest months of life takes the form of matching facial and vocal expressions of emotion (Field, Woodson, Greenberg, & Cohen, 1982; Hay, Nash, & Pedersen, 1981). Thus, overt imitation (for example, crying when another person cries) is one of the first signs of responsiveness to the emotional life of others, which later becomes elaborated in phenomena such as social referencing (Campos & Stenberg, 1981; Feinman, 1982) and acquisition of a feeling state vocabulary (Dunn et al., 1987).

It has recently been argued that attainments indicating the emergence of the very young child's theory of mind, which have been attributed to the development of a "metarepresentational capacity" revealed in domains such as pretense (Leslie, 1987; Perner, this volume), in fact derive directly from this earlier emotional responsiveness (Hobson, in press). If so, how exactly does the child move from the early responsiveness to emotions to an understanding of thought, knowledge, and belief? Based on our work, we argue that the missing link in this sequence of events is in the realm of motivation and conation and that one vehicle for development is the flexible use of imitation. The missing link is desire. By observing others, infants begin to realize that other people have desires, and they begin to organize their own physiologically and psychologically based perceptions of internal states and external circumstances in terms of the socially agreed-on notions of want and need.

We come to this conclusion because our analysis of the mother's and child's use of mental state terms (Hay et al., in preparation) in turn forced us to reconceptualize our earlier studies of behavioral imitation. Not only are 1-year-olds and their mothers talking about what they want; the infants' responses to our experimental manipulations can similarly be conceptualized as thoughtful and creative attempts to figure out what we, as experimenters, want. For example, infants who observed that an unfamiliar woman appeared delighted when another adult put a hat on her foot then chose to interact with her in this tried-and-true manner (Hay et al., 1985). Imitation in this admittedly special case was a means of providing another human being with something that she seemed to want.

This analysis of the observational learning paradigm in terms of the observer's task being to identify other people's desires then sheds light on the finding that, even in the second year of life, modelling is not necessarily more effective than instruction and may under some circumstances, be less effective. Modelling is simply not the most accurate and succinct way of indicating one's desires. Expressing a desire through words or gestures may be much more informative (Hay & Murray, 1982; Hay et al., 1985; Murray, 1986). Long before they themselves are verbally fluent, infants betray a clear understanding of symbolic gestures, such as pointing and the outstretched hand that signal what another person finds interesting and wants. The salience of such signals probably derives from the earlier responsiveness to emotions, and so the process moves from emotional to motivational referencing. That there may then be a clear link between awareness of one's own and another's motivation and awareness of that person's thoughts is indicated by the observed association between the child's expression of desire and the mother's expression of her thoughts. This link requires further exploration.

If we posit that 1-year olds, by observing others' indications of what they want, by receiving numerous inquiries from their caregivers about what they themselves want, and by thus gaining a shared vocabulary with respect to wants and needs, begin to name and comprehend the phenomenon of desire, can we say that they have begun to construct a theory of mind? And, if so, how does this development then proceed? For example, is there decalage? Do metarepresentational capacities emerge in the province of desire before they do in the realm of thought (see, e.g., Wellman & Woolley, 1990)? Perhaps 3-year-old children's very difficulties with paradigms such as the false belief task (Wimmer & Perner, 1983) represent negative transfer from their mental operations within the realm of desire; there is no truth value with respect to desire as there is with belief, and a response to the desires of others requires dealing in probabilities, not facts.

In the natural caregiving setting, children's expressions of their own wants are frequently at odds with caregivers' assessments of the children's needs; caregivers' expression of their own wants and needs are sometimes modified under pressure from children. Thus, in this initial exposure to a particular class of intentional mental states, children learn that mental states are fluid and negotiable. It may come as some surprise to learn that other mental states are fixed and either true or false.

All of these possibilities with respect to developmental sequence deserve more explicit examination. For the time being, however, it is sufficient to conclude that, at least in the second year of life, imitation is frequently a manifestation of one's own desire and responsiveness to the desires of others. At the same time, 1-year olds' expressions of their own desires, though socially influenced, are not instances of mindless mimicry. Rather, behavioral imitation is imbued with meaning—that is, in the dictionary sense, bound up with one's own and others' intentions and purposes—and an understanding of shared meaning is at least partially advanced through the process of observational learning. What we have is not perhaps so much an individual's construction of a theory of mind but a meeting of minds in the conative realm between thought, feeling, and action.

ACKNOWLEDGMENTS

Work on this chapter was supported by grants from the Bethlem Maudsley Fund and the MacArthur Foundation. We are grateful for comments from the editors of this volume and for additional comments from Adrian Angold, Simon Baron-Cohen, and Peter Hobson.

REFERENCES

Abravanel, E., & Sigafoos, A. (1984). Exploring the presence of imitation in early infancy. *Child Development, 55,* 381–392.

Baldwin, J. M. (1906). *Social and ethical interpretations in mental development* (4th ed.). New York: MacMillan.

Bandura, A. (1977). *Social learning theory.* Englewood Cliffs, NJ: Prentice-Hall.

Berry, C. S. (1908). An experimental study of imitation in cats. *Journal of Comparative Neurology and Psychology, 18,* 1–26.

Cairns, R. B. (1979). *Social development: The origins and plasticity of interchanges.* San Francisco: Freeman.

Campos, J., & Stenberg, C. (1981). Perception, appraisal and emotion: The onset of social referencing. In M. E. Lamb & L. R. Sherrod (Eds.), *Infant social cognition.* (pp. 273–314). Hillsdale, NJ: Lawrence Erlbaum Associates.

Church, R. M. (1957). Transmission of learned behavior between rats. *Journal of Abnormal and Social Psychology, 54,* 163–165.

Dunn, J., Bretherton, I., & Munn, P. (1987). Conversations about feeling states between mothers and their young children. *Developmental Psychology, 23,* 132–139.

Feinman, S. (1982). Social referencing in infancy. *Merrill-Palmer Quarterly, 28,* 445–470.

Field, T., Woodson, R., Greenberg, R., & Cohen, D. (1982). Discrimination and imitation of facial expressions by neonates. *Science, 218*, 179–181.

Galef, B. J., Jr., & Clark, H. H. (1971). Social factors in the poison avoidance and feeding behavior of wild and domestic rat pups. *Journal of Comparative and Physiological Psychology, 75*, 341–347.

Hay, D. F. (1977). Following their companions as a form of exploration for human infants. *Child Development, 48*, 1624–1632.

Hay, D. F. (1979). Cooperative interactions and sharing between very young children and their parents. *Developmental Psychology, 15*, 647–655.

Hay, D. F. (1981). Multiple functions of proximity-seeking in infancy. *Child Development, 51*, 636–645.

Hay, D. F., & Murray, P. (1982). Giving and requesting: Social facilitation of infants' offers to adults. *Infant Behavior and Development, 5*, 301–310.

Hay, D. F., Murray, P., Cecire, S., & Nash, A. (1985). Social learning of social behavior in early life. *Child Development, 56*, 43–57.

Hay, D. F., Nash, A., & Pedersen, J. (1981). Responses of six-month-olds to the distress of their peers. *Child Development, 52*, 1071–1075.

Hobson, R. P. (1990). On acquiring knowledge about people, and the capacity to pretend: A response to Leslie. *Psychological Review, 97*, 114–121.

Home, H. J. (1966). The concept of mind. *International Journal of Psychoanalysis, 47*, 42–49.

Kohlberg, L. (1982). Moral development. In J. M. Broughton & D. J. Freeman-Moir (Eds.), *The cognitive developmental psychology of James Mark Baldwin* (pp. 277–325). Norwood, NJ: Ablex.

Leslie, A. M. (1987). Pretense and representation: The origins of "theory of mind." *Psychological Review, 94*, 412–426.

Meltzoff, A. N., & Moore, M. K. (1983). The origins of imitation in infancy: Paradigm, phenomena, and theories. In L. P. Lipsitt (Ed.), *Advances in infancy research*. (Vol. 2, pp. 266–301). Norwood, NJ: Ablex.

Murray, P. A. (1986). *Infants' responsiveness to modeling vs. instruction*. Unpublished doctoral Thesis, State University of New York at Stony Brook.

Neuringer, A., & Neuringer, M. (1974). Learning by following a food source. *Science, 184*, 1005–1008.

Piaget, J. (1962). *Play, dreams, and imitation in childhood*. New York: Norton.

Rheingold, H. L. (1982). Little children's participation in the work of adults, a nascent prosocial behavior. *Child Development, 53*, 114–125.

Rheingold, H. L., Hay, D. F., & West, M. J. (1976). Sharing in the second year of life. *Child Development, 47*, 1148–1158.

Rosenblatt, J. S., & Schneirla, T. C. (1962). The behavior of cats. In E. S. E. Hafez (Ed.), *The behavior of domestic animals* (pp. 453–488). Baltimore: Williams & Wilkins.

Searle, J. R. (1980). Minds, brains, and programs. *The Behavioral and Brain Sciences, 3*, 417–457.

Sears, R. R., Maccoby, E. E., & Levin, H. (1957). *Patterns of child rearing*. New York: Harper.

The Shorter Oxford English Dictionary on Historical Principles. (1973). Oxford: Clarendon Press.

Wellman, H. M., & Woolley, J. D. (1990). *From desires to beliefs: The early development of everyday psychology. Cognition, 35*, 245–275.

Wimmer, H., & Perner, J. (1983). Beliefs about beliefs: Representation and constraining function of wrong beliefs in young children's understanding of deception. *Cognition, 13*, 103–128.

CHAPTER 8

On Representing That: The Asymmetry Between Belief and Desire in Children's Theory of Mind

Josef Perner
Sussex University

Belief and desire are sometimes treated as equivalent components in theories of action (Aristotle's practical syllogism) or like symmetrical mirror images among the different mental states (Searle, 1983). On the basis of such analyses, one might expect that belief and desire should be understood by young children at about the same time; however, there is accumulating evidence that children understand the role of desire much earlier than that of belief, even in well-controlled contexts of apparently equal complexity.

One result in particular that puzzled me started with a study by Nicola Yuill (1984). She showed 3-year olds pictures of a boy with a ball. A think bubble indicated that the boy wanted to throw the ball to the girl in the picture, not to the other boy. Children were extremely good at judging that the boy would be quite pleased if, as intended, the girl caught the ball but not so pleased if the other boy caught it. Julie Hadwin (Hadwin & Perner, in press) replicated these results and designed structurally matching stories with the only difference being that the think bubble was interpreted as what the boy thinks, and children had to judge the boy's surprise as he found out what was really the case. Even most 5-year-olds had difficulty understanding that, when the belief was confirmed, the boy would not be as surprised as when his belief was violated (e.g., he found out that the boy had the ball when he had thought that the girl was holding it).

I try to explain this difference between belief and desire by looking at how these mental states represent. As it turns out, my explanation does not put belief (what people think) on one side and desire (what people want) on the other. Rather, it cuts right through different uses of the word *think*. It separates *thinking that something is the case* (belief) from *thinking of something* (pure thought). With this distinction, I can also explain why children find some stories involving the word *think* easier to understand than others (e.g., Wellman & Bartsch, 1988).

In order to make these necessary distinctions, I first set up my target, that is, the case for symmetry between belief and desire. Then, excursions into the concept of representation and into the distinction between *thinking of* and *thinking that* follow. The results from these analyses allow me to make my case against symmetry. In the final section, I work out the implications for development.

THE CASE FOR SYMMETRY

Searle (1983) emphasized that belief and desire differ as to how they relate to the world but they have in common that both have propositional content which stipulates the *conditions of satisfaction* (propositional content). For instance, "John thinks the car is in the garage," and "John wants the car in the garage" are both *satisfied* if the car is, in fact, in the garage. However, the way in which this fit between the world and the propositional content is to be achieved differs. This idea is well illustrated in an example by Elizabeth Anscombe (1957, p. 56), expressed here in John Searle's (1979b) elegant elaboration:

> Suppose a man goes to the supermarket with a shopping list given him by his wife on which are written the words 'beans, butter, bacon, and bread.' Suppose as he goes around with his shopping cart selecting these items, he is followed by a detective who writes down everything he takes. As they emerge from the store both shopper and detective will have identical lists. But the function of the two lists will be quite different. In the case of the shopper's list, the purpose of the list is, so to speak, to get the world to match the words; the man is supposed to make his actions fit the list. In the case of the detective, the purpose of the list is to make the words match the world; the man is supposed to make the list fit the actions of the shopper. This can be further demonstrated by observing the role of 'mistake' in the two cases. If the detective gets home and suddenly realizes that the man bought pork chops instead of bacon, he can simply erase the word 'bacon' and write 'pork chops.' But if the shopper gets home and his wife points out he has bought pork chops when he should have bought bacon he cannot correct the mistake by erasing 'bacon' from the list and writing 'pork chops'." (pp. 3, 4)

This difference in *direction of fit* between the two lists can be extended to the *causal relations* between lists and the shopper's actions. The wife's list governs (causes) the shopper's actions, whereas it is the shopper's actions that govern what words the detective puts on his list. These two lists illustrate the difference between mental states. The shopper's list is analogous to desire, which is the causal root for intentional changes in the world and the world is supposed to be made to fit the desire. The detective's list is analogous to belief or knowledge. It is caused by the actions in the world, and it is supposed to fit the state of the world. The first two rows in Table 8.1 summarize this symmetry in direction of fit and causality between belief and desire.

Now, what about representation? It is reasonable to say that the words on each list *represent* the items bought. Notice that this holds true for *both* lists—belief and desire, as it were—violating the otherwise clean mirror-image symmetry in terms of direction of fit and causality. If one wanted to preserve the symmetry for representation, the least objectionable way might be to claim that, in the case of the shopper's list, it is the items bought that "represent" the words on the list. But even this would be an absurd solution.

The interesting consequence of this observation is that the *direction of representation* does not coincide either with the direction of fit or with the direction of causality. This fact is remarkable insofar as both of these relationships have been thought to be critical for representation. My aim is to elaborate this asymmetry to argue that belief and intention throw up different representational problems. Before I can make this argument, however, an excursion into the concept of representation is necessary.

THE CONCEPT OF REPRESENTATION

I first run through some old arguments for why correspondence and causality do not suffice for defining representation. With this discussion

TABLE 8.1. The Symmetry Between Belief and Desire and the Problem With Representation

Criterion	Belief	Desire
Direction of Fit	mind → world	mind ← world
Direction of Causality	mind ← world	mind → world
Direction of Representation	mind → world	mind → world
Situations Represented	sense + referent	sense only
Misrepresentation	possible	impossible

I want to prepare the ground for the argument that it is the function of *standing in for* something else that determines whether something is a representation, and that belief and intention differ in terms of what they stand in for.

Correspondence and Causality

For there to be representation, we need two things that can take on different states. One I call the representational medium, the other the world. Obviously, there must be correspondence between the states of the medium and the states of the world. For instance, if I am filming with a video camera, the visible changes in the world are reflected in changes on the screen (representational medium). However, the question is whether such correspondence is, in itself, sufficient to establish a relationship of representation between world and medium. That it is not sufficient can be seen by the following "philosophical" consideration: Correspondence is a symmetrical relation, whereas representation is not. If the state of the medium corresponds to the state of the world, then the state of the world corresponds to the state of the medium. In contrast, the medium represents the world, but the reverse is not true.

In any case, an important question is what establishes the correspondence between medium and world. A traditional answer was "resemblance." This seems intuitively quite appealing. For instance, the patterns on my video monitor represent the filmed scene, because the patterns on the screen look like the scene. Ever since Goodman's (1976) critique of this "copy theory of representation," the concept of "resemblance" has lost its appeal as an explanation for representation. Fodor (1984) provided a very crisp summary of different points of critique. I mention just one problem: *Resemblance* is a symmetrical relation. It can, therefore, not make clear why it is that the video screen represents the filmed scene but the filmed scene does not represent the patterns on the screen, even though the scene is as similar to the patterns on the screen as these are similar to the filmed scene.

More recently, causality has been suggested as the means by which the correspondence between world and representational medium has to be established. For instance, it is the video screen that represents the filmed scene, because the changes in the scene cause the changes on the screen and not vice versa. Or, in case of the mind's perceptual states, it is the mechanism of perception that causes perceptual states to correspond to, hence represent, the perceived surroundings, rather than the other way around (Dretske, 1981; Fodor, 1987). So, we see that causality has one advantage over resemblance: It can account for the asymmetry of the representational relationship between medium and represented world (Fodor, 1984).

However, defining representation in terms of causality does not solve all problems. We have already encountered one problem. We would like to say that the content of a desire (the items on the wife's shopping list) represents the desired state of the world (the items to be purchased), but the causal relationship is the opposite than what is required. Because it is the desire that is causally involved in producing the desired state, we would be forced to say that the desired state "represents" the desire — that is, the items purchased represent(?) the words on the list — an absurd consequence.

Another problem is that anything that is causally influenced by something else would count as a representation of it. To use a famous example, smoke in the air represents the fire that causes it. Admittedly, we are getting close to representation, inasmuch as the smoke is often referred to as a *sign* of fire; or, it is said that smoke *means* fire. However, the purely causal relationship of fire producing smoke cannot account for "meaning," because then, as Dretske (1986b) pointed out *misrepresentation* would be impossible.

If causality were a defining feature of representation, that is, if the smoke represented the fire because it was caused by the fire, then there would be no misrepresentation, because the smoke without fire would, by definition, not represent the fire, as it was not caused by it. Yet, the possibility of misrepresentation is characteristic of typical representational systems. If we are using a faulty map that shows a lake in an area where there has never been a lake, then this map still represents *that there is a lake in that area*, even though the blue patch on the map symbolizing the lake could not have been caused by there being a lake, because that state of affairs never existed.

"Standing-In For" and Interpretive Systems

It is intuitively obvious that what is missing from these accounts of representation is an *interpretive system*. The smoke "means" fire, and the map "represents" that there is a lake, because the interpreter interprets them in that way. What has exercised philosophers is the question of whether the notion of interpretation can be explicated by means of natural processes, like causality, which do not circularly presuppose an intentional (interpretive) system like the human mind.

A possible story that is emerging from these considerations (Dennett, 1987, ch. 8; Dretske, 1986a; Fodor, 1984; Millikan, 1984) is that representation occurs only in biological systems. Millikan, in particular, has argued that representation occurs only within self-replicating systems whose organs and processes are replicated or repeated because they serve an important function. The function of representation is to correspond to aspects of the world. The importance of this function lies in the fact that the organism can use the representation to *stand in for* the real world. This is important for the frequently arising case where the organism's actions should ideally be governed by a distant aspect of the real world or by aspects of a not-yet-existing beneficial future state. Because distant aspects and nonexisting states cannot causally affect action directly, biology's trick is to use representations of these states instead. Because the function of the representation is to correspond to the states of the world, these states can then govern the organism's behavior via their representations.

The definition of representation should therefore contain two elements: (a) there must be a correspondence between states of the representational medium and states of the represented world, and (b) this correspondence must be exploited by an interpretive system so that the representation is used as a stand-in for the represented. It is this stand-in function that determines the asymmetry between representational medium and represented world; not the causal relationship.[1] Causality, however, plays an important role in establishing reliable correspondence. Without a causal relationship, there would not be an enduring, reliable correspondence. Yet, despite the importance of causality in establishing reliable correspondence, a particular representational state does not have to be caused by its corresponding state of the world in every single instance. This would have to be the case if representation were directly defined in causal terms. For the functional approach, there only needs to be enough causal regularity to establish correspondence under *normal* circumstances—often enough to serve its (biological) function (Millikan, 1984, ch. 1). In fact, it is on those occasions when the normal causal relationship breaks down that misrepresentation occurs. For instance, blue areas on maps mean lakes because, normally, when there is a blue patch, there is a lake. This usually reliable correspondence holds because of a causal, albeit complicated and intricate, connection between there being a lake, the

---

[1]A representational relationship can also exist between medium and world, where the state of the world does not cause the corresponding state of the representational medium but where a common cause is responsible for their reliable co-occurence.

cartographic process, and, finally, the map. Once this normal use of blue patches has been established, the occasional deviation leads to misrepresentation for an interpretive system working on the established correspondence. Similarly, a system for which there is normally a reliable relationship between smoke being caused by fire will misinterpret smoke as a sign of fire when it is actually caused by a smoke bomb. If these occurrences become frequent, then the system will revise its interpretation of smoke.

Misrepresentation and the Sense-Reference Distinction

In the case of misrepresentation, there is a division of what the representation stands in for. Let us say my faulty map is of Death Valley. In search of a nice place to swim, my driving behavior is governed by this map, because I take it to stand for the actual situation in Death Valley. In other words, it is a *representation of (refers to)* the actual situation in Death Valley, but it *represents this situation as* there being a lake in Death Valley. Following Dretske (1988), I call the actual situation in Death Valley without a lake the *referent* of my representation and the counterfactual situation where there is a lake in Death Valley the *sense* of my cartographic representation which is determined by the usual meaning of the combination of marks on the map.

Both situations — sense and referent — are represented by the map in the sense that I take the map to stand in for them. If I did not take it as a stand-in for the actual situation (referent), I would not actually drive there in desperation for a swim, and if I did not take it as standing for a situation where there was a lake in Death Valley (sense), I would not sweat out the futile drive to that place either.

In short, the map misrepresents because the meaning of its symbols describe a different situation (sense: lake in Death Valley) than the situation it refers to (referent: actual situation where there is only desert in Death Valley). All representations whose role it is to inform about the state of the world, including all epistemic mental states like perceptions, beliefs, knowledge, and so forth, have a referent and sense. But there are also other, derivative uses of representation that have only sense and no referent (one could say they do not really stand in for anything — they only stand for something, namely their sense).

Mere thoughts are good examples. When I am merely thinking of a valley with a lake, this thought only has sense (the situation where there is a valley with a lake in it) but no real situation as its referent. A bit touchier is the thought of there being a lake in Death Valley. Of course, the expression "Death Valley" has a referent, but the situation I am thinking of does not. Certainly, the real situation is not its referent, because, being a mere thought rather than a serious belief, I do not take this thought to stand in for the real situation. I only take it to stand for the hypothetical, thought-of situation. The distinction between idle thoughts and beliefs is brought out in natural language by the particle "that."

SAYING "THAT" IN MENTAL STATE REPORTS

Mental state terms are often called *propositional attitudes* (Russell, 1914), because, in those reports mental states are expressed as a relation between a person and a proposition. For example, "You think I am lying on a Mediterranean beach." In this report on your thoughts, the word think relates you to the proposition (or situation) of me being on a Mediterranean beach. To understand the report, one has to know something about how think relates you to the proposition, that is, what consequences this link has on you. I cannot give a complete analysis of these consequences, but, certainly, it should have some effect on your behavior. For instance, if somebody asks you where I am, you will answer "on a Mediterranean beach," which you would not do if you did not think that I was there. Also, you would not give this answer if you were linked by *want* to the proposition of me lying on a Mediterranean beach. In that case, you would answer "on a Mediterranean beach" when I asked you, "Where should I be lying this summer?".

In view of the preceding discussion about reference and sense, we have to ask what precisely it is that *think* relates you to. The answer to this question depends on whether we are talking about *thinking of* or *thinking that*:

1. You think *of* me lying on a Mediterranean beach.
2. You think *that* I am lying on a Mediterranean beach.

The difference between these sentences is important. The first describes a very nice thought of yours, whereas the second expresses a serious misconception about my work ethic (a particularly annoying misconception when I am, in fact, sitting here in rainy England trying to compose this chapter). Why is there this difference between the two sentences?

The difference arises because *think of* and *think that* relate you differently to situations. *Think of* in sentence 1 relates you only to the situation where I am lying on a Mediterranean beach (sense). *Think that* in sentence 2 relates you to two situations: to the situation of me lying on a Mediterranean beach as the *sense* of your belief and to the real situation of me sitting in rainy England as the *referent* of your belief.

We are now equipped with the distinction between sense and referent and the understanding that the referential use of mental terms is marked by *that*. With this distinction, I return to the question of the representational nature of desire.

THE CASE AGAINST SYMMETRY

To discuss the representational status of desire, it is useful to remember Anscombe's example of the two lists with identical content but different uses. One of them was the detective's list, which corresponded to epistemic states like belief and knowledge. Its representational status is straightforward. It represents the items that the man took off the shelves. It allows for misrepresentation. When the detective marks down "bacon" when the man had taken pork chops, then the sense of his list consists of the items: beans, butter, *bacon*, bread, and so forth, whereas the referent of his list consists of the items: beans, butter, *pork chops*, bread, and so on.

The more interesting question is what the man's shopping list, which is taken to illustrate desire, represents. Could we not say it represents exactly the same as the detective's list? Its sense consists of the items: beans, butter, bacon, bread, and so on, and its referent of the actual items: beans, butter, pork chops, bread, and so forth. Let us check this claim by testing whether the man used the list as standing for these situations. We clearly can agree that he used it as standing for the sense situation. It is this situation that ideally should govern his actions. Unfortunately, a hypothetical future situation has no causal power to govern action, and so a representation of that situation has to take its role. In contrast, it is not clear in which sense the list functioned as a stand-in for the (by error) actually achieved situation, which includes the unwanted pork chops. The actually achieved situation neither did cause his actions, nor should have caused them. So the representation was not a stand-in for the actually achieved situation. The only situation that the shopping list did stand for is the situation with the items he should have bought; the goal situation. It is, therefore, the only situation that the shopping list (desire) represents.

Also, our linguistic intuition confirms that the actually achieved situation could not be the referent for the shopping list, because we would not say that, due to the man's mistake, his shopping list "misrepresents" what he actually bought. The list does not represent that situation at all. It simply represents a different situation: the one the man should have achieved but, by mistake, did not achieve. This intuition is further strengthened by the fact that, at least in English, the word *want* does not lend itself to forming an equivalent construction to *think that*.

The bottom part of Table 8.1 summarizes this asymmetry in representational function between belief and desire. I now want to use this asymmetry to explain why children seem so much more proficient in understanding and reasoning about wants than about beliefs (thinking that).

DEVELOPMENTAL IMPLICATIONS

Children as young as 2 years old are, in some respects, quite competent social reasoners, and so they must have some kind of "theory of mind." Yet, at the same time, they fail to understand other, very basic aspects of the mind. Not before they are about 4 years old do they understand that a person can entertain a false belief (Wimmer & Perner, 1983) and can distinguish between appearance and reality (Flavell, Flavell, & Green, 1983). To explain this discrepancy, I ventured to propose that, before the age of 4, the young child interprets mental states as relations to situations directly. Only later does the child reconceptualize them as relations to representations of situations (Perner, 1988).

By conceiving of mental states as relations to situations, the young child gains an already quite powerful theory of action. The child can understand that different mental attitudes toward a situation have different implications. For instance, if a person has the attitude "want" towards a nonexisting situation, then that person might do something to bring about that situation, whereas if the person is just thinking of that situation, he or she will not act (unless he or she also wants to respond in relation to that situation, as, for instance in pretence, or "thinking aloud"). Or, if that person is afraid of that situation, then he or she will do something to prevent it from becoming reality.

The difference to the later developing conception of mental states as representations is that the young child derives the person's actions as if people were governed by situations directly, without representations having to stand in for these situations to do the causal work.[2] It becomes necessary to bring in representations as stand-ins for situations in order to understand cases of misrepresentation, because there it becomes essential to differentiate between sense and reference. This explains the late understanding of false belief (Wimmer & Perner, 1983) and of the appearance–reality distinction (Flavell et al., 1983).

Without conception of mental states as representations the child cannot understand *thinking that*. The child has a theory of *thinking* but can only, at best, assimilate *thinking that* to *thinking of*. This inability to understand *thinking that* provides the basis for understanding why children find wants so much easier to understand than beliefs. Understanding most relevant behavioral and emotional implications of desire does not need the understanding of *that*. For belief, this understanding is essential.

This difference between desire and belief helps me understand why 3-year-olds in the study by Yuill (1984) could give near-perfect judgments of pleasedness, which involve the contrast between what a person wants and what the person achieves. These children were shown a picture of a boy holding a ball and facing another boy and a girl in some distance. A think bubble over the boy's head made clear what he wanted to achieve, that is, that the girl catch the ball. Then, a subsequent picture showed what actually happened, that is, either the girl caught the ball or the other boy caught it. Even the younger 3-year-olds all judged correctly that the thrower would feel more pleased when the girl caught the ball than when the other boy caught it.

It is important to realize that, for this understanding, the boy's goal need not be understood as mental representation but can be interpreted

---

[2] I have to clarify this proposal in the hope of avoiding a common misunderstanding. When I presented the idea at the SRCD workshop at Yale that young children do not understand mental states as relations to representations but as relations to situations, I discerned some rumblings of discontent. It was thought ridiculous that I tried to describe 3-year-olds as behaviorists. This charge arose, I think, because I characterized the young child's theory as a theory of behavioral dispositions. That is, in order to understand the psychological relevance of a person's thinking of a situation, one has to understand that the thought disposes the person to act in relation to that situation. It is important to realize that the situation need not be a real situation but can be—and, in the case of wants, almost always is—a counterfactual, merely *thought-of* or *desired* situation. Behaviorists, in my understanding, would not allow for behavior being governed by nonexisting situations. My theory, therefore, does not characterize the young child as a behaviorist but rather as something like the Aristotelian finalists, who explain behavior as directed or aimed at nonexisting ideals (causa finalis). Such a conception is not only not behaviorist but is also thoroughly incompatible with current scientific explanation at large. In fact, conceptualizing mental states as representations is partly motivated by the need to find a scientifically acceptable way of explaining how "nonexisting" situations can exert influence on real behavior (Fodor, 1985).

as a hypothetical future situation. To gain a more concrete picture of the child's reasoning processes, one may imagine the child viewing the actor within a landscape of possible situations that stretch from past to present to the future. The child knows which situation is the actual present situation, that is, that the protagonist has the ball. The child can also imagine relevant possible future situations, for example, the other boy catches the ball, or the girl catches the ball. The protagonist's goal can be represented as one of those possible future situations, namely, that the girl catches the ball. To mark that this situation is the protagonist's goal, a link "goal" is introduced between the protagonist and that possible situation. Now the protagonist throws the ball, the boy catches it, and the subject is asked how pleased the protagonist will feel about that result. In the subject's representation of events, the originally possible future situation "boy catches ball" has become reality. This situation is not the one that was designated the protagonist's goal, and so he will not feel particularly pleased. Had the goal situation become reality, he would feel much more pleased.

As this analysis shows, there is no need to interpret the goal as a representation of the achieved outcome. Pleasedness can simply be judged at the level of situations. If the goal situation is the same as the actually achieved situation, then the actor is pleased. If the two situations are different, then the actor is not so pleased. It is for this reason, I think, that this task is so easy for 3-year-olds. The interesting question is whether this task would stay so easy if it involved the match between a belief and a real situation. To test this, we have to move from judgments of pleasedness to judgments of surprise.

Julie Hadwin (Hadwin & Perner, in press) extended Yuill's test of understanding pleasedness to incorporate a test of understanding surprise in a structurally analogous situation. The set-up was slightly modified so that the protagonist was separated from the other two characters by a tall wall. Otherwise, the pleasedness test was the same as Yuill's. In the surprise stories, the protagonist was shown as *thinking that* the girl had the ball. When he looked behind the wall, he saw that reality either matched his expectation (the girl did have the ball) or violated his expectation (the other boy had the ball), in which case the thrower should be relatively surprised.

It is worthwhile to sketch again the similarity between this case and the one about pleasedness. In both cases, the protagonist has a mental state (goal or belief) that he later finds out either does or does not match reality (after his throw or after looking behind the wall) and, consequently, he feels either more or less pleased or surprised. However, despite this clear similarity, it is not possible, as it was with goals, to interpret the content of belief as a possible situation.

Interpreting belief as a direct relation to a possible situation would not allow differentiation from *thinking of*. That is, the protagonist would be understood as thinking of the girl holding the ball. If the protagonist were, in fact, just thinking of her holding it and not thinking that she had it, then finding out that the boy had it would not be terribly surprising. (It would be as little surprising as if you saw me sitting at my terminal typing this chapter after thinking of me lying on a Mediterranean beach.) You would only be surprised about me sitting here if you had thought *that* I was at the beach. In other words, simply having the possibility in mind and finding out that the world is different is not surprising. So, to understand surprise, one has to be able to understand misrepresentation, namely that the person represents the actual situation (referent) as different from how it really is.

The necessity to understand thinking *that* for judging surprise is my explanation for why Hadwin's children found surprise judgments difficult. Not before the age of 5 or even 6 years were a substantial proportion able to give consistent judgments. This is surprising, considering that, in a structurally almost identical task, 3-year-olds had no difficulty giving correct judgments of pleasedness.

There is a variety of results about children's understanding of desire and the word *think* that fit this analysis. Three-year-olds can be very proficient in understanding how a person will act depending on what that person wants or thinks, provided that the person's action can be correctly predicted based on *thinking of*. If an understanding of "*thinking*" as *thinking that* is essential (as in Hadwin's surprise task), then it becomes difficult for 3-year-olds.

There are now several studies that have demonstrated children's ability to understand the significance of what a person wants. For instance, Wellman and Woolley (in press) reported that 3-year-olds find it easy to predict that a boy who wants to take his dog to the park will do so once he has found the dog but will keep searching if he found his cat instead. Shultz (1980) summarized a series of studies showing that 3-year-olds can judge whether a person meant to do something or not, depending on whether the result of the action matches or mismatches the person's stated goal.

Wellman and Bartsch (1988, Experiments 2 and 3) demonstrated that 3-year-olds are also pretty good at predicting that a person's action depends on what that person thinks. The authors used eight different stories, of which I analyze here only one, Wellman and Bartsch's (1988) Discrepant Belief Story: "Look, there are bananas in the cupboard and bananas in the refrigerator. Jane wants a banana. Jane thinks there are only bananas in the cupboard; she doesn't think there are bananas in the refrigerator. Where will Jane look for bananas?" (p. 258). On three such tasks, 14 of 15 three-year-olds predicted at least twice that Jane would look in the cupboard rather than in both locations or the refrigerator. Wellman and Bartsch concluded from that finding that 3-year-olds understand belief. Apart from several other plausible strategies (see Perner, 1989) that might have led children to the correct answer, I consider here only the question of how children would respond if their only available interpretation of "think" is in the sense of thinking of.

The following gloss might give some impression of how the story might come across to these children: " . . . Jane thinks only of the bananas in the cupboard; she doesn't think [much] of the bananas in the refrigerator. Where will Jane look for bananas?" Even if one assumes that Jane is fully aware of the fact that there are bananas in both locations (i.e., no false belief considered), one still would predict that she will look in the cupboard for bananas. In short, even children without an understanding of *thinking that* (belief) are likely to give a correct answer to this kind of story.

Now take, in contrast, Wellman and Bartsch's (1988) Explicit False Belief Story: "Jane wants to find her kitten. Jane's kitten is really in the playroom. Jane thinks her kitten is in the kitchen. Where will Jane look for her kitten?" (p. 258). Again, one can gloss the *"think"* sentence in terms of *thinking of*, but it remains unclear what one should predict. It all depends on what the point is supposed to be. Should one predict what Jane really wants to do as the more plausible option or what she wants to do in her thoughts the less likely option—but not altogether implausible, because why else would the speaker bother to mention what Jane is thinking of? I do not know what children think about this story, but the fact is that 3-year-olds opted only 16% of the time for the less plausible (but correct) option. One can only understand that this answer is correct if one understands *thinking that*. This understanding emerges after the age of 4 years: 31% of 4;4-year-olds and 86% of 4;5-year-olds got it right (Wellman & Bartsch, 1988, Exp. 3, Fig. 4).

So, we see that tasks involving *"thinking"* can be easy or difficult depending on whether *"think"* has to be interpreted as a mental representation (i.e., belief, *thinking that* which requires the content-referent distinction) or simply as a relationship to a situation (i.e., *thinking of*). In contrast, tasks involving *"want"* do not appear to require a representational interpretation. But, is that true? Could we not find a task involving *"want"* where a representational interpretation becomes necessary?

In fact, not all aspects of desire and intention are easy to understand for 3-year-olds. For instance, there is the finding by Gopnik and Seager (1988) that children who know that one book is for adults and the other for children still do not seem to understand that the adult will, therefore, choose the book for adults. Also, there is the finding by Shultz (1980) that 5-year-olds, but not 3-year olds, can judge the intentionality of reflexes. As Janet Astington (this volume) has pointed out, children seem good at understanding intentionality when a person's goal has been explicitly specified and their judgments can be based on a match/mismatch strategy. Difficulty arises, Astington argues, when children have to understand the causal relationship between events in the world, desires, and action. Because the causal relationship between desire and action is constitutive of the concept of intention, Astington focuses on children's understanding of that concept.

I think we all agree that the 3-year-old understands that there are desirable situations and that people work their way towards those situations (e.g., Wellman & Woolley, in press), and that if a person is successful, then he or she meant (Shultz, 1980) to do what he or she did and is pleased (Yuill, 1984). This understanding also allows for simple "causal" reasoning, like pointing out that somebody did something because he or she wanted to (Hood & Bloom, 1979).

However, for understanding intentional causation more is required. The child has to understand that the action towards the desired situation has to be caused by a mental representation of itself (Searle, 1979a). Now, the 3-year-old could not make do by substituting that mental representation of the planned action with a thought-of action, because a thought-of action cannot cause a real action. It is only the act of representing the thought-of action that can cause it.

Why would a child need to understand anything as complex as that in Shultz's experiment to understand that the leg movement caused by the knee-jerk reflex was not intended? Because the child is not given the description of a "desired action," he or she cannot judge intentionality by the match/mismatch between actual and desired action. The child needs the idea, in principle, that an intentional action must be caused by some internal representation of it. Without that idea, the child would not even know where to look for an answer.

CONCLUSION

I started with the puzzle of why children find problems involving a person's wants easier than problems involving thinking. My analysis of thinking of and thinking that has shown that what young children find easy and difficult is actually based on a different distinction, namely whether the mental states involved have to be construed as mental representation (e.g., belief and, possibly, intention) or whether it is sufficient to understand them as a relationship to a situation (thought and desire).

ACKNOWLEDGMENTS

The preparation of this chapter was greatly helped by a Social Science Fellowship from the Nuffield Foundation and a Research Scholarship from the Alexander-von-Humboldt Foundation.

REFERENCES

Anscombe, G. E. M. (1957). *Intention*. Cambridge, England: Cambridge University Press.

Dennett, D. C. (1987). *The intentional stance*. Cambridge, MA: Bradford Books/MIT Press.

Dretske, F. (1981). *Knowledge and the flow of information*. Cambridge, MA: Bradford Books/MIT Press.

Dretske, F. (1986a). Aspects of cognitive representation. In M. Brand & R. M. Harnish (Eds.), *The representation of knowledge and belief* (pp. 101–115). Tucson: The University of Arizona Press.

Dretske, F. (1986b). Misrepresentation. In R. Bogdan (Ed.), *Belief* (pp. 17–36). Oxford: Oxford University Press.

Dretske, F. (1988). *Explaining behavior: Reasons in a world of causes*. Cambridge, MA: MIT Press/Bradford Books.

Flavell, J. H., Flavell, E. R., & Green, F. L. (1983). Development of the appearance-reality distinction. *Cognitive Psychology, 15*, 95–120.

Fodor, J. A. (1984). Semantics, Wisconsin style. *Synthese, 59*, 231–250.

Fodor, J. A. (1985). Fodor's guide to mental representation: The intelligent auntie's vade-mecum. *Mind, 94*, 76–100.

Fodor, J. A. (1987). *Psychosemantics: The problem of meaning in the philosophy of mind*. Cambridge, MA: Bradford Books/MIT Press.

Goodman, N. (1976). *Languages of art*. Indianapolis: Hackett Publishing Co.

Gopnik, A., & Seager, W. (in press). Young children's understanding of desires. *Child Development*.

Hadwin, J., & Perner, J. (in press). Pleased and surprised: Children's cognitive theory of emotion. *British Journal of Developmental Psychology*.

Hood, L., & Bloom, L. (1979). What, when, and how about why: A longitudinal study of early expressions of causality. *Monographs of the Society for Research in Child Development, 44*, (6, Serial No. 160).

Millikan, R. (1984). *Language, thought, and other biological categories: New foundations for realism*. Cambridge, MA: MIT Press.

Perner, J. (1988). Developing semantics for theories of mind: From propositional attitudes to mental representation. In J. Astington, P. L. Harris, & D. R. Olson (Eds.), *Developing theories of mind* (pp. 141–172). New York: Cambridge University Press.

Perner, J. (1989). Is "thinking" belief?: A reply to Wellman and Bartsch. *Cognition, 33*, 315–319.

Russell, B. (1914). *Our knowledge of the external world*. London: Allen and Unwin.

Searle, J. R. (1979a). The intentionality of intention and action. *Cognitive Science, 4*, 47–70.

Searle, J. R. (1979b). A taxonomy of illocutionary speech acts. In J. Searle (Ed.), *Expression and meaning* (pp. 1–29). Cambridge, England: Cambridge University Press.

Searle, J. R. (1983). *Intentionality: An essay in the philosophy of mind*. Cambridge, England: Cambridge University Press.

Shultz, T. R. (1980). The development of the concept of intention. In A. Collins, (Ed.), *Minnesota symposium on child psychology*, (Vol. 13, pp. 131–164). Hillsdale, NJ: Lawrence Erlbaum Associates.

Wellman, H. M., & Bartsch, K. (1988). Young children's reasoning about beliefs. *Cognition, 30*, 239–277.

Wellman, H. M., & Woolley, J. D. (in press). *From simple desires to ordinary beliefs: The early development of everyday psychology. Cognition*.

Wimmer, H., & Perner, J. (1983). Beliefs about beliefs: Representation and constraining function of wrong beliefs in young children's understanding of deception. *Cognition, 13*, 103–128.

Yuill, N. (1984). Young children's coordination of motive and outcome judgments of satisfaction and morality. *British Journal of Developmental Psychology, 2*, 73–81.

CHAPTER 9

Intention in the Child's Theory of Mind

Janet W. Astington
University of Toronto

> *A 3-year-old girl was helping to feed her baby brother. After spooning in a few mouthfuls of cereal, she took another spoonful and simply dumped it on the baby's head. Then she turned quickly to her very angry mother and claimed, "I didn't do it on purpose."*
> —Shultz, (1980, p. 157)

It is anecdotes such as this that enliven one's reading of the developmental literature. But what are we to make of it? At least this: The little girl's use of *not on purpose* does not conform to adult usage. Why not? That is the question I attempt to answer in this chapter.

On purpose is one of the ways in which we denote intentional action in contrast to accidental behavior, along with *was trying to, planned to, meant to, intended to,* and so on. We also use some of these terms to refer to future actions, for example, *plans to, means to, intends to,* and so forth. A complete understanding of intention must include both of these aspects. As Bratman (1987) put it: "We do things intentionally, and we intend to do things. Our commonsense psychology uses the notion of intention to characterize both our actions and our mental states" (p. 111).

CHILDREN'S METAREPRESENTATIONAL ABILITIES

The child's acquisition of this commonsense psychology, or theory of mind, has recently become a lively area of research in cognitive

157

development. The child's theory of mind is the understanding children have of their own and others' minds and of the relation between the mind and the world. This understanding enables children to predict and explain actions by ascribing mental states, such as beliefs, desires, and intentions, to themselves and to other people.

Currently, there is some controversy over the age at which it is appropriate to attribute a theory of mind to the child. Like most theories, the child's theory of mind is not acquired overnight; there is considerable, gradual development during the years from infancy to school age and even into the adolescent years (Astington, Harris, & Olson, 1988). In all of this controversy, one thing is clear: Important developments occur at about 4 years of age. There is a crucial change in the child's understanding at this time, resulting in a new conception of the representational capacities of the mind (Flavell, 1988; Forguson & Gopnik, 1988; Perner, 1988).

Infants form representations of reality that are veridical representations of what is perceived, but they don't consider them as representations. Significant changes in the child's representational abilities occur after 18 months of age with the development of the child's symbolic capacities. By 2 years of age, children are not limited simply to forming representations of reality; they can also form representations of absent and nonexistent situations. For example, they can form hypothetical representations, as in pretend play (Leslie, 1988). Soon after this, they can talk about these representations using mental terms, such as *think, know, remember, pretend, want,* and so on (Bretherton & Beeghly, 1982; Shatz, Wellman, & Silber, 1983). They can also distinguish these representations from reality; as Wellman and Estes (1986) have shown, 3-year olds distinguish appropriately between real objects and mental entities that are remembered, imagined, dreamed of, or thought about. They can even make *simple* predictions about a person's actions, based on the person's wants and beliefs (Wellman & Bartsch, 1988).

Thus, 2- and 3-year-olds have a fairly rich and impressive set of abilities in this area. However, there is some debate whether we should refer to these abilities as *metarepresentational.* The term was used by Pylyshyn (1978) as characterizing the "ability to represent the *representing relation* itself" (p. 593). Perner (1988) argued that 2- and 3-year-olds' abilities are not truly metarepresentational, because children of this age do not conceptualize the representational process. They represent situations, including hypothetical and counterfactual situations, and they can associate people with these situations. Thus, they interpret mental states as relations to situations; they do not yet conceptualize them as relations to representations of situations, because they do not conceptualize the other person's representational process (Perner, this volume). Forguson and Gopnik (1988), on the other hand, have argued that 2- and 3-year-olds metarepresent all nonepistemic mental states, such as desires, intentions, pretence, and so forth. For them, the fundamental change that occurs at 4 years of age is in the child's ability to metarepresent epistemic mental states as well, that is, to realize that real things are represented, as are hypothetical, counterfactual, and absent things and states of affairs.

A "WATERSHED" AT FOUR YEARS OF AGE

Despite disagreement concerning whether it is appropriate to characterize 2- and 3-year-olds' abilities as metarepresentational, there is agreement that their theory of mind is a rather limited theory. There is some sort of watershed at about 4 years of age, leading to a whole new range of abilities. There are many experimental tasks that 3-year-olds cannot do that 4- and 5-year-olds can do. In all of these tasks, the older children's success appears to depend on a new understanding of the representational capacities of the mind, whatever the precise nature of that new understanding is.

The false belief paradigm is a well-known example of these tasks (Hogrefe, Wimmer, & Perner, 1986; Perner, Leekam, & Wimmer, 1987; Wimmer & Perner, 1983). Perner, Wimmer, and their colleagues have clearly shown that, after about 4 years of age, children recognize that other people may hold beliefs that are different from their own; they understand that a person may believe something that they know to be false, and they can anticipate that the person will act on the basis of that false belief. At the same age, children first understand the distinction between reality and appearance, that is, the distinction between what something is and what someone might believe it to be (Flavell, Flavell, & Green, 1983). Further, children's understanding of false belief and of the appearance-reality distinction are related to one another and also to children's understanding of change in their own beliefs (Gopnik & Astington, 1988). Four-year-olds, but not 3-year-olds, recognize that their own beliefs may change over time, and they can remember and report their earlier beliefs. Four-year-olds also understand the role of perception (Wimmer, Hogrefe, & Sodian, 1988) and point of view (Flavell, Everett, Croft, & Flavell, 1981) in belief formation, and they can identify and remember the sources of their beliefs (Gopnik & Graf, 1988).

A striking point is that all these abilities depend on changes in the child's understanding of belief. There is a fundamental difference between 3- and 4-year olds' understanding of others' beliefs, their own beliefs, belief change, and belief formation. This supports Forguson and Gopnik's argument that the crucial change at 4 years of age is a change in the child's understanding of epistemic mental states, that is to say that 4-year-olds acquire the ability to metarepresent beliefs, in addition to the earlier ability to metarepresent desires and intentions. Perner's view, also, is not unsupported by these data, but his argument is more radical; he contends that children do not conceptualize the representational process at all until 4 years of age. This conceptualization can explain their newfound success on tasks involving false belief, appearance-reality, representational change, and so on. But further, Perner's argument predicts that there will also be changes in children's understanding of nonepistemic mental states, because these states, too, are not metarepresented until 4 years of age.

INTENTION IN THE CHILD'S THEORY OF MIND

Obviously, to decide between these two possibilities, we need to look at children's understanding of nonepistemic mental states. Can 2- and 3-year-olds' abilities be explained without the assumption that intentions and desires are metarepresented? And, further, is there some change in the child's understanding of intention and desire at 4 years of age? If so, does the nature of that change support Perner's view that children do not metarepresent intentions and desires before 4 years?

Developmentalists have given less attention to children's concepts of intention and desire, at least in the context of their theory of mind. Perhaps one reason for this is the assumption that these concepts are less problematic and are acquired earlier than the concept of belief. Premack and Woodruff (1978), investigating the chimpanzee's theory of mind, concluded that "of all possible guesses, we find the most compelling one to be that inferences about motivation will precede those about knowledge, both across species and across developmental stages" (p. 526). Their critics pointed out that, logically, beliefs and desires are equally important in predicting action. Nonetheless, it may be the case that, psychologically, desires appear more prominent because beliefs are often shared. Certainly, developmentalists have assumed that children are aware of others' intentions and desires from a very young age (e.g., Dunn, this volume).

Because it is so obvious that people want different things, we assume that it must be obvious to young children too, and we assume that they can easily predict that people will, therefore, do different things. On the other hand, because beliefs are generally shared, a person's actions can be predicted without considering his or her belief, because there is usually no difference between the person's representation of the world and the world itself (Perner, 1988). That is, young children do not need to have an understanding of belief to predict another's action, because they can use their own knowledge of the world in place of the other's belief. No difficulty arises unless the other holds a false belief, and, as we have seen, not until 4 years of age can children predict that others' actions would be determined by their false beliefs, that is by their *representation* of the world, not by the way the world really is. And not until then are children considered to have a concept of belief as a person's mental representation of the world.

It is my argument that this applies a stricter criterion to the concept of belief than to the concept of intention; indeed, some authors (Chandler, 1988; Wellman & Bartsch, 1988) have argued that it may be too strict a criterion, which is not my point. Until children demonstrate an understanding of false belief, we do not really know if they have a concept of belief, because we cannot test their understanding of true belief, because no distinction can be made between the true belief and the way the world is. Thus, my point is this: In the case of intention, do young children really understand that people have different intentions, or do they just know that people do different things? The question is: When do children metarepresent intentions and conceptualize intentions as mental representations, at 2 or at 4 years of age?

An Analysis of the Concept of Intention

Putting the question in Bratman's (1987) terms, quoted at the beginning of this chapter ("we do things intentionally and we intend to do things"), we can ask: At what age do children use the notion of intention to characterize both actions and mental states? Searle made a distinction similar to Bratman's (Anscombe, 1957, is the source for both). Searle (1983) pointed out that sometimes intention and action occur simultaneously—what Searle has called an intention-in-action. This sort of action is not premeditated, it is simply performed; even so, it is intentional (see Fig. 9.1). The intention and the movement, occurring together, constitute the action. At other times, the action may be planned in advance. Here, belief and desire lead to the formation of what Searle has called a *prior intention*, and this is the everyday use of the term *intention*: some plan to perform an action in the future. This is a purely mental state, which represents the intended action prior to its performance. Intentional performance of the intended action then

PRIOR INTENTION (1)	causes—>	INTENTION -IN-ACTION (2)	causes—>	BODILY MOVEMENT (3)
1 + 2 + 3		= prior intention that is carried out		
2 + 3		= unplanned intentional action		
1 alone		= unfulfilled prior intention		
1 + 2, or 2 alone		= failed effort		
3 alone		= movement, but not action		

FIG. 9.1. Relations between intention, action, and movement (Data from Searle, 1983, p. 94; adapted by permission.

includes intention-in-action, but the performance may, in fact, never take place if the intention is unfulfilled. In that case, there is only mental representation. Thus, Searle's intention-in-action corresponds to Bratman's acting intentionally, and Searle's prior intention corresponds to Bratman's intending to do something.

CHILDREN'S UNDERSTANDING OF INTENTION

The question, then, becomes: Do young children have a concept of intention as a mental state, representing an intended action? Applying the same criterion to the concept of intention that is applied to the concept of belief, one would have to show that children understand intentions *separate from* actions in the world. Unfulfilled intentions are the parallel case to false beliefs. In the case of unfulfilled intention, there is no subsequent action; it is simply a mental representation, with no instantiation in the world because its satisfaction conditions are not met. Thus, it is crucial to see whether children conceptualize intentions as mental states that accompany actions (intentional action), that may precede actions (prior intention), and that may occur and not lead to any action (unfulfilled intention).

Research has focused on the first of these aspects, that is, on children's ability to distinguish between intentional and unintentional action, especially in the context of their moral judgments, from which understanding of intention may only be inferred, not assessed directly. In addition, very little of the moral judgment research has looked at the 3- to 5-year-old period, critical to the present issue, and so I do not review it here.

Shultz has investigated children's understanding of intentional action directly in various real situations and has included children as young as 3 years of age. In one experiment (Shultz, Wells, & Sarda, 1980), a number of actions were elicited from subjects in such a way that they sometimes made mistakes; for example, a shiny and a dull penny were put on the table in front of a child who was then asked to point to the shiny one. Sometimes, subjects wore prism spectacles, reversing left and right so that they pointed to the dull penny by mistake. They were then asked, "Did you mean to do that?", or an observer child was asked, "Did he mean to do that?". Shultz et al. showed that children as young as 3 years of age could, in this way, distinguish intentional actions from unintentional ones, both for their own behavior and for the observed behavior of others. It might be suggested that the children were basing their distinction simply on the unwanted consequences of the mistake. However, in another experiment, Shultz and Wells (1985) used an electronic target-shooting game, rigged so that the experimenters could control the outcome without the subjects' knowledge. The child had to choose a colored card and then attempt to shoot that colored section of the target. Unlike the shiny penny case, any particular color was sometimes the wrong one and sometimes the right one, depending on the particular card chosen. Shultz and Wells showed that 3-year-olds could identify outcomes that matched goals as intended and ones that did not match as unintended, even though the outcome was the same in both cases.

Yuill (1984) also demonstrated 3-year-olds' ability to recognize successful outcomes (Perner, this volume). She presented picture stories to children 3 to 7 years of age. In the stories, a child's motive (for example to throw a ball to a particular other child) was depicted in a "think bubble"; actions and outcomes were also illustrated (for example, the child who caught the ball). In different stories, the same outcome picture might represent a successful or an unsuccessful outcome. Yuill showed that even 3-year-olds judged a character who wanted and brought about a certain outcome to be more pleased than one who did not want but nonetheless brought about that same outcome. Similarly, Bruchkowsky (1984, cited in Case, 1985) showed that 3-year-olds could judge which of two puppets might be sad when both wanted a bicycle for a birthday present, and one received a bicycle and the other received a different, but equally desirable, toy. Wellman and Bartsch's (1988) recent studies also show that young children can reliably distinguish between characters who want the same thing but get different things or who get different things but wanted the same thing. That is to say, a number of different studies show that children understand unfulfilled intentions and unsatisfied desires before the age at which they understand false beliefs. Again, these data support Forguson and Gopnik's view that children metarepresent intentions and desires before the age at which they metarepresent beliefs.

CHILDREN'S USE OF A MATCHING STRATEGY

It might be possible to explain the 3-year-olds' success on these tasks without assuming that they have metarepresentational ability. Do these young children conceptualize a person's intention or desire as his or her representation, or do they simply associate the person with the goal situation (Perner, this volume)? If the goal situation and the actually achieved situation match, children say that the action was done on purpose or that the person will be pleased with the outcome, and if they do not match, children say that the action was not done on purpose or that the person will not be pleased with the outcome. It is possible that 2- and 3-year-olds, who are credited with understanding desires and intentions, are simply matching goals and outcomes and then labelling matches as intended or desired, using *meant to, on purpose, pleased, happy*, and so on, and labelling mismatches as not intended or not desired, using *didn't mean to, not on purpose, not pleased, sad*, and so on. Even from 18 months of age, children can match goals and outcomes, at first using, for example, *there* to mark a match and, for example, *uh-oh* to mark a mismatch (Gopnik, 1982). In a similar fashion, Shultz's (1988; this volume) computer model employs matching as the most primitive strategy.

The crucial question is: Does the successful employment of a matching strategy require metarepresentational ability, that is, does it require a concept of representation? Perner has been criticized for denying 3-year-olds a concept of representation (Forguson, 1989) because DeLoache (1987) has shown that children just 3 years of age are able to use a model as a representation. They can use the position of a small toy dog hidden in a model room as an indication of the location of a big toy dog in a real room with furniture and layout similar to that of the model. Perner (1988) has suggested that this achievement marks the beginning of children's conceptualization of representation; at this stage, children understand external representations, but they do not understand internal mental representation, which is required for success on the false belief task. However, Zaitchik (1990) has recently shown that 3-year-olds do not understand the relationship of falsity for external representations either. It might be that 3-year olds have no concept of representation. In the DeLoache task, children might not need to treat the model as a representation at all; they could perform successfully by using a matching strategy. A matching strategy requires them to compare a model and a situation, but it does not require them to conceptualize the model as a representation. This suggestion is supported by the fact that the children found it as easy to use the location of the big toy in the room to find the small toy in the model, as they did to perform the reverse operation of using the model to locate the toy in the room (Campbell & Olson, in press). So what is represented, and what is representation; or is it simply a two-way matching process?

THE CONCEPT OF INTENTION
AFTER FOUR YEARS OF AGE

The 3-year-old's ability to match goals and outcomes may not indicate the possession of a metarepresentational conception of intention. It is still an open question whether, at 4 years of age, there is some change in children's understanding of intention comparable to the change in their understanding of belief. For example, 3-year-olds do not understand the causal links between the world and a person's beliefs about the world (Wimmer, Hogrefe, & Sodian, 1988); similarly, they may not understand that people's intentions cause their actions—what Searle (1983) referred to as the causal self-referentiality of intention. In addition, 3-year-olds do not understand that a person's false belief is his or her representation of the world; similarly, they may not understand that an intention is a person's representation of the intended action. In both of these cases, there is some evidence that 3-year-olds lack understanding that is possessed by 4-year-olds.

Understanding the Causal Nature of Intention

First, it is not clear that 3-year-olds can always distinguish between intentional and unintentional action where the outcome in the world is the same for both the intended and the unintended action. For example, Shultz et al., (1980) reported that 5-year-olds, but not 3-year-olds, could distinguish intentional actions from reflexes and passive movements, for example, intentionally kicking the leg up versus its moving due to the knee-jerk reflex; that is, cases where the actual event in the world is the same for both intended and unintended behavior, but the cause is different. It is perhaps unclear how this case differs from the target-shooting example discussed earlier (Shultz & Wells, 1985), where children could distinguish between intended and unintended action when the outcome in the world was the same. One difference is that in the reflex kick case the child was told to try not to move his or her leg, that is, the goal was to do nothing, whereas in the target shooting case the goal was to shoot another, different color (Perner, this volume). It may, however, be simply that the reflex kick case is less comprehensible to young children than the target shooting is, for reasons other than their understanding of intention. Parenthetically, a small point is that, in the target-shooting experiment, the effect for the 3-year-olds was much less than for 7-year-olds (the next age group tested), and the age of the 3-year-old group ranged up to 4;5, so these results could be due to a change occurring at about 4 years. Of course, the data are also consistent with lower performance generally in the 3-year-old group, still sufficient to yield a significant effect.

Thus, it is possible that 3-year-olds do not understand the causal self-referentiality of intention. The representation of an intention is more than the representation of a goal. It is not *X happens*, nor even *I do X*, but *I do X by way of carrying out this intention*, that is to say, *I do X in order to fulfill this intention* (Searle, 1983). To assess understanding of such a concept would require a case where the goal and the outcome in the world are the same in both cases, but only one is intentional. That is, the end is the same, but the means differ. Such is the contrast between a deviant causal chain and an intentionally caused action that Shultz (this chapter) refers to. Could 3-year-olds distinguish these two cases? A difficult empirical problem is how to describe such cases in a way that 3-year-olds would understand. It may be that 3-year-olds can distinguish intended versus unintended outcomes but do not understand that the intention causes the outcome, and so they may confuse an intended outcome and fortuitous success. On the other hand, 5-year-olds may understand this causal link between intention and outcome. Somewhat similar are scenarios where the same outcome results from the same action, but in one instance it is intended and in the other it is unintended. Cases of this sort usually involve false belief. For example, Lyons-Ruth (1981) told children a story in which a character put a book into a friend's lunch box; in one version he wanted to give it to the friend, and in another version he thought it was his own lunch box. The youngest children tested (mean age 4;4) did not distinguish between the two cases, although one might expect that children of this age would understand false belief. Thus, it is not yet clear whether 3- and 4-year-olds do understand the causal link between intention and action.

Recognizing Prior Intention

Secondly, it is not clear that 3-year-olds recognize intention as a person's representation of the intended subsequent action. The distinction between the intention and the action is most clearly seen in the case of an unfulfilled intention, because then there is only intention and no subsequent action. However, in the case of a prior intention, there is a temporal separation between the two; the intention precedes the action. I have designed a task to assess 3- to 5-year-olds' ability to recognize prior intention. Children were shown a pair of pictures; in one picture, a child was performing some action (e.g., a girl painting, a boy swinging), and, in the other picture, another child was not performing that action but was getting ready to or was in a position where it could be performed (e.g., a girl standing by a table that had painting materials on it, a boy running to an empty swing) (see Fig. 9.2). The pictures were adapted from a children's book (Kent, 1974). The aim of the task was to see if children would make different choices in answer to questions about actions, such as "Which girl's painting?", "Which boy's swinging?", and questions about intentions, such as "Which girl's gonna paint?", "Which boy thinks he'll swing?". Children were shown eight different pairs of pictures, and for each pair they were asked a single question. Four of the questions were about actions, and four of the questions were about intentions. A different intention term was used in each of the four questions about intentions: *gonna, thinks (s)he'll, wants to, and would like to*, which are terms that children of this age use to express their own intentions.

All the children tested were always correct for the questions about actions, pointing appropriately to the picture showing the child performing the action. For the questions about intentions, the preferred reading of these questions is to choose the other picture, that is, the one that showed the child not performing the action but preparing to do so or in a position where it could be performed. Obviously, one cannot actually depict an intention. Taking that picture as the correct choice for intention questions, a majority of 5-year-olds but few 3-year-olds showed recognition of prior intention by pointing to the picture of the child preparing to act: 13% of 3-year-olds, 44% of 4-year-olds, and 61% of 5-year-olds ($X^2 = 8.50$, $p < .01$, $df = 2$) chose four out of four correctly for intention questions.

It must be acknowledged that it is not incorrect to choose the action picture for the intention questions, for example, "Which boy's gonna swing?". It's the boy who is swinging; he's swinging now, and he's gonna carry on swinging. However, usually when we talk about what someone intends to do (or *is going to do, thinks he'll do, would like to*, or *wants to do*), we are referring to his future action. As Bratman (1984) said, "There is a tension in saying that I intend to do what I am now doing: talk of what I intend to do seems normally reserved for my attitude towards my future conduct" (p. 379). It is interesting that in the task described here, 5-year-olds but not 3-year-olds were aware of the

Which girl is painting?

Which girl...   's gonna ...... paint?
                  thinks she'll ..
                  wants to ....
                  would like to ..

Which boy is swinging?

Which boy ...   's gonna ...... swing?
                  thinks he'll ...
                  wants to ....
                  would like to ..

Fig. 9.2. Sample test items for task assessing recognition of prior intention.

future-directness of talk about intention. And this awareness is not an experimental artifact produced by the contrast between questions about intention and questions about action. The order of the eight pairs of pictures and of the eight questions were counterbalanced across subjects. Half of the children were asked an action question first and the other half an intention question first, and there was no difference in the number of children in the two halves who scored four out of four correctly for intention questions.

Why cannot 3-year-olds succeed on this task using the same strategy that they use in tasks that require them to distinguish between intentional and unintentional action? I argued earlier that they were successful on those tasks because they compared a model of the goal situation with the actual situation in the world and differentially labelled matches and mismatches. In the present task, however, the child has to distinguish between intentions and goals, that is, between means and ends. A goal is the desired end state, whereas an intention is a person's representation of the means to that end; that is, the intention is not the goal. In the present task, the correct picture can be chosen only if the intention is understood separately from the goal, as a representation. If you ask children, "Which boy wants to swing?", 3-year-olds will associate person and desired end-state, and so they will choose the picture of the boy on the swing. On the other hand, 5-year-olds will metarepresent the intention and will recognize it as the boy's mental representation of the means to the end, not the end itself and so will choose the other picture—just as they metarepresent beliefs, and thus understand false belief. The children tested here were also given a simple false belief task, and their scores on the two tasks were compared.

The false belief task was similar to that used by Perner et al., (1987). Children were shown a closed crayon box; when asked what they thought was inside it, they all responded with the usual contents. Then, the box was opened, and they saw that it actually contained birthday cake candles. When the candles were put back out of sight, they could all remember the actual contents. Then, they were given a typical false belief question, asking what another child would think was inside the box when he or she first saw it. Three quarters of the children passed both the intention and the false belief task, or failed both, indicating parallel development of understanding prior intention and false belief.

CONCLUSION

It is likely that children's conception of intention does change at about 4 years of age just as their conception of belief does, leading to their understanding of prior intention and false belief. Before this age, the child's use of expressions of intention is tied to actions and outcomes in the world. When children first use *there* and *uh-oh*, then later *meant to*, *didn't mean to*, *on purpose*, *not on purpose*, and so on, as described earlier, they are referring to actions and outcomes in the world, that is, to consequences. In Bratman's terms, they are using the notion of intention to characterize actions, not mental states. Recall the anecdote quoted at the beginning of this chapter, in which a little girl spooned cereal onto her baby brother's head and then said that she didn't do it on purpose. What the little girl meant, perhaps, is that that was an undesirable consequence; it was hardly an unintentional action. It is even possible that the early use of *not on purpose* is a plea to escape punishment. One young child told me that *not on purpose* meant "I'm sorry," which reminds me of Dunn's (this volume) example of the 2-year-old who responded to her mother's protest, "You're hurting me!" with "Sorry. Sorry. I don't mean to."

Thus, the point I make is that this early talk, which seems to be about intentions, may be about unanticipated or unwanted events in the world. It might be that unexpected consequences of children's own intended actions helps lead them to an understanding of intention as *separate* from consequence or, in other words, to distinguish between means and ends. It is then that children will be able to distinguish between intentional and unintentional action, not just wanted and unwanted consequences, and to conceptualize prior intention and understand that intentions cause actions. Children acquire such a concept of intention at about the same time that they acquire a concept of false belief. This supports the argument that there is a general change in children's understanding of mental states at about 4 years of age, indicating the acquisition of metarepresentational ability and the development of a representational theory of mind.

ACKNOWLEDGMENTS

I thank Lynd Forguson, Alison Gopnik, David Olson, Daniela O'Neill, Josef Perner, and the editors for their helpful comments. I also acknowledge the support of the Natural Sciences and Engineering Research Council of Canada and the Social Sciences and Humanities Research Council of Canada.

REFERENCES

Anscombe, G. E. M. (1957). *Intention*. Oxford: Blackwell.

Astington, J. W., Harris, P. L., & Olson, D. R. (Eds.). (1988). *Developing theories of mind.* New York: Cambridge University Press.

Bratman, M. E. (1984). Two faces of intention. *The Philosophical Review, 93,* 375-405.

Bratman, M. E. (1987). *Intentions, plans, and practical reason*. Cambridge, MA: Harvard University Press.

Bretherton, I., & Beeghly, M. (1982). Talking about internal states: The acquisition of an explicit theory of mind. *Developmental Psychology, 6,* 906-921.

Bruchkowsky, M. (1984). *The development of empathic understanding in early childhood.* Unpublished masters thesis, University of Toronto (OISE).

Campbell, R. N., & Olson, D. R. (in press). Children's thinking. In M. Hughes & R. Grieve (Eds.), *Understanding children*. Oxford: Blackwell.

Case, R. (1985). *Intellectual development: Birth to adulthood*. Orlando, FL: Academic Press.

Chandler, M. (1988). Doubt and developing theories of mind. In J. W. Astington, P. L.

Harris, & D.R. Olson (Eds.), *Developing theories of mind* (pp. 387-413). New York: Cambridge University Press.

DeLoache, J. S. (1987). Rapid change in the symbolic functioning of very young children. *Science, 238,* 1556-1557.

Flavell, J. H. (1988). The development of children's knowledge about the mind: From cognitive connections to mental representations. In J. W. Astington, P. L. Harris, & D. R. Olson (Eds.), *Developing theories of mind* (pp. 244-267) New York: Cambridge University Press.

Flavell, J. H., Everett, B. A., Croft, K., & Flavell, E. R. (1981). Young children's knowledge about visual perception: Further evidence for the Level 1 - Level 2 distinction. *Developmental Psychology, 17,* 99-103.

Flavell, J. H., Flavell, E. R., & Green, F. L., (1983). Development of the appearance-reality distinction. *Cognitive Psychology, 15,* 95-120.

Forguson, L. (1989). *The book of common sense.* London: Croom Heim.

Forguson, L., & Gopnik, A. (1988). The ontogeny of common sense. In J.W. Astington, P. L. Harris, & D. R. Olson (Eds.), *Developing theories of mind* (pp. 226-243). New York: Cambridge University Press.

Gopnik, A. (1982). Words and plans: Early language and the development of intelligent action. *Journal of Child Language, 9,* 303-318.

Gopnik, A., & Astington, J. W. (1988). Children's understanding of representational change and its relation to the understanding of false belief and the appearance-reality distinction. *Child Development, 59,* 26-37.

Gopnik, A., & Graf, P. (1988). Knowing how you know: Young children's ability to identify and remember the sources of their beliefs. *Child Development, 59,* 1366-1371.

Hogrefe, G.-J., Wimmer, H., & Perner, J. (1986). Ignorance versus false belief: A developmental lag in attribution of epistemic states. *Child Development, 57,* 567-582.

Kent, J. (1974). *Hop, skip and jump book.* New York: Random House.

Leslie, A. M. (1988). Some implications of pretense for mechanisms underlying the child's theory of mind. In J. W. Astington, P. L. Harris, & D. R. Olson (Eds.), *Developing theories of mind* (pp. 19-46). New York: Cambridge University Press.

Lyons-Ruth, K. (1981). Developing a language of human action: Subjective goal as semantic component of the verb "give." *Child Development, 52,* 866-872.

Perner, J. (1988). Developing semantics for theories of mind: From propositional attitudes to mental representation. In J. W. Astington, P. L. Harris, & D. R. Olson (Eds.), *Developing theories of mind* (pp. 141-172). New York: Cambridge University Press.

Perner, J., Leekam, S. R., & Wimmer, H. (1987). Three-year-olds' difficulty with false belief: The case for a conceptual deficit. *British Journal of Developmental Psychology, 5,* 125-137.

Premack, D., & Woodruff, G. (1978). Does the chimpanzee have a theory of mind? *The Behavioral and Brain Sciences, 4,* 515-526.

Pylyshyn, Z. W. (1978). When is attribution of beliefs justified? *The Behavioral and Brain Sciences, 1,* 592-593.

Searle, J. R. (1983). *Intentionality: An essay in the philosophy of mind.* Cambridge, England: Cambridge University Press.

Shatz, M., Wellman, H. M., & Silber, S. (1983). The acquisition of mental verbs: A systematic investigation of the first reference to mental state. *Cognition, 14,* 301-321.

Shultz, T. R. (1980). The development of the concept of intention. In A. Collins, (Ed.), *Minnesota symposium on child psychology* (Vol. 13, pp. 131-164). Hillsdale, NJ: Lawrence Erlbaum Associates.

Shultz, T. R. (1988). Assessing intention: A computational model. In J. W. Astington, P. L. Harris, & D. R. Olson (Eds.), *Developing theories of mind* (pp. 341-367). New York: Cambridge University Press.

Shultz, T. R. & Wells, D. (1985). Judging the intentionality of action-outcomes. *Developmental Psychology, 21,* 83-89.

Shultz, T. R., Wells, D., & Sarda, M. (1980). The development of the ability to distinguish intended actions from mistakes, reflexes, and passive movements. *British Journal of Social and Clinical Psychology, 19,* 301-310.

Wellman, H. M., & Bartsch, K. (1988). Young children's reasoning about beliefs. *Cognition, 30,* 239-277.

Wellman, H. W., & Estes, D. (1986). Early understanding of mental entities: A reexamination of childhood realism. *Child Development, 57,* 910-923.

Wimmer, H., Hogrefe, G.-J. & Sodian, B. (1988). A second stage in children's conception of mental life: Understanding informational accesses as origins of knowledge and belief. In J. W. Astington, P. L. Harris, & D. R. Olson (Eds.), *Developing theories of mind* (pp. 173-192). New York: Cambridge University Press.

Wimmer, H., & Perner, J. (1983). Beliefs about beliefs: Representation and constraining function of wrong beliefs in young children's understanding of deception. *Cognition, 13,* 103-128.

Yuill, N. (1984). Young children's coordination of motive and outcome in judgements of satisfaction and morality. *British Journal of Developmental Psychology, 2,* 73-81.

Zaitchik, D. (1990). When representations conflict with reality: The preschooler's problem with false beliefs and "false" photographs. *Cognition, 35,* 41-68.

CHAPTER 10

The Development of the Language of Belief: The Expression of Relative Certainty

Chris Moore
Dalhousie University

David Furrow
Mount St. Vincent University

Not very long after children produce recognizable words, they start to employ words that convey mental attitudes: at first desires, later beliefs. Although many linguistic expressions convey mental attitudes (see, e.g., Olson & Astington, 1986), the acquisition of terms such as *know*, *think*, and *guess* is of particular relevance to the child's developing theory of mind, because these terms make direct reference to internal cognitive states. In this chapter, we review what previous studies of the language of mental state have taught us about the child's theory of mind, and we then report our own work investigating children's understanding of the expression of the mental states of certainty and uncertainty. The review is not detailed, because a number of good reviews already exist (e.g., Johnson, 1982; Olson & Astington, 1986); however, we highlight certain issues and findings from this body of work in order to establish a framework for our investigations. We then discuss the pragmatics of mental terms and describe a series of studies that we have recently conducted on this topic. Finally, we consider how the development of aspects of the child's understanding of mental terms may relate to the development of a theory of mind. Whereas previous work has examined children's understanding of the existence of true and false beliefs and of how those beliefs can be acquired, our interest here goes in a somewhat different direction to examine children's understanding of the fact that beliefs can be held with differing degrees of certainty. Certainty and degrees of uncertainty may be considered as weights that are attached to beliefs and, as such, are integral aspects of beliefs.

PREVIOUS EXPERIMENTAL STUDIES

The aspect of mental terms that has been studied most extensively is that of presupposition, which has been understood in two main ways. On the one hand, presupposition has been taken to be a property of the mental verb, whereas on the other hand, it is taken to refer to the beliefs of the speaker of the utterance. With respect to verb presupposition, most authors have followed the analysis provided by Kiparsky and Kiparsky (1970). Those authors argued that certain verbs, including some mental verbs such as *know* and *remember*, presuppose the truth of the complement statement, whereas other verbs, including mental verbs such as *think* and *guess* do not. To illustrate, Sentence 1 (following) presupposes the truth of Sentence 3, whereas sentence 2 does not. Verbs of the former kind are called *factives*, and those of the latter kind are called *nonfactives*.

1. John knows that it is raining.
2. John thinks that it is raining.
3. It is raining.

Kiparsky and Kiparsky (1970) provided a number of tests for factivity; the most commonly used is the negation test (Abbeduto & Rosenberg, 1985; Hopmann & Maratsos, 1978; Macnamara, Baker, & Olson, 1976; Scoville & Gordon, 1980). By this test, a verb may be considered a factive if the truth of the complement remains constant even when the verb is negated. Thus, sentence 4 also implies the truth of Sentence 3.

4. John does not know that it is raining.

A number of studies have examined children's ability to recognize this property of mental verbs. Most of the earlier attempts to assess the understanding of the factive-nonfactive distinction in children presented sets of complex sentences containing a main verb and a complement sentence (Harris, 1975; Hopmann & Maratsos, 1978; Scoville & Gordon, 1980). Both the main verb and the complement verb could be either in the positive or in the negative form. The children were then asked to decide whether the complement sentence was true or not. The most commonly studied mental verb was *know*, and results appeared to show that the factive status of this verb was not understood until 7 to 11 years of age.

It has been argued (e.g., Abbeduto & Rosenberg, 1985) that part of the difficulty for younger children in the studies just mentioned is the unnaturalness of the tasks, whereby test sentences are presented in isolation. Other studies have attempted to provide some sort of meaningful context for the presentation of the stimulus sentences. Using a story context, Macnamara et al., (1976) found that 4-year-old children understood the implications and presuppositions of the verbs *pretend* and *forget* while having much more difficulty with *know*. Most recently, Abbeduto and Rosenberg (1985) presented test sentences with only a minimal context. For example (adapted from Abbeduto & Rosenberg, 1985, p. 626),

context: I have a friend named Mary. Mary has a cat.

test sentence: Mary knows that the cat is slow.

presupposition question: Is the cat slow?

The subjects were required to answer the test question either "yes," "no," or "don't know." The researchers reported that by 4 years of age, children recognize the factive versus nonfactive presuppositions of the terms *know, think, remember*, and *forget*.

Tests for factivity, such as the constancy of the truth value of the complement under negation, are logical tests; however, the definition of presupposition used both by the Kiparskys (see Kempson, 1975, p. 66) and by language acquisition researchers influenced by their account (e.g., Abbeduto & Rosenberg, 1985; Scoville & Gordon, 1980) is not itself strictly logical. Presupposition is also used to refer to the beliefs of the speaker of the sentence containing the mental verb. According to this kind of analysis, use of a factive term such as *know* implies that the speaker believes that the subject of the verb has unambiguous evidence, either perceptual, inferential, or stored in memory as to the truth of the complement. Alternatively, use of a nonfactive such as *think* implies that the speaker believes that the subject of the verb has no such evidence.

Another body of studies has examined this feature of mental terms (Abbeduto & Rosenberg, 1985; Bassano, 1985; Johnson & Maratsos, 1977; Johnson & Wellman, 1980; Miscione, Marvin, O'Brien, & Greenberg, 1978; Wellman & Johnson, 1979). The general strategy has been to request children to select the mental term that best describes a person's mental orientation (either their own or that of some story protagonist) towards a particular statement or event. In fact, this work may be considered to have had two main objectives (see, e.g., Johnson, 1982).

Firstly, it was aimed at examining whether young children recognized the mental nature of the referents of mental terms. On the basis of some of the earliest studies (e.g., Johnson & Wellman, 1980; Miscione et al., 1978), it was claimed that children up to about 5 years old did not recognize that mental terms referred to internal, nonmaterial processes, but were associated only with external observable events. So, for example, in a task in which the child was required to find a hidden object, the success or failure in the search determined the term that the child deemed appropriate to describe the event and was independent of variations in informational and prior knowledge conditions: If the search was successful, then the child "knew," "guessed," or "remembered"; if unsuccessful, then the child "forgot." Other experimental work (e.g., Johnson & Maratsos, 1977), as well as observational work described hereafter (Shatz, Wellman, & Silber, 1983), has shown that it is not the case that children younger than 4 or 5 years do not recognize the existence of mental states; rather they have difficulty in coordinating together prior informational conditions, present informational conditions, and actual outcomes in order to determine the appropriate mental term to select (see review by Johnson, 1982).

The other main focus of this body of research has been to investigate whether the different speaker presuppositions of the various terms are recognized. These studies have varied the informational conditions of an individual by providing either direct perceptual or inferential evidence as to the truth of a statement or no such evidence. The child's task is typically to decide which mental term best describes the individual's mental state. Results over a number of studies are not entirely consistent. Johnson and Maratsos (1977) reported that 4-year-olds, but not younger children differentiate *know* and *think* appropriately on the basis of their informational conditions. On the other hand, Abbeduto and Rosenberg (1985) reported difficulty with the informational conditions of *think* but not *know* at 4 years. Bassano (1985) reported an equivalent pattern of difficulty for the French terms *croire* and *savoir*. Johnson and Wellman (1980) found that 4 and 5-year-olds did not understand the informational conditions of *know* and *guess*. The differences in the age at which mental term understanding has been shown are probably due to task differences. Johnson and Maratsos' (1977) study is really closer to a study of verb presupposition, in that the children were being tested on whether they understood that the complement of a complex sentence with *think* as the main verb can be false, whereas the complement of a complex sentence with *know* as the main verb must be true. As noted previously, the factive-nonfactive distinction for *know* and *think* appears to be understood by the age of four. The other studies examining informational conditions and speaker presuppositions are more complex, in that they present a variety of conditions that have to be differentiated.

In sum, experimental studies of children's understanding of the presuppositions of mental terms have shown that the terms *know, think,* and *guess* do not start to be differentiated until 4 years of age. At this age, children appear to be able to distinguish the terms by allocating different truth values to the complement sentences. From this time on, the various mental terms start to be differentiated on the basis of the informational conditions required for their appropriate use in sentences.

OBSERVATIONAL STUDIES

Although the majority of work on the acquisition of mental terms has been done experimentally, a relatively small number of naturalistic observational studies have examined the spontaneous occurrence of the words of interest. One of the first of these was carried out by Bretherton and her colleagues (Bretherton & Beeghly, 1982; Bretherton, McNew, & Beeghly-Smith, 1981). Bretherton and colleagues were, in fact, interested in a rather broader range of lexical items: those referring to all internal states, including perceptual, physiological, volitional, moral, and affective terms, as well as mental (or, as they labeled them, cognitive) terms. Using maternal report, they found that internal state words start to appear during the second year of life. However, the mental category was not well represented until the middle to end of the third year. The most common mental verbs were *know, think, remember, forget,* and *pretend.* The interpretation given to these findings by the authors is that the appearance of such words in the productive vocabularies of 2-year-old children indicates that, in at least an implicit sense, the children must have a theory of mind (see also Bretherton, this volume).

This view was modified slightly by Shatz et al. (1983), who pointed out that mental terms need not be used functionally to refer to mental state but could play more conversational roles and, therefore, that the mere appearance of mental terms in the productive lexicon of a child need not signify any understanding of mental entities or processes (see also Wellman & Estes, 1987). They conducted a functional analysis of the mental state language of a number of children and, on the basis of a conservative categorization, showed that the earliest uses of mental terms did seem to be conversational. For example, the term *know* would be used in the idiomatic expression "I don't know," or in the expression "You know what?" to introduce information. Nevertheless, by the end of the third year of life, they reported that their subjects were using mental terms for true mental state reference, for example, "Before I thought this was a crocodile; now I know it's an alligator" (Shatz et al., 1983, p. 309). Because the child explicitly contrasts two mental states in this example, it is taken to be a valid index that the child can involve mental states as the topic of conversation. Shatz et al. (1983) concluded that an understanding of some aspects of mental state is present by 3 years of age, although this does not imply that an adult-like understanding has developed by this stage. In any case, Shatz et al.'s (1983) work serves to highlight an overlooked component of mental terms— their pragmatic function. It is the pragmatics of mental terms that we focus on in this chapter.

THE PRAGMATICS OF MENTAL TERMS

Pragmatics is the study of the use of language in context, usually focusing on the intentional communicative purposes that utterances serve in daily use. A common pragmatic function of mental terms is to mark the degree of certainty with which a statement is made (Richards, 1982; Urmson, 1963). For Urmson (1963), these terms can express degrees of certainty and can even be arranged on a scale of reliability ranging from *know* to *believe* (and presumably *think*, although it is not mentioned) to *guess*. For example, the speaker of sentence 5 (following) expresses more certainty that the book is in the garden than does the speaker of sentence 6. This function was recognized by Shatz et al. (1983) in their observational study and was called "modulation of assertion." The role of this function in the overall acquisition of mental terms has been considered in the previous literature. For example, Johnson and Wellman (1980) proposed that children may first recognize mental terms as reliability or certainty indicators and only later recognize them as logically different types. However, to date, this issue has not been studied experimentally.

5. I know the book is in the garden.
6. I think the book is in the garden.

In a series of studies, we have investigated children's understanding of the use of mental terms to express differential degrees of certainty by using a task that requires the child to find a hidden object. What we wanted to achieve in designing this task was to move away from methodologies in which the child has to make a linguistic judgment, either about truth values or about the suitability of different mental terms in different sentences. Instead, the child has to show understanding of the language by interpreting the communicative intent and behaving appropriately. The task requires the child to find a hidden object, which can be in one of two boxes. The only clues the child has are two statements, one referring to each box. The statements, presented by the experimenter using two puppets, contrast only in the mental term used. In this way, the child has to judge the location of the object by the relative certainty expressed by the two statements containing contrasting mental terms.

In the first experiment of the series (Moore, Bryant, & Furrow, 1989), children were presented with the three terms, *know, think,* and *guess.* The terms were presented in all three possible combinations. Sixty-nine children in five age groups participated. There were 14 children at each of 3, 4, 5, and 8 years of age, and 13 at 6 years of age. The mean ages were at about the middle of the year in each age group.

Children were tested individually. Each child was introduced to the task and told that he or she was going to play a hiding game, in which he or she had to find a candy that was hidden in one of two boxes. The child was advised that two monkeys, hand-puppets manipulated by the female experimenter, would help him or her find the candy. At least three practice trials were then conducted to ensure that the child understood the point of the game. In each trial, two small boxes, one red and the other blue, were placed in front of the child. The child was told that there was a candy in one of them and that he or she should listen carefully to the two monkeys who would help him or her find it. The puppets each made a statement in turn indicating one of the boxes. For the practice trials, one puppet would say, "it's really in the red/blue box," and the other would say, "I'm pretending it's in the blue/red box." The child was then told to find the candy, and she would search. The contrast between really and pretend, was used for the practice trials because the distinction between reality and pretense is understood very early (see, e.g., Flavell, 1988; Leslie, 1987). If the child failed any of the practice trials, these trials continued until he or she was correct on three consecutive trials. No child took more than six trials to reach criterion.

Following successful practice, each child received a total of 12 test trials. The child was presented with two statements, each containing one of the mental terms *know, think,* or *guess.* For example, one puppet would say, "I think it's in the red box," and the other would say, "I know it's in the blue box." In these trials, the child was not allowed to search after the statements but was told to point to the box with the candy and then he or she could see how many candies he or she had won at the end. In this way, there was no feedback as to correctness through the session. Trials were presented in four sets of three, such that each set contained one of each of the possible pairwise contrasts between the three mental terms. The order of the contrasts in each set was predetermined randomly, and the four sets were presented in four different orders according to a Latin square design.

For analysis, responses were scored according to the range of certainty first proposed by Urmson (1963). A response was given a score of one if the child went with the statement including *know* in preference to the statements including *think* and *guess*, and if the child went with the statement including *think* in preference to that including *guess*. Each contrast, therefore, yielded a possible score of zero to four. A two-way repeated measure ANOVA was performed on the data, with age as a between-subjects variable and contrast as a within-subjects variable. The results showed a main effect for age ($F(4,64) = 7.55$, p $< .0001$), a main effect for contrast ($F(2,128) = 71.85$, $p < .0001$), and a contrast by age interaction ($F(8,128) = 6.30$, $p < .0001$). Univariate tests of the contrast main effect revealed that the *think-guess* contrast was significantly more difficult than the *know–think* contrast and than the *know–guess* contrast, which did not differ ($F(1,64) = 81.21$, $p < .0001$; $F(1,64) = 85.06$, $p < .0001$, respectively). One-way ANOVAS with age as the independent variable performed for each contrast revealed a main effect for age for the *know–think* ($F(4,68) = 13.55$, $p < .0001$) and for the *know–guess* ($F(4,68) = 11.66$, $p < .0001$) contrasts, but not for the *think–guess* contrast. The means are shown in Fig. 10.1. The 3-year-olds performed

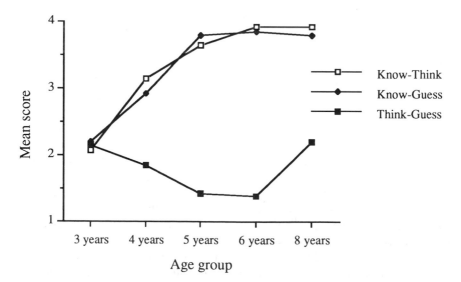

FIG. 10.1.   Mean score (out of 4) for each contrast at each age in ther first experiment.

at chance level for all three contrasts. For the *know–think* contrast, the 3-year-olds performed significantly worse than all the other age groups (all *ps* < .001), and the 4-year-olds performed significantly worse than the 6- and 8-year-olds (*ps* < .05). For the *know–guess* contrast, the 3-year-olds performed significantly worse than all the other groups (*ps* < .05), and the 4-year-olds performed significantly worse than all older age groups (*ps* < .001). No other differences were significant.

The results from the first experiment provide evidence that the understanding of the use of mental terms to express differential degrees of certainty develops over the preschool years. By 4 years of age, these children have some understanding that *know* expresses more certainty than *think* and *guess*. This understanding appears complete by 5 years of age. The distinction between *think* and *guess* was not well understood at any age studied in this experiment.

From this experiment, we have data on children's understanding of three of the mental verbs that have been studied most often in earlier experimental studies. How do these findings compare with those from previous semantic studies? We find that at 4 years of age, children are beginning to differentiate *know* from *think* and *guess*. By 5 years, these two contrasts appear to be at ceiling. These results fall at the low end of the range of previous estimates (cf Abbeduto & Rosenberg, 1985; Johnson & Maratsos, 1977). As stated earlier, Abbeduto and Rosenberg (1985) have shown an understanding of the factive-nonfactive distinction for the verbs *know, think, remember* and *forget* at 4 years, but no clear evidence of the understanding of the different informational conditions of *know* and *think* until 7 years. Johnson and Maratsos (1977) demonstrated an understanding of the *know–think* difference at 4 years, the earliest previously shown. To our knowledge, the distinction between *think* and *guess* has not been previously studied. We find no clear differentiation between these terms at any of the ages studied.

The point of these studies, of course, is not to try to find evidence of an understanding of mental terms at ever earlier ages but to understand something about how these terms are understood by the child and what they tell us about the child's developing theory of mind. A number of issues present themselves in this context, and in the rest of this chapter we discuss and attempt to resolve three of these issues. Firstly, it appears that the development of semantic and pragmatic competence occurs at around the same time in development. This result immediately raises a few questions: What is the relation between these two types of understanding? Secondly, what does the understanding of the expression of certainty through the use of mental terms tell us about children's understanding of mental state? Thirdly, spontaneous production of utterances containing mental terms used for marking certainty has been noted at significantly younger ages than those reported for success in experimental comprehension tasks; is there an explanation for this discrepancy?

FACTIVITY OR CERTAINTY?

Results from the most recent experimental studies on the comprehension of mental terms, including the one reported here, point to the years from 3 to 5 as being the important ones in the acquisition of competence. At 3 years, there is essentially random performance on all tasks; beginning understanding is seen at 4 years, and by 5 years children are performing adequately on a number of tasks. From these tasks, as well as from earlier studies (cf Johnson, 1982), there is no evidence that children first acquire pragmatic competence and only later logical or semantic competence as some have suggested (e.g., Johnson & Wellman, 1980; Limber, 1973). What, then, is the relation between performance on the pragmatic task described here and the previous tasks? One possibility is that the children are making their choice in the hidden object task on the basis of the words' semantic properties. Specifically, *know* is a factive, whereas *think* and *guess* are nonfactives. This possibility is implied by the analysis of Shatz et al. (1983), who pointed out that expressing degrees of certainty or modulation of assertion using mental terms is based on the factive/nonfactive properties of these terms. Conceivably, the children make their judgment on the basis of whether or not the truth of the complement ("It's in the red/blue box") is presupposed by the main verb. Such a strategy would lead them to be correct for the contrasts involving one factive and one nonfactive (*know–think, know–guess*) but to have difficulty for the case involving two nonfactives (*think–guess*). As we have seen, this pattern is exactly the one that has been obtained with 5-year-olds.

In order to examine this issue, we conducted an experiment along the same lines as before, using a case of a mental term that is nonfactive but conveys a high degree of certainty, *sure* (Moore & Davidge, 1989). *To be sure* is generally considered to be a nonfactive construction—it does not presuppose the truth of a complement sentence (e.g., Scoville & Gordon, 1980); however, it clearly does convey a high degree of certainty. We were, therefore, able to compare a nonfactive of high certainty with a factive of high certainty (*know*) and a nonfactive of lower certainty (*think*).

Sixty children participated in the experiment. There were 15 at each of four age groups, 3, 4, 5, and 6 years, with mean ages at around the middle of each year. The experiment was designed and carried out exactly as before, with 12 test trials, four of each pair of the three mental terms. There were also the same practice trials, and all children reached criterion within six practice trials. Responses were scored as correct if the child chose the box indicated by *know* over that indicated by *sure* and *think*, and if the child chose the box indicated by *sure* over that indicated by *think*.

A two-way ANOVA with age as between-subjects variable and contrast as within-subjects variable revealed a significant main effect for age ($F(3,56) = 4.97$, $p < .005$), a significant main effect for contrast ($F(2,112) = 7.83$, $p < .001$), and a significant age by contrast interaction ($F(6,112) = 4.05$, $p < .005$). One-way ANOVAS conducted on each contrast showed main effects for age for the *know–think* and *sure–think* contrasts only ($F(3,56) = 7.53$, $p < .001$; $F(3,56) = 5.02$, $p < .005$, respectively). The results are shown in Fig. 10.2. Comparisons of least square means revealed that for the *know–think* contrast, the 3-year olds performed significantly worse than all other age groups ($ps < .01$). For the *sure–think* contrast, the 3-year-olds performed significantly worse than the 5- and 6- year-olds ($ps < .01$). No other differences were significant.

The developmental finding with respect to the *know–think* contrast was again replicated in this experiment. By 4 years of age, children recognize the greater reliability of *know* over *think*. In addition, this experiment has provided evidence on the development of the understanding of the *be sure* construction. Previous work on *be sure* had been limited to an examination of factivity and nonfactivity in the grade

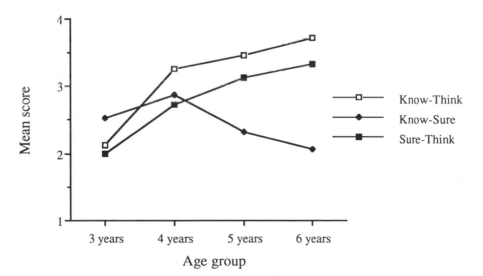

FIG. 10.2.   Mean score (out of 4) for each contrast at each age in the second experiment (from Moore & Davidge, 1989).

school years (e.g., Scoville & Gordon, 1980). This study shows that an understanding of *be sure* as an expression of certainty starts to be acquired in the preschool years, along with *know* and *think*.

The more important finding from this experiment, however, is that the results using this hidden-object search task cannot be explained in terms of an understanding of the factive-nonfactive distinction. Here, the children differentiate the two nonfactives, *sure* and *think*, but make no differentiation between the factive *know* and the nonfactive *sure*. It seems, then, that an explanation in terms of the understanding of relative certainty is more appropriate. The two terms expressing high certainty were confused, but both were differentiated from the term expressing less certainty.[1]

Can this approach help us any further? We believe that it can. It may be argued that the apparent semantic properties of mental terms are, in fact, better understood in terms of the pragmatics of their use. Kempson (1975) has argued that the presupposition account of factive verbs does not work in general, and she has provided a Gricean analysis of the factive-nonfactive distinction in terms of whether or not the proposition expressed by the complement sentence is part of the shared background knowledge between speaker and hearer. According to this analysis, verbs that are termed *factives* imply that the complement is part of the shared background and thus is *assumed* to be true by speaker and hearer. This analysis appears to work well for simple utterances involving a mental verb with third-person subject; for example, if the speaker believes that "Casablanca" is playing at the Paramount theater and believes that the listener also knows this, then either Sentence 7 or Sentence 8 (following) would be an appropriate utterance, depending

---

[1]The finding that, even at 8 years of age, some of the pairs of mental terms studied in these experiments are not clearly differentiated raises the question of what should be taken as "correct" performance. As noted, this issue has been considered by some authors (e.g., Johnson & Wellman, 1980; Urmson, 1963), however their views appear to be based entirely on intuition or informal observation. As far as we know, there have been no direct empirical studies of adult use or comprehension of mental terms to express degrees of certainty. We have examined this issue by testing 80 adults on the same mental term contrasts as we used with children. The contrasts were presented in much the same way as for the children except that two adults replaced the puppets as speakers. For the adult subjects, the *know–sure* and *think–guess* contrasts were the most difficult. The results revealed that the only contrast for which there was any difference between the adults and the 8-year-olds in the first two experiments was the *think–guess* contrast. The mean for the adults for the *think–guess* contrast was significantly different from chance, with *think* chosen as more reliable. However, questioning of the adults as to their views on the *think–guess* distinction revealed two opinions. A majority replied that *think* was more certain than *guess*, but some claimed that there was no difference. Therefore, at present, it is unclear whether the difference between 8-year-olds and adults on the *think–guess* contrast is a developmental one or the result of sample differences.

on John's belief. This analysis also explains why background knowledge or familiarity with the propositional content of the task can influence children's (and adults') processing of the complement in verb presupposition tasks (e.g., Harris, 1975; Hopmann & Maratsos, 1978; Olson & Torrance, 1986). The important point, as Kempson (1975) indicated, is that this implication that the complement is shared knowledge "is context-dependent and as such is not a semantic property [of the verbs]" (p. 191).

1. John knows that "Casablanca" is playing at the Paramount theater.
2. John does not know that "Casablanca" is playing at the Paramount theater.

Utterances with first-person subjects, as is the case with the studies reported here, present a somewhat different situation. Here, the complement is not shared; rather, the speaker is using the mental term to assert something about his or her subjective certainty about the complement and is thereby attempting to influence the hearer's own subjective certainty about the complement (c.f. Richards, 1982). Nevertheless, we claim that in both first- and third-person cases, the distinctions between the various mental terms are best analyzed in terms of communication.

CERTAINTY AS A MENTAL STATE

As the reader may have noticed, so far in this chapter we have studiously avoided the question of the extent to which appropriate responses to the utterances used in these studies implies an understanding of mental state. We can do so no longer. Does the child represent the speaker as being in a state of more or less certainty when interpreting these statements? Even if we assume that the child is willing to enter fully into the role-playing context of the task, it is clear that some would answer no. Urmson (1963), for example, claimed that mental verbs used in this "parenthetical" way are "not psychologically descriptive" (p. 233), and so presumably do not require any understanding of the speaker's mental state for interpretation. Shatz et al. (1983) appear to have followed Urmson on this point, describing modulation of assertion as a conversational function distinct from true mental state reference.

On the other hand, it seems to us that certainty and degrees of uncertainty are validly designated as intentional states, or mental orientations towards some object or event in reality, and that the expressions examined in these experiments are (some of) the verbal expressions of those states. An utterance such as, "I think John went to the store," is conveying (at least) two things. It conveys an explanation of John's movements or absence, and it conveys that the speaker is not convinced of the truth of that explanation. From this perspective, correct interpretation of the use of mental verbs to modulate an assertion clearly indicates an understanding of relative certainty.

There is a way to investigate this issue empirically, however. Modulation of assertion is also achieved in natural language through the use of "modal" terms, such as *must, might, could,* and so on. If children start to understand the expression of degrees of certainty using modal terms at about the same time as they understand the same function expressed through the use of mental terms, then one might be more confident that it is a general understanding of relative certainty that is developing. The final experiment to be described here included a comparison between modal terms that differ in expressed certainty.

In addition, it is noteworthy that the point at which children seem to start showing an understanding of the expression of certainty corresponds closely with the age that has been shown to be important for the development of an understanding of other aspects of mental state. Evidence from a number of areas isolates the 4-year mark as the important point in the establishment of a theory of mind. Studies on children's understanding of false belief (see Perner, Leekham, & Wimmer, 1987), representational change (see Gopnik & Astington, 1988), and the appearance-reality distinction (see Flavell, Flavell, & Green, 1983) have all found a marked shift in understanding at about 4 years of age. What the studies that we have reported so far in this chapter show is that the understanding that beliefs can be held with greater or lesser degrees of certainty also appears to develop at about the same age.

This similarity, between these different tasks, in the age at which children perform successfully may not be coincidental. Perner (1988a) has proposed that the 3-year-old's problem in false-belief tasks is that she does not treat mental states as attitudes towards representations of reality but merely as attitudes towards reality itself. Thus, the 3-year-old is not able to perform well in situations where there are conflicting *representations* of the same aspect of reality. By 4 years, the child can typically treat mental states as representational and thereby perform correctly. Astington and Gopnik (1988) have argued that such an account can explain children's performance on false-belief, representational change, and appearance-reality tasks. In their study (see also Gopnik & Astington, 1988), they showed that performance on all of these tasks is intercorrelated, implying that the same underlying development is accounting for changes in performance. Our task also requires the child to be able to entertain two conflicting representations of the same reality, and thus would appear to require a representational theory of mind. Following the logic of the previous studies, then, we would predict that performance on our hidden-object task would be correlated with performance on other tasks requiring a representational theory of mind, namely the various belief tasks of Perner et al. (1987), Gopnik and Astington (1988), and Flavell et al. (1983). In this study, therefore, we presented children with false-belief, representational change, and appearance-reality tasks, as well as with mental term and modal term contrasts in our hidden-object task (Moore, Pure, & Furrow, 1990, Exp. 2).

Twenty-six 4-year-olds recruited from Halifax preschools participated. The average age was 4;2, with a range from 4;0 to 4;7. Each subject was presented with 12 trials of the hidden-object task and three trials for each of the tasks assessing the understanding of representational change, false belief, and appearance-reality. The hidden-object trials were presented together, as were the belief tasks, with order of type of task (hidden-object vs. belief) counterbalanced across subjects. In the hidden-object trials, there were six trials involving the terms *must* and *might*, and six involving the contrast between *know* and *think*. These trials were presented in random order, with all other aspects of the task counterbalanced (e.g., order of statements, the puppet that made each statement, and the box to which each statement referred). In the belief tasks, the order of the three types of tasks (false-belief, representational change, appearance reality) in each trial was determined according to a Latin square.

The hidden-object task was presented in the same way as in Experiment 1, including the use of the same practice trials and criterion for inclusion as a subject. No subjects were excluded for failing the practice trials. Subjects received six trials using the *must–might* contrast and six using the *know–think* contrast. The wording for the mental term trials was the same as in the first two experiments, and for the modal term trials it was, "It must be in the red/blue box," and, "It might be in the blue/red box."

The belief tasks involved three trials, each one using a misleading object. There was a Smartie (candy) box that actually contained crayons (after Perner et al., 1987), an eraser that resembled a small book, and a candle that resembled an apple. The two latter objects were extremely realistic and fooled a number of adults to whom they were shown prior to their use in the experiment. In addition, there was a practice trial, presented before any of the belief tasks, also modelled after one used by

Gopnik and Astington (1988). A closed box was shown to the child and then opened, revealing a toy. The toy was then replaced by a different toy, and the box was closed again. The child was asked, "When you first saw the box, before we opened it, what was inside it?". This task was originally used by Gopnik and Astington (1988) as a control task to assess the children's ability to answer questions about changes in reality rather than changes in representations of reality. We included it as an introduction to the kind of task the children would be receiving. All children were successful on this task.

The three kinds of test objects were presented to the children in the same way. Initially, the object was placed on the table in full view of the child but just out of reach, and the child was told to "look at what I've brought." They were then given the object and allowed to examine it and/or open it and were asked "What is (in) it?". The few errors were corrected by the experimenter. The child was then asked three kinds of questions following the wording used by Gopnik and Astington (1988, Exp. 2, Form B) and presented in detail in the appendix to their paper. The wording for the eraser/book trial is presented here as an example. In the false belief question, the child was asked what he or she thought another child, on seeing the object in its original state, would think it was (or, in the case of the Smartie box, was in it): "X hasn't touched this. What will (s)he think it is before (s)he touches it?". In the representational change question, the child was asked what he or she thought the object was (or what was in the box) when he or she had first seen it: "What did you think this was before you touched it?". The appearance-reality question had two parts: *appearance*—"What does this look like? Does it look like an eraser, or does it look like a book?"; and *reality*—"What is this, really? Is it really an eraser, or is it really a book?". The order of all questions and parts of questions was randomized within subjects.

Responses were given a score of one for each correct answer. For the hidden-object task, correct answers were choosing *must* over *might* and *know* over *think*. For the false-belief and representational change tasks, a correct answer was responding on the basis of their own or the other's false belief: for example, for the eraser/book trial, saying that they thought it was a book and that the other person would think it was a book. A correct response in the appearance-reality task entailed answering the appearance question according to what the object looked like (e.g., a book) and answering the reality question according to what the object actually was (e.g., an eraser). Thus, subjects could score from zero to six in the modal term and in the mental term trials, and from zero to three in the other three types of questions. Partial correlations of scores among the five tasks (modals, mental terms, false belief, representational change, and appearance-reality) were calculated, controlling for age. The results are shown in Table 10.1, where it can be seen that significant positive correlations for all task combinations except modals and representational change were found. A number of results should be noted. Firstly, performance with the modal terms was highly correlated with performance with the mental terms. This result confirms the view that 4-year-olds are indeed developing an underlying understanding of the mental states of relative certainty, rather than specific lexical distinctions. Secondly, performances on all of the belief tasks were intercorrelated. This replicates the effect found first by Gopnik and Astington (1988), who showed the close resemblance between these different kinds of belief tasks. Thirdly, for the most part, performance on the hidden-object tasks was correlated with performance on the belief tasks. The subjects who could use mental and modal term distinctions to find the hidden object also tended to be able to distinguish appearance from reality and to answer questions on the basis of beliefs rather than reality. Furthermore, the correlations were not due to a nonspecific effect of age. This result implies that these effects are all manifestations of the development of some underlying understanding of the nature of beliefs.

PRODUCTION AND COMPREHENSION OF THE EXPRESSION OF CERTAINTY

One final issue remains to be considered. Although we have pointed to the 4-year mark as the important one in children's understanding of

TABLE 10.1

Partial correlations, controlling for age, among five types of
task in Experiment 3 (from Moore, Pure, & Furrow, 1990)

	Mean Scores (and Standard Deviation)	Modal Terms	False Belief	Representational Change	Appearance-Reality
Mental terms	4.58 (1.27)	.78***	.67***	.52**	.53**
Modal terms	4.77 (.99)		.55**	.23	.41*
False belief	2.15 (1.15)			.82***	.74***
Representational change	2.50 (.86)				.75***
Appearance-reality	2.42 (.90)				

Note. Scores for mental and modal terms out of 6; scores for belief tasks out of 3.
***$p < .001$ (1-tailed); **$p < .005$ (1-tailed); *$p < .05$ (1-tailed).

mental state, there is evidence from a variety of observational studies that, in more natural, familiar, and perhaps emotionally charged contexts (see Bloom, Rispoli, Gartner, & Hafitz, 1989; Bretherton & Beeghly, 1982; Dunn, this volume; Shatz et al., 1983), somewhat younger children appear to show in their use of language an understanding of a variety of mental states. Most significantly in the present context, Bloom et al. (1989) and Shatz et al. (1983) have reported that their subjects towards the end of the third year of life were using mental terms such as *think* and *know* productively to modulate assertions, that is, to express differential degrees of certainty. There are a number of differences between these studies and our experiments. Firstly, there are the obvious methodological differences. Their studies are observations made in naturalistic contexts; ours are experiments. Both kinds of methodologies tend to attract criticism. On the one hand, observational evidence is often ambiguous and more open to reductive explanations (Perner, 1988b). On the other hand, experiments tend to be artificial and may, therefore, be more likely to underestimate competence. These issues, of course, are ever present in developmental research and cannot easily be resolved.

Although the possibility of interpretive problems in either or both approaches is real, it seems to us more likely that both effects are genuine. Probably a more significant difference between our studies and previous observational ones is that, whereas Bloom et al. (1989) and Shatz et al. (1983) reported the productive use of mental terms to express certainty, we are examining comprehension of this same function. The difference between comprehension and production is likely to be of importance here. It is possible that productive and comprehensive performance may require different levels of understanding. The crucial question is whether the subjects in the Bloom and Shatz studies, when using the expressions of certainty or uncertainty, *intend* that the hearer will *recognize* that they are expressing those mental states. It is possible that the child may hold a belief with certainty or uncertainty and express it, without intending at all to express the relative certainty to the hearer. It could, therefore, be argued that the mere linguistic expression of degrees of certainty, as noted by Bloom et al. (1989) and by Shatz et al. (1983), shows no reflective understanding of the mental states of certainty or uncertainty. Indeed, Shatz et al. (1983) admitted to as much by characterizing modulation of assertion as a conversational function and not as true mental state reference. On the other hand, the systematic comprehension of modulation of assertion in our task would require the ability to reflect on the different degrees of certainty of the mental attitudes expressed—something that may well be beyond the capabilities of the 3-year old. As Feldman (1988) has pointed out in an analysis of the linguistic expressions of mental states, although part of having a theory of mind is having the appropriate linguistic devices available, there is more to it. The child must not only be able to express mental attitudes but must also be able to achieve recursion, or treat mental attitudes as a topic. Recursion or embedding is also considered by Shultz (this volume) to be important in his production system modelling of older children's understanding of intentional states. We are not in a position to decide this issue now; however, the study of the use of mental terms in the 3-year-old's linguistic environment and the child's response to those utterances may be the route to the resolution of this question.

CONCLUSION

Children start to appreciate the use of mental state language to express differing degrees of certainty at about 4 years of age. In this chapter, we have argued that this development is tied to the child's growing theory of mind and supports the view that what develops at this time is the recognition that mental states are representational. Because the child can now appreciate mental states as representations of reality, he or she can also recognize not only that beliefs can be true or false but that one expressed belief may more accurately reflect reality than another.

ACKNOWLEDGMENTS

Preparation of this chapter was supported by grant # 410-87-1315 from the Social Sciences and Humanities Research Council of Canada. We are grateful to Dana Bryant, Jane Davidge, and Kiran Pure for their work on the project and to the staff and children of the preschools and elementary schools that participated in the research.

REFERENCES

Abbeduto, L., & Rosenberg, S. (1985). Children's knowledge of the presuppositions of know and other cognitive verbs. *Journal of Child Language, 12,* 621–641.
Astington, J. W., & Gopnik, A. (1988). Knowing you've changed your mind: Children's understanding of representational change. In J. W. Astington, P. L. Harris, & D. R.

Olson (Eds.), *Developing theories of mind* (pp. 193–206). New York: Cambridge University Press.

Bassano, D. (1985). Five-year olds' understanding of "savoir" and "croire." *Journal of Child Language, 12,* 417–432.

Bloom, L., Rispoli, M., Gartner, B., & Hafitz, J. (1989). Acquisition of complementation. *Journal of Child Language, 16,* 101–120.

Bretherton, I., & Beeghly, M. (1982). Talking about internal states: The acquisition of an explicit theory of mind. *Developmental Psychology, 18,* 906–921.

Bretherton, I., McNew, S., & Beeghly-Smith, M. (1981). Early person knowledge expressed in gestural and verbal communication: When do infants acquire a "theory of mind"? In M. Lamb & L. Sherrod (Eds.), *Infant social cognition* (pp. 333–373). Hillsdale, NJ: Lawrence Erlbaum Associates.

Feldman, C. F. (1988). Early forms of thought about thoughts: Some simple linguistic expressions of mental state. In J. W. Astington, P. L. Harris, & D. R. Olson (Eds.), *Developing theories of mind* (pp. 126–137). New York: Cambridge University Press.

Flavell, J. H. (1988). The development of children's knowledge about the mind: From cognitive connections to mental representations. In J. W. Astington, P. L. Harris, & D. R. Olson (Eds.), *Developing theories of mind* (pp. 244–267). New York: Cambridge University Press.

Flavell, J. H., Flavell, E. R., & Green, F. L. (1983). Development of the appearance-reality distinction. *Cognitive Psychology, 15,* 197–207.

Gopnik, A., & Astington, J. W. (1988). Children's understanding of representational change and its relation to the understanding of false belief and the appearance-reality distinction. *Child Development, 59,* 26–37.

Harris, R. (1975). Children's comprehension of complex sentences. *Journal of Experimental Child Psychology, 19,* 420–433.

Hopmann, M. R., & Maratsos, M. P. (1978). A developmental study of factivity and negation in complex syntax. *Journal of Child Language, 5,* 295–309.

Johnson, C. N. (1982). Acquisition of mental verbs and the concept of mind. In S. Kuczaj (Ed.), *Language development. Vol.1. Syntax and semantics* (pp. 445–478). Hillsdale, NJ: Lawrence Erlbaum Associates.

Johnson, C. N., & Maratsos, M. P. (1977). Early comprehension of mental verbs: Think and know. *Child Development, 48,* 1743–1747.

Johnson, C. N., & Wellman, H. M. (1980). Children's developing understanding of mental verbs: Remember, know, and guess. *Child Development, 51,* 1095–1102.

Kempson, R. M. (1975). *Presupposition and the delimitation of semantics.* Cambridge: Cambridge University Press.

Kiparsky, P., & Kiparsky, C. (1970). Fact. In M. Bierwisch & K. Heidolph (Eds.), *Progress in linguistics* (pp. 143–173). The Hague: Mouton.

Leslie, A. M. (1987). Pretense and representation: The origins of "theory of mind." *Psychological Review, 94,* 412–426.

Limber, J. (1973). The genesis of complex sentences. In T.E. Moore (Ed.), *Cognitive development and the acquisition of language* (pp. 169–185). New York: Academic Press.

Macnamara, J., Baker, E., & Olson, C. L. (1976). Four-year-olds' understanding of pretend, forget, and know: Evidence for propositional operations. *Child Development, 47,* 62–70.

Miscione, J. L., Marvin, R. S., O'Brien, R. G., & Greenberg, M. T. (1978). A developmental study of preschool children's understanding of the words "know" and "guess." *Child Development, 49,* 1107–1113.

Moore, C., Bryant, D., & Furrow, D. (1989). Mental terms and the development of certainty. *Child Development, 60,* 167–171.

Moore, C., & Davidge, J. (1989). The development of mental terms: Pragmatics or semantics? *Journal of Child Language, 16,* 433–441.

Moore, C., Pure, K., & Furrow, D. (1990). Children's understanding of the modal expression of certainty and uncertainty and its relation to the development of a representational theory of mind. *Child Development, 61,* 722–730.

Olson, D. R., & Astington, J. W. (1986). Children's acquisition of metalinguistic and metacognitive verbs. In W. Demopoulos & A. Marras (Eds.), *Language learnability and concept acquisition* (pp. 184–199). Norwood, NJ: Ablex.

Olson, D. R., & Torrance, N. G. (1986). Some relations between children's knowledge of metalinguistic and metacognitive verbs and their linguistic competencies. In I. Gopnik & M. Gopnik (Eds.), *From models to modules: Studies in cognitive science from the McGill workshops* (pp. 66–81). Norwood, NJ: Ablex.

Perner, J. (1988a). Developing semantics for theories of mind: From propositional attitudes to mental representation. In J. W. Astington, P. L. Harris, & D. R. Olson (Eds.), *Developing theories of mind* (pp. 141–172). New York: Cambridge University Press.

Perner, J. (1988b). Higher order beliefs and intentions in children's understanding of social interaction. In J.W. Astington, P.L. Harris, & D.R. Olson (Eds.) *Developing theories of mind* (pp. 271–294). New York: Cambridge University Press.

Perner, J., Leekam, S. R., & Wimmer, H. (1987). Three-year-olds' difficulty with false belief: The case for a conceptual deficit. *British Journal of Developmental Psychology, 5,* 125–137.

Richards, M. M. (1982). Empiricism and learning to mean. In S. Kuczaj (Ed.), *Language development. Vol.1. Syntax and semantics* (pp. 365–396). Hillsdale, NJ: Lawrence Erlbaum Associates.

Scoville, R. P., & Gordon, A. M. (1980). Children's understanding of factive presuppositions: An experiment and a review. *Journal of Child Language, 7,* 381–399.

Shatz, M., Wellman, H. M., & Silber, S. (1983). The acquisition of mental verbs: A systematic investigation of the first reference to mental state. *Cognition, 14,* 301–321.

Urmson, J. O. (1963). Parenthetical verbs. In C. E. Caton (Ed.), *Philosophy and ordinary language* (pp. 220–246). Urbana: University of Illinois Press.

Wellman, H. M., & Estes, D. (1987). Children's understanding of mental verbs and what they mean. *Discourse Processes, 10,* 141–156.

Wellman, H. M., & Johnson, C. N. (1979). Understanding of mental processes. A developmental study of "remember" and "forget." *Child Development, 50,* 79–88.

CHAPTER 11
Modelling Embedded Intention

Thomas R. Shultz
McGill University

This chapter focuses on my recent and current work on the computational modelling of selected aspects of children's theories of mind. The choice of a computational approach to these problems was made for fairly standard reasons. I wanted to achieve precise and computationally sufficient models and to be able to forge theoretical connections to general reasoning processes. Most of the research on early theory of mind phenomena has been based on verbal theorizing and diagnostic empirical studies. At this point, a fair amount is known about what concepts precede what other concepts, but very little is known about how children actually reason with these concepts and how they progress to more advanced levels. Understanding the mechanisms of reasoning and transition is what is needed, and computational approaches are likely to provide some insight into the nature of such mechanisms.

The chapter begins with a brief review of my recent work on first-level awareness of intentionality and then focuses somewhat more speculatively on the modelling of embedded intentional phenomena. Three examples of embedded phenomena are considered in some detail: false belief in children, deception in vervet monkeys, and strategic game playing in children.

FIRST LEVEL AWARENESS OF INTENTIONALITY

My computational work on children's theories of mind began with an attempt to model first-level awareness of intention in the narrow sense.

The essential issue is how the child or system decides whether an action or outcome of an action is intended. The result was a computer program called JIA, for Judging the Intentionality of Action (Shultz, 1988). JIA was originally designed to model the performance of young children in psychological experiments in which they were asked to decide whether a piece of behavior emitted by themselves or by someone else or an outcome of the behavior was intended or not intended (Shultz, 1980). In doing so, the JIA program used the same heuristics that children are known to use, including matching, valence, monitoring, and discounting.

The initial matching algorithm was quite simple: The content of what was intended was matched against the observed outcome. It soon became obvious, however, that this was far too simple an approach to deal with the wide variety of classic philosophical puzzles about judging intention. Many of these puzzles were, in fact, designed to confound overly simple theories of intention. Such puzzles were of two main types: multiple descriptions of actions and outcomes (the so-called *accordion* effect) and *deviant causal chains*.

An example of the accordion effect is provided by the case of the assassination of the Archduke Ferdinand of Austria by Gavrilo Princip (Searle, 1983). This event was widely considered to have triggered the First World War. Princip enacted a plan to shoot and kill the Archduke, the presumptive heir to the Austrian empire, in order to hurt Austria and thus avenge his own country, Serbia, for Austrian oppression and interference. In cases such as this, multiple true descriptions can be made concerning the many actions in a complex plan. Like the folds of an accordion, alternative true descriptions of an action can easily be expanded or contracted. Correct answers to the question, *"What did Princip do?"*, include *"He pulled his finger," "He fired a gun," "He shot the Archduke," "He killed the Archduke," "He hurt Austria," "He started WW1,"* and so on. Only some of these multiple action descriptions may have been intended. Such cases are considered puzzling, because it is unclear how many actions had actually been performed and how the intentionality of each should be assessed.

Deviant causal chains create even more complex puzzles for theories of intention. In these cases, an intended event is produced but not in the manner planned. In one such classic case, an individual tries to kill someone by shooting him. The shot misses, but it alarms a herd of wild pigs, which trample the victim to death (Davidson, 1973; Searle, 1983). Such cases are difficult, because the plan can become very detailed and can be enacted much as intended. Even so, the causal chain is probably deviant enough to make observers question the intentionality of the killing.

What sort of reasoning algorithm could deal with these puzzling cases and with the more pedestrian cases from child development literature (Shultz, 1980)? The basic architecture of the JIA system is illustrated in Fig. 11.1. The case or problem to be analyzed is presented in the form of two input networks, one representing the actor's plan and another representing the actual sequence of events. A particular event is singled out for analysis to determine whether or not it was intended. JIA can approach such a problem in either of two ways, by retrieving a previously computed answer from its knowledge frames or by constructing a new answer based on application of its reasoning heuristics. JIA tries the retrieval strategy first. If retrieval yields an ambiguous answer or an unambiguous answer that is corrected by feedback from the program's user, then control is directed to the constructive strategy. Here, the various reasoning heuristics are applied. Matching the event (and the causal sequence by which it was produced) against the actor's plans will be attempted if any elements of the plan are known. If the actor's plan is completely unknown, then the more objective heuristics are applied: discounting, monitoring, and valence. Sufficiently strong

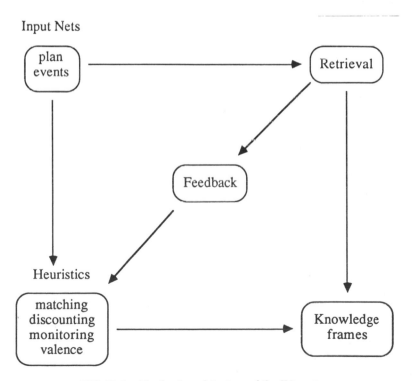

FIG. 11.1. The basic architecture of the JIA system.

conclusions drawn from application of the heuristics are stored in JIA's knowledge frames for later possible use by the retrieval strategies.

Most of the reasoning done by JIA is implemented in the form of a production system operating on the plan and event networks. Once it has been decided to use constructive heuristics, JIA undertakes a decision about which ones to use. In conformity with the bias shown by human subjects (Shultz & Wells, 1985), JIA selects the matching heuristic whenever possible, that is, whenever at least some aspect of the actor's plan is known. Such is likely to be the case in judging one's own action-outcomes and when another's plan is either stated publicly or constrained by context. If none of the actor's plan of action is known, JIA resorts to the objective heuristics.

The matching heuristic is, perhaps, the most interesting part of the program. An event is intended only if it is part of the actor's plan and is caused as planned (Davidson, 1973; Goldman, 1970; Woodfield, 1976). To determine whether an event is part of actor's plan, JIA undertakes a breadth-first search, within the plan net, from the root or highest level plan to the event in question. If that search can be successfully completed, then the event is indeed part of the plan; otherwise, it is not a part of the plan. If the event is judged to be part of the plan, then JIA attempts to determine whether it was caused as planned. To do this, it compares the portions of the plan and events nets from the event node down. JIA computes the proportion of by-means-of and effect-of relations that the two portion nets have in common using Tversky's (1977) ratio model. This similarity metric is then scaled up by the vagueness of the plan: degree of match = similarity + [(similarity * vagueness) * (1 - similarity)]. Plan vagueness is, in turn, calculated as 1 - plan complexity, where plan complexity is depth of plan/depth of events. As with human subjects, JIA is relatively certain of any conclusions emerging from the matching heuristic (Shultz & Wells, 1985).

EMBEDDED INTENTIONAL PHENOMENA

The previous section dealt with intention in the narrow sense, as a mental state that guides and directs behavior. It also dealt with first-level awareness of those narrowly defined mental states, as in awareness of one's own or another's intentional state. More generally, though, intention can refer to any mental state. Definitionally, general intentional states have the property of *aboutness* (Dennett, 1987); that is, they are states of mind that refer to something else. In this broad sense, states of knowledge, belief, intention, feeling, seeing, and hearing, for example, are all intentional. They are all states about other things. One does not simply *know, believe, intend, want, feel, see,* and *hear*. Rather, one *knows something, believes something, intends something, wants something, feels something, sees something,* or *hears something*.

Such general intentional phenomena also exhibit *referential* opacity (Dennett, 1987). This means that they are expressed in clauses for which the normal substitution rule does not hold. Normally, if one substitutes a synonymous term for another, the truth or falsity of the clause is preserved. For example, one can say either *"Brian Mulroney spent the weekend at Meech Lake"* or *"The prime minister of Canada spent the weekend at Meech Lake"*, with no change in truth value, because Brian Mulroney is the prime minister of Canada, and no intentionality is involved. Consider, however, *"John believes that Brian Mulroney spent the weekend at Meech Lake."* If John is unaware that Brian Mulroney is the prime minister of Canada, then it does not follow that *John believes that the prime minister of Canada spent the weekend at Meech Lake*. The reason for this lack of substitutability is that the substituted clauses are intentional states.

Intentional states, in this general sense, can also be embedded. The clause *"Brian Mulroney spent the weekend at Meech Lake"* can be the embedded *X* in *John believes X*. Moreover, the degree of embeddedness can be arbitrarily deep, as in *"John thinks that Brian believes that . . . "*

In the following sections, I consider some of the special problems posed by these general characteristics of intention for computational modelling and propose some solutions to them. A major problem is that the truth boundaries between levels of embeddedness need to be preserved. For example, merely believing that *Brian Mulroney is the president of Canada* does not make it so. Canada, in fact, has no president. Truth values at an embedded level cannot be directly transferred to the embedding level.

Building on Fauconnier's (1985) theory of mental spaces, Dinsmore (1987) showed that certain propositional functions (which include, but are not limited to, intentional states) can be used to relate truth across levels of embeddedness. In particular, the truth of some proposition in a mental space (i.e., at some degree of embeddedness) corresponds to the truth of a proposition in the real world. For example, if John's belief is that *Brian Mulroney is the president of Canada*, then it is true, in the real world (i.e., at the top level of embeddedness), that *John believes that Brian Mulroney is the president of Canada*.

I examine several issues about representing embedded intentional phenomena while considering three well-known phenomena from the literature on intentionality: false belief, deception, and strategic game playing. Each topic is seen to raise special problems of its own, and it shall be of interest to determine whether the solutions have any degree of generality. Although the presented programs do run, they should not be regarded as complete simulations. Rather, the chapter should be regarded as a feasibility study for the computational modelling of intentional phenomena.

FALSE BELIEF

Perner (1988) and others have shown that young children have particular difficulty in understanding the false beliefs of others. Consider the following story used by Perner (1988):

There is an ice-cream van stationed at the church, but Mary was told it was in the park. Mary is leaving the house to go to the ice-cream van. Where is she going?

The young child, who typically answers *To the church*, may be following this production rule:

(p false-belief:younger

    (s ^agent <person> ^action want ^object <goal> ^embed-in
     nil)

    (s ^agent <goal> ^action at ^object <location1> ^embed-in
     nil)

    (s ^agent <person> ^action at ^object { <location2> < >
     <location1> } ^embed-in nil)

    →

    (make s ^agent <person> ^action approach ^object
     <location1>))

Translated into English, production rule *false-belief:younger* says that if person wants a goal, that goal is at a particular location, and the person is at another location, then the person is likely to approach the first location.

Some Notational Details

In order that readers can read such production rules and appreciate some of the details of the programming, some notational background is now given. All of the production rules presented here are written for an interpreter called OPS5 (Official Production System; Forgy, 1981). OPS5 allows the use of both primitive and compound data types. Primitive data types are either numbers or symbolic atoms. Among the most useful compound data types in OPS5 is the element class. An element class is declared as follows:

> (literalize class
>
>   attribute$_1$
>
>   attribute$_2$
>
>   . . .
>
>   attribute$_n$)

Literalize is an OPS5 command, *class* refers to the name of the element class, and then come the names of the various attributes of this class. The programmer specifies both the class and the names of attributes. As instances of element classes get created in working memory, each attribute will take a value, in the form of a primitive data type (i.e., a number or symbolic atom). Readers familiar with frame data structures might recognize that OPS5 element classes are fairly simple frames, without the elaborations that one often finds in complete frame representation languages (e.g., Roberts & Goldstein, 1977).[1]

In my work on modelling embedded intentional phenomena, I have found it sufficient to use a single, uniform element class that I call s, for *sentence*. Each sentence is composed of three principal syntactic components: *agent*, *action*, and *object*. The agent and action components are required, but the object component is optional. Actions are constants, represented as symbolic atoms, but agents and objects can be constants or can be elaborated as another sentence. This provides for the possibility of embedded representations, which are critical to the successful modelling of intentional phenomena. To keep track of the semantics of this embedding, I add two other attributes to the sentence class, *id* and *embed-in*. The id attribute provides each sentence with a unique name, which in actual data elements will be rendered as the name of sentence's action followed by a unique number. In case of embedding, the embed-in attribute assumes the value of the id of the embedding sentence. Otherwise its value is nil, to indicate that the sentence is not embedded but rather exists at the top level. Comments in OPS5 code are preceded by the ; symbol. Comments are not read by the program but

---

[1]In most frame systems, the class name is known as the frame name, and the attributes are called slots.

can be informative to human readers. Following is the commented declaration of the element class s.

> (literalize s   ;sentence
>
>   id   ;action + unique#; needed only with embedding
>
>   agent   ;name of agent or id of embedded sentence
>
>   action   ;name of action
>
>   object   ;name of object or id of embedded sentence
>
>   embed-in) ;nil or id of embedding sentence

Returning to the production *false-belief:younger*, one can see that OPS5 productions consist of an OPS5 command *p* (for production), a unique name, a left-hand side that consists of one or more condition elements, the symbol →, and a right-hand side that consists of a sequence of actions. In our models, each condition element consists of a sentence as just defined.[2] The attribute values in each such sentence are either constants or variables. Constants are represented as symbolic atoms. Variables are surrounded by angled brackets < >. Each such condition specifies a pattern that is to be matched against information in working memory. When all the condition elements of a production are simultaneously satisfied with consistent variable bindings, the production is said to be instantiated. If an instantiated production is selected for firing, then all of the OPS5 commands on the production's right-hand side are executed in order. The only command used in the present programs is the *make* command. *Make* takes a sentence as its argument and creates a new element in working memory that has the class and attribute values of this sentence.[3] Any variables in this sentence are bound to values consistent with those in the production's left-hand side before the new element is deposited in working memory.

Thus, for production *false-belief:younger* to be instantiated, there would need to be three sentences in working memory with consistent variable bindings: (a) some person wanting a particular goal, (b) that goal being at a particular location, and (c) the person being at another particular location, which is not the same as the first location. If this instantiated production were then selected for firing, a new sentence would be deposited in working memory that says that the person approaches the first location.

---

[2]Sentences, whether working memory elements or condition elements in production rules, employ the ^ symbol as a prefix to attribute names.

[3]It is actually more correct to state that *make* takes as arguments an element class name and a sequence of attribute-value pairs.

A production rule such as *false-belief:younger* may well model the behavior of young children on Perner's items, but eventually it would fire when it should not, producing a false-positive error. A more discriminating production, such as *false-belief:older* will avoid such false-positive errors and produce conclusions that are typical of those of older children.

(p false-belief:older

   (s ^agent <person> ^action want ^object <goal> ^embed-in nil)

   (s ^id <id1> ^agent <person> ^action believe ^object <id2> ^embed-in nil)

   (s ^id <id2> ^agent <goal> ^action at ^object <location1> ^embed-in <id1>)

   (s ^agent <person> ^action at ^object {<location2> < > <location1>} ^embed-in nil)

   →

   (make s ^agent <person> ^action approach ^object <location1>))

This rule states that if a person wants a goal, and the person believes that that goal is at a particular location, and the person is at another location, then one can predict that the person will approach the first location. A key difference between this production and the former one is the presence of an embedded intentional state. The third condition element (the goal being at location 1) is embedded within the second condition element (the person's belief). The syntactic object of the person's belief is that the goal is at a particular location. The ability of the child (or system) to comprehend such embedded intentional states will be critical to the formation of such rules.

What is important to note from this example is that a false-belief phenomenon can be modelled with production system programming in such a way that both reproduces the performance of older and younger children and constrains the search for developmental mechanisms capable of managing the transition between the major stages. A successful transition mechanism must at least be able to modify production *false-belief:younger* by replacing the sentence that specifies the location of the goal with an embedding sentence that describes the goal's location as a belief of the person. A secondary point from this example is that cognition regarding false-belief phenomena cannot be modelled solely by considering embedded intentional states. It is also critical to have some sense of the domain in which false beliefs are being studied. In the present example, we needed to know about pursuit of goals in particular locations. Modelling other false-belief phenomena will require different domain-specific knowledge.

DECEPTIVE COMMUNICATION

In a fascinating attempt to apply intentional analyses to cognitive ethology, Dennett (1983) noted the possibly deceptive use of alarm calls in vervet monkeys. Seyfarth, Cheney, and Marler (1980) had reported that vervets in the wild emit different alarm calls to different kinds of predators, such as leopards, eagles, and snakes. Recordings of alarm calls played back when predators were absent caused vervets to run into the trees for leopard alarms, look up for eagle alarms, and look down for snake alarms.

Dennett (1983) suggested accounting for such communication in terms of intentionality and proposed that the degree of embeddedness of intentional states was a deep mark of intelligence that would be valid across species. I found it instructive to represent the varying degrees of embeddedness contained in some of Dennett's hypothetical examples of vervet communication. Consider the case of one vervet, Tom, emitting a leopard call in the presence of another vervet, Sam. Dennett pointed out that this communicative effort can be interpreted in a number of competing ways, with varying degrees of embeddedness. Degree of embeddedness can be easily represented in our sentence notation. A zero-order interpretation would be that Tom emits a leopard call.

(make s ^agent tom ^action emit ^object leopard-call)

A first-order interpretation would be that Tom wants Sam to run into the trees.

(make s ^id want1 ^agent tom ^action want ^object run1)

(make s ^id run1 ^agent sam ^action run ^object trees ^embed-in want1)

A second-order interpretation would be that Tom wants Sam to believe that there is a leopard present.

(make s ^id want2 ^agent tom ^action want ^object believe2)

(make s ^id believe2 ^agent sam ^action believe ^object is2
  ^embed-in want2)

(make s ^id is2 ^agent leopard ^action is ^object present ^
  embed-in believe2)

A third-order interpretation would be that Tom wants Sam to believe
that Tom wants Sam to run into the trees.

(make s ^id want3 ^agent tom ^action want ^object believe3)

(make s ^id believe3 ^agent sam ^action believe ^object want4
  ^embed-in want3)

(make s ^id want4 ^agent tom ^action want ^object run3
  ^embed-in believe3)

(make s ^id run3 ^agent sam ^action run ^object trees ^embed-in
  want4)

Embeddedness can be arbitrarily deep, but let's terminate with the
fourth-order interpretation that Tom wants Sam to recognize that Tom
wants Sam to believe that there is a leopard present.

(make s ^id want5 ^agent tom ^action want ^object recognize5)

(make s ^id recognize5 ^agent sam ^action recognize ^object
  want6 ^embed-in want5)

(make s ^id want6 ^agent tom ^action want ^object believe5
  ^embed-in recognize5)

(make s ^id believe5 ^agent sam ^action believe ^object is5
  ^embed-in want6)

(make s ^id is5 ^agent leopard ^action is ^object present ^
  embed-in believe5)

Thus, OPS5 linked data structures do appear adequate for handling the
sorts of embedded intentional interpretations suggested by Dennett
(1983). Such techniques are not sufficient for the modelling of reasoning,
however, because by themselves, the sentences don't do anything. They
are declarative but not procedural. Procedural knowledge, represented
as production rules, could be used to explain cognitive inferences and
action. Consider the following zero-order rule to account for the
emission of leopard calls.

(p vervet:zero-order

    (s ^agent <vervet> ^action at ^object <location> ^embed-in
    nil)

    (s ^agent <vervet> ^action is ^object vervet ^embed-in nil)

    (s ^agent <leopard> ^action at ^object <location> ^embed-
    in nil)

    (s ^agent <leopard> ^action is ^object leopard ^embed-in nil)

    →

    (make s ^agent <vervet> ^action emit ^object leopard-call))

Production *vervet:zero-order* says that if a vervet and a leopard are in the
same location, one can expect the vervet to emit a leopard-call. The
second- and fourth-condition elements check to make sure that the first
animal is a vervet and the second is a leopard. Animal types are of
critical importance in rules that deal with alarm calls.

But because lone male vervets, on seeing a leopard, silently seek
refuge in trees (Dennett, 1983), a first-order rule might be more
appropriate.

(p vervet:1st-order

    (s ^agent <vervet1> ^action at ^object <location> ^embed-in
    nil)

    (s ^agent <vervet2> ^action at ^object <location> ^embed-in
    nil)

    (s ^agent <vervet1> ^action is ^object vervet ^embed-in nil)

    (s ^agent <vervet2> ^action is ^object vervet ^embed-in nil)

    (s ^id <id1> ^agent <vervet1> ^action want ^object <id2>
    ^embed-in nil)

    (s ^id <id2> ^agent <vervet2> ^action run ^object trees
    ^embed-in <id1>)

    →

    (make s ^agent <vervet1> ^action emit ^object leopard-call))

This rule says that if two vervets are in the same location, and one of
them wants the other to run into the trees, the first vervet should emit

a leopard call.[4] Anecdotes suggest that such a deeper interpretation may
be correct. Seyfarth (in Dennett, 1983) reported that one vervet band
was losing ground to another band in a territorial skirmish when one of
the losing side emitted a leopard alarm. All of the vervets took up the cry
and headed for trees. This created a truce, allowing the original caller's
side to regain the territory they had lost. A second-order interpretation
would also be consistent with these data.

(p vervet:2nd-order

    (s ^agent <vervet1> ^action at ^object <location> ^embed-in
     nil)

    (s ^agent <vervet2> ^action at ^object <location> ^embed-in
     nil)

    (s ^agent <vervet1> ^action is ^object vervet ^embed-in nil)

    (s ^agent <vervet2> ^action is ^object vervet ^embed-in nil)

    (s ^id <id1> ^agent <vervet1> ^action want ^object <id2>
     ^embed-in nil)

    (s ^id <id2> ^agent <vervet2> ^action believe ^object
     <id3> ^embed-in <id1>)

    (s ^id <id3> ^agent <leopard> ^action at ^object
     <location> ^embed-in <id2>)

    (s ^agent <leopard> ^action is ^object leopard ^embed-in nil)

    →

    (make s ^agent <vervet1> ^action emit ^object leopard-call))

The second-order rule says that if two vervets are in the same location,
and one vervet wants the other to believe that a leopard is present, the
first vervet will emit a leopard call. As Dennett (1983) pointed out, it is
a difficult challenge to unequivocally support any particular interpretation of such wild primate behaviors. In most cases, any number of
interpretations will apply with equal validity in the absence of further
information. He proposed an interesting *Sherlock Holmes* technique for
sorting out which interpretations are most likely to be appropriate. The

---

[4]Although one could write a zero-order production to handle the emission of leopard
calls only in the presence of other vervets, it would not really explain the role of the other
vervets in the caller's decision to make the call.

main point I would like to add is that this sort of diagnostic enterprise will be aided by a rigorous, computationally sufficient formulation of the competing interpretations.

PRODUCTION SYSTEMS

Even production rules do nothing on their own. In order to function, they must be processed by an interpreter. For those who are unfamiliar with such programs, it may be useful to provide an overview of how production systems work—OPS5, in particular. Production systems typically have three main components: a rule base, a working memory, and an interpreter. The interpreter works in a three-phase cycle of matching, selecting, and acting. In the matching phase, working memory elements are examined to determine which instantiations of which production rules are capable of firing. The firable instantiations are those that match with consistent bindings as described before. This set of instantiations forms a conflict set, from which one instantiation is selected for firing.

The selection phase in the present programs uses the LEX (for LEXicographic) conflict resolution strategy. LEX applies three principles to select an instantiation for firing: refraction, recency, and specificity. Refraction specifies that an instantiation cannot be fired more than once, unless it has been modified in some way.

After removing previously fired instantiations from the conflict set, LEX orders the remaining instantiations in the conflict set on the basis of the recency with which the matching working memory elements entered working memory. Then, if there is still more than one instantiation in the conflict set, the specificity principle favors the most specific production. The most specific production is the one with the greatest number of tests on its left-hand side.

The selection principles used by LEX do have some degree of psychological validity. Refraction prevents an instantiation from firing continuously in an infinite loop in those cases where the production does not remove from working memory some element that the production needs as a condition element. Recency ensures a data-driven order to the way conclusions are generated. That is, the system stays with a particular aspect of information in working memory until no additional processing can be done on it. Specificity implements a well-known psychological principle, known as the *priority of the specific*: specific information has priority over more general information (Locksley, Borgida, Brekke, & Hepburn, 1980; McClelland & Rumelhart, 1985).

STRATEGIC GAME PLAYING

Strategic actions are those designed to disguise one's intentions from one's opponents. As such, strategic actions are a reliable indicator of embedded awareness of intention (Schmidt, 1976). In the simplest case, this embedded awareness is at the second level, as when person A is aware that person B is aware of person A's intentions. Without such awareness, person A would have no reason to behave strategically.

Because strategic actions ordinarily involve deception, their assessment, especially in children, raises a variety of practical and ethical issues. Fortunately, there is a natural, harmless context for strategic deception—game playing. Shultz and Cloghesy (1981) designed a simple card game for this purpose, modelled after Premack's (1976) procedures with chimpanzees. The adult experimenter, who was the child's opponent, began by removing one black and one red card from a deck, placing them face up in front of child. The experimenter kept the deck and looked at the top card. She then pointed to either a black or a red exposed card as an indication to the child whose job it was to guess the color of that top card. If the child guessed correctly, he or she won that top card. If not, the experimenter won the top card. The object of the game was to win as many cards as possible from the other player.

Each child played the game under two conditions, once as guesser and once as pointer. The experimenter started by playing straight but changed to a deceptive strategy when the child won four consecutive cards. The game continued for 30 tricks. The results indicated no embedded awareness of intention in 3-year-olds, but this awareness increased with age in children of 5, 7, and 9 years. The question I pursue in this section is whether one could develop a rule-based computational model of children's reasoning and behavior in this game. Two production rules, one for guessing and another for pointing, could be said to be given by the rules of the game:

```
(p cards:guess

    (s ^agent <top-card> ^action is ^object new ^embed-in nil)

    (s ^agent <player> ^action is ^object guesser ^embed-in nil)

    (s ^agent <opponent> ^action point ^object <color>
        ^embed-in nil)

    - (s ^agent <opponent> ^action is ^object untruthful ^embed-
        in nil)

    →

    (make s ^agent <top-card> ^action has-color ^object
        <color>))
```

Production *cards:guess* specifies that if the top card is new, the player is in the role of guesser, the opponent points to a particular color, and there is no evidence that the opponent is untruthful, then the expectation is that the top card is of that color.[5]

    (p cards:point

        (s ^agent < top-card > ^action is ^object new ^embed-in nil)

        (s ^agent < player > ^action is ^object pointer ^embed-in nil)

        (s ^agent < top-card > ^action has-color ^object < color >
          ^embed-in nil)

      →

        (make s ^agent < player > ^action point ^object < color >
          ^embed-in nil))

Production *cards:point* specifies that if a player is in the role of pointer, and the top card has a particular color, then the player should point to that color. These two rules enable the system to play a straight game, but a system relying on them will start to lose as soon as the opponent begins to play deceptively. To begin to play deceptively, the system needs rules to detect the opponent's veracity:

    (p detect-truth1

        (s ^agent < person > ^action make ^object < statement >
          ^embed-in nil)

        (s ^agent < statement > ^action is ^object true ^embed-in nil)

      →

        (make s ^agent < person > ^action is ^object truthful))

Production *detect-truth1* says that if a person makes a statement, and that statement is true, then expect that person to be truthful. A companion production, detect-false, detects falsity by specifying that if a person makes a statement, and that statement is false, then expect that the person is untruthful.

    (p detect-false

        (s ^agent < person > ^action make ^object < statement >
          ^embed-in nil)

---

[5]Initially, this production would probably lack the last, negated condition element. But eventually, it will need this negated condition element so that it defers to production cards:guess:modified. (See discussion of defaults and preferences hereafter.)

(s ^agent <statement> ^action is ^object false ^embed-in nil)

- (s ^agent <person> ^action believe ^embed-in nil)

→

(make s ^agent <person> ^action is ^object untruthful))

Production *default-truth* deals with cases in which there is no evidence about the veracity of the person's statement. It says that if a person makes a statement, and there is no evidence that the statement is either true or false, then assume that the statement is true and that the person is truthful.

(p default-truth

    (s ^agent <person> ^action make ^object <statement>
    ^embed-in nil)

    - (s ^agent <statement> ^action is ^object true ^embed-in nil)

    - (s ^agent <statement> ^action is ^object false ^embed-in nil)

    →

    (make s ^agent <statement> ^action is ^object true)

    (make s ^agent <person> ^action is ^object truthful))

Production *detect-truth2* deals with the case of false belief. It specifies that if a person makes a statement, and that statement is false, but the person believes that the statement is true, then expect that the person is truthful. This would correct some of the false-positive errors created by the firing of production *detect-truth1*.

(p detect-truth2

    (s ^agent <person> ^action make ^object <statement>
    ^embed-in nil)

    (s ^agent <statement> ^action is ^object false ^embed-in nil)

    (s ^id <id1> ^agent <person> ^action believe ^object
    <id2> ^embed-in nil)

    (s ^id <id2> ^agent <statement> ^action is ^object true
    ^embed-in <id1>)

    →

    (make s ^agent <person> ^action is ^object truthful))

This sample set of productions to detect veracity would, of course, have more general applicability than this particular card game. This is an example of more general knowledge being called upon to aid in dealing with a particular specific domain.

To some extent, these truth-detecting productions compete with each other, because they share many of the same condition elements but have contradictory conclusions. Having productions with contradictory conclusions fire would tend to create confusion or even chaos. One solution is for some productions to defer to other productions with more specific knowledge. One way to implement this is to build negative tests into the left-hand sides of the deferring productions. For example, production *default-truth* defers to production *detect-truth1*. Both of these productions attempt to conclude something about the truthfulness of a person by noting that the person made a statement. But *detect-truth1* requires, in addition, information about the truth of the person's statement, whereas production *default-truth* does not. This provides the former production with somewhat greater validity but still enables the latter production to generate adaptive conclusions by default, that is, in the absence of information about the veracity of the person's statement.

One cannot rely on the specificity principle of conflict resolution to prefer the more specific production over the default production. This is because specificity will only tend to postpone the firing of the default production until after the more specific production has fired; specificity alone will not prevent the default production from firing eventually and thus creating confusion. The negative tests that are the second and third condition elements of production *default-truth* prevent this production from firing whenever there is information about the veracity of the person's statement.

In a similar way, production *detect-false* defers to production *detect-truth2*. Both productions employ a condition element referring to the falsity of the person's statement, yet one concludes that the person is untruthful and the other that the person is truthful. Production *detect-truth2* is to be preferred because of its use of specific privileged information regarding the beliefs of the person. Again, this preference is assured by the presence of a negative test in the left-hand side of production *detect-false*. In this case, the test looks for the absence of evidence about the person's beliefs.

These productions for detecting a person's veracity will, of course, require the presence of still other productions that detect either the veracity of statements or the contents of a person's beliefs. Needless to say, both of these could pose challenging computational and psychological problems. But the explicitness of this approach at least makes it clear what is known and what is still to be solved. The conclusions of these productions for detecting a person's veracity will appear as condition elements in more sophisticated guessing and pointing productions. An example is provided by a modified guessing rule:

(p cards:guess:modified

    (s ^agent <top-card> ^action is ^object new ^embed-in nil)

    (s ^agent <player> ^action is ^object guesser ^embed-in nil)

    (s ^agent <opponent> ^action point ^object <color1> ^embed-in nil)

    (s ^agent <opponent> ^action is ^object untruthful ^embed-in nil)

    →

    (make s ^agent <top-card> ^action does-not-have-color ^object <color1>))

This production says that if the top card is new, the player is in the guesser role, the opponent points to a color, and there is a feeling that the opponent is untruthful, then anticipate that the top card is not the color pointed to by the opponent. The original pointing rule also needs to be similarly modified to create deceptive pointing. Even with such deceptive guessing and pointing rules in place, however, the system would play only a fairly good reactive game. If its opponent knows that the system is playing with *rule-guess-modified*, the system can easily be beaten. To play more actively and stay a step ahead of its opponent, the system should anticipate, rather than simply react. I am not yet sure what such anticipatory rules would look like.

This exercise in devising rule-based reasoning mechanisms for strategic game playing has made it clear that the achievement of this sort of reasoning is extremely subtle and complex. At the same time, the exercise suggests that such modelling may be quite fruitful in identifying reasoning mechanisms and even in suggesting possible developmental mechanisms. Clearly, the system will at least need procedural knowledge for the detection of truth and falsity in order to advance to more effective strategies. Now that we have examined some of the representational and processing issues for three embedded intentional phenomena, we are in a somewhat better position to think about the issue of development.

TRANSITION MECHANISMS

In the present context, it is clear that the search for transition mechanisms can be constrained to mechanisms capable of creating or modifying production rules. Artificial intelligence researchers are experimenting with a variety of techniques for learning production rules, and at least some of these techniques may be good candidates for psychological transition mechanisms.

Production Modification

Techniques for modifying productions include discrimination, generalization, composition, compilation, and strength adjustment. Discrimination increases the specificity of a rule's left-hand side, usually by adding condition elements or instantiating variables (Anderson, 1983; Langley, 1987). There is mounting evidence that children's knowledge does become increasingly differentiated as they mature (Smith, Carey, & Wiser, 1985). Examples of the increasing specificity of productions were provided by all three of the embedded intentional phenomena examined here. Thus, a discrimination mechanism could figure importantly in explaining cognitive development.

Generalization accomplishes the opposite of discrimination, in that it makes a production more general in its application (Anderson, 1983). Typically, this is done by deleting condition elements or by changing constants to variables. Generalization may also have a place in cognitive development, although it may be less useful overall than is discrimination. A single example is an algebra-learning program that generalizes its procedures from specific numbers to variables that can assume a range of values (Neches, Langley, & Klahr, 1987).

The composition process collapses a series of productions that typically fire in sequence (Anderson, 1983; Lewis, 1987). It thus creates a macro production that includes the condition elements of the first production on the left-hand side and all of the other condition and action elements on the right-hand side. Composition accelerates skilled performance, because it reduces the amount of matching that needs to be done. And, unlike discrimination and generalization, composition can function without the benefit of corrective feedback.

Compilation of productions is another technique for reducing the relatively expensive matching process. It functions by replacing variables with constants, normally in frequently used productions that continually match to the same set of values (Anderson, 1983, 1986).

Strength adjustment concerns the modification of a numerical index associated with a rule. These indices typically reflect the tendency of a rule to be considered or the certainty of the rule's conclusions (Anderson, 1983; Holland, Holyoak, Nisbett, & Thagard, 1986). In most such schemes, positive feedback increases these quantitative indices, and negative feedback lowers them.

Production Creation

The creation of productions is usually considered to be a more difficult problem than that of modification in the sense that the creation mechanism has less relevant knowledge to work with. Creation is important, however, because the system may function in novel domains. Creation could be more general than modification, because a good creation scheme may obviate the need for rule modification. If new rules can be created from scratch, why modify old ones? The principal creation techniques studied so far include induction, analogy, and chunking.

Inductive techniques attempt to abstract the necessary and sufficient conditions for some action by analyzing examples or instances (Holland et al., 1986; Mitchell, Utgoff, & Banerji, 1983). There is some doubt that humans have the working-memory capacity for this sort of creative process, at least with large numbers of complex examples.

Analogy involves remembering a similar problem where the rules are known, mapping these rules to the novel target problem, and then tweaking the rules to adjust for possible differences between the old and new problems (Winston, 1980). Despite some promising work on analogical mapping (Gentner, 1983), the problems of analogy retrieval and tweaking remain difficult and obscure. We know that at least some humans sometimes use analogy effectively, but we do not yet understand how they do it.

Chunking is a technique for saving the results of so-called weak problem-solving techniques, such as search. The Soar architecture is a relatively seamless implementation of search techniques and procedural knowledge that is coded as productions (Laird, Rosenbloom, & Newell, 1987). Soar uses production knowledge whenever it can, and it searches through relevant problem spaces when its knowledge runs out. Then it chunks the results of the search, forming new productions. Soar has been successfully applied to a variety of both toy- and realistic-sized problems, and a few investigators are becoming interested in its possible application to cognitive development. Because Soar uses much of the OPS5 code, its knowledge representation methods are fairly compatible with those used in the productions presented here.

CONCLUSIONS

Consideration of these three well-known phenomena from the psychological literature on embedded intentional states suggests that it is feasible to simulate such states with conventional symbolic modelling tools, such as production rules. Although none of the three phenomena was fully modelled here, exploration of the possibilities did not uncover any insurmountable obstacles to such modelling.

In particular, the major problem of representing and reasoning with varying degrees of embeddedness can be handled quite naturally within OPS5 productions, using linked data representations.

This chapter also suggested a number of candidates for transition mechanisms that might be capable of generating the procedural knowledge for reasoning about embedded intentional states. These included modification principles such as discrimination and creation principles such as chunking. Interestingly, such learning mechanisms are not completely idiosyncratic to embedded intention but are known to be generally useful in getting production systems to modify their own rule base (Klahr et al., 1987).

Although the present explorations are certainly encouraging in these senses, time and future research will tell whether the general approach outlined here truly has merit.

ACKNOWLEDGMENTS

Portions of the work reported here were supported by a grant from the Natural Sciences and Engineering Research Council of Canada and by the McGill-IBM Cooperative Project.

REFERENCES

Anderson, J. R. (1983). *The architecture of cognition*. Cambridge, MA: Harvard University Press.

Anderson, J. R. (1986). Knowledge compilation: The general learning mechanism. In R. S. Michalski, J. G. Carbonell, & T. Mitchell (Eds.), *Machine learning: An artificial intelligence approach* (Vol. 2, pp. 289–310). Los Altos, CA: Morgan Kaufman.

Davidson, D. (1973). Freedom to act. In T. Honderich (Ed.), *Essays on freedom of action* (pp. 139–156). London: Routledge & Kegan Paul.

Dennett, D. C. (1983). Intentional systems in cognitive ethology: The "Panglossian Paradigm" defended. *Behavioral and Brain Sciences, 6*, 343–355.

Dennett, D. C. (1987). *The intentional stance*. Cambridge, MA: MIT Press.

Dinsmore, J. (1987). Mental spaces from a functional perspective. *Cognitive Science, 11*, 1–21.

Fauconnier, G. (1985). *Mental spaces: Aspects of meaning construction in natural language*. Cambridge, MA: MIT Press.

Forgy, C. L. (1981). *OPS5 user's manual* (Tech. Rep. No. CMU-CS-81-135). Pittsburgh: Carnegie-Mellon University, Department of Computer Science.

Gentner, D. (1983). Structure mapping: A theoretical framework for analogy. *Cognitive Science, 7,* 155–170.

Goldman, A. I. (1970). *A theory of human action.* Princeton, NJ: Princeton University Press.

Holland, J. H., Holyoak, K. J., Nisbett, R. E., & Thagard, P. R. (1986). Induction: *Processes of inference, learning, and discovery.* Cambridge, MA: MIT Press.

Laird, J. E., Rosenbloom, P. S., & Newell, A . (1987). Chunking in Soar: The anatomy of a general learning mechanism. *Machine Learning, 1,* 11–46.

Langley, P. (1987). A general theory of discrimination learning. In D. Klahr, P. Langley, & R. Neches (Eds.) *Production system models of learning and development* (pp. 99–162). Cambridge, MA: MIT Press.

Lewis, C. (1987). Composition of productions. In D. Klahr, P. Langley, & R. Neches (Eds.) *Production system models of learning and development* (pp. 329–358). Cambridge, MA: MIT Press.

Locksley, A., Borgida, E., Brekke, N., & Hepburn, C. (1980). Sex-stereotypes and social judgment. *Journal of Personality and Social Psychology, 39,* 821–831.

McClelland, J. L., & Rumelhart, D. E. (1985). Distributed memory and the representation of general and specific information. *Journal of Experimental Psychology: General, 114,* 159–188.

Mitchell, T. M., Utgoff, P. E., & Banerji, R. (1983). Learning by experimentation: Acquiring and refining problem-solving heuristics. In R. S. Michalski, J. G. Carbonell, & T. Mitchell (Eds.), *Machine learning: An artificial intelligence approach* (pp. 163–190). Palo Alto, CA: Tioga Publishing Co.

Neches, R., Langley, P., & Klahr, D. (1987). Learning, development, and production systems. In D. Klahr, P. Langley, & R. Neches (Eds.), Production system models of learning and development (pp.1–53). Cambridge, MA: MIT Press.

Perner, J. (1988). Developing semantics for theories of mind. In J. Astington, P. Harris, & D. Olson (Eds.), *Developing theories of mind* (pp. 141–172). New York: Cambridge University Press.

Premack, D. (1976). Language and intelligence in ape and man. *American Scientist, 64,* 674–683.

Roberts, R., & Goldstein, I. (1977). *The FRL manual* (Artificial Intelligence Laboratory Memo 409). Cambridge, MA: MIT.

Schmidt, C. F. (1976). Understanding human action: Recognizing the plans and motives of other persons. In J. S. Carroll & J. W. Payne (Eds.), *Cognition and social behavior.* Hillsdale, NJ: Lawrence Erlbaum Associates.

Searle, J. R. (1983). *Intentionality: An essay in the philosophy of mind.* Cambridge, England: Cambridge University Press.

Seyfarth, R., Cheney, D. L., & Marler, P. (1980). Monkey responses to three different alarm calls: Evidence of predator classification and semantic communication. *Science, 210,* 801–803.

Shultz, T. R. (1980). Development of the concept of intention. In W. A. Collins (Ed.), *Development of cognition, affect, and social relations. The Minnesota Symposia on Child Psychology* (Vol. 13, pp. 131–164). Hillsdale, NJ: Lawrence Erlbaum Associates.

Shultz, T. R. (1988). Assessing intention: A computational model. In J. Astington, P. Harris, & D. Olson (Eds.), *Developing theories of mind* (pp. 341–367). New York: Cambridge University Press.

Shultz, T. R., & Cloghesy, K. (1981). Development of recursive awareness of intention. *Developmental Psychology, 17,* 465–471.

Shultz, T. R., & Wells, D. (1985). Judging the intentionality of action-outcomes. *Develop-*

mental Psychology, 21, 83–89.

Smith, C., Carey, S., & Wiser, M. (1985). On differentiation: A case study of the development of the concepts of size, weight, and density. *Cognition, 21,* 177–237.

Tversky, A. (1977). Features of similarity. *Psychological Review, 84,* 327–352.

Winston, P. H. (1980). *Learning and reasoning by analogy: The details.* AIM 520, (Artificial Intelligence Laboratory Memo 520). Cambridge, MA: MIT.

Woodfield, A. (1976). *Teleology.* Cambridge, England: Cambridge University Press.

Author Index

Page numbers in *italics* denotes complete biographical information.

Subject Index

W

Word learning, 84

Z

Zone of proximal development, 132–133